ARMAMENT AND HISTORY

J. F. C. FULLER

ARMAMENT AND HISTORY

The Influence of Armament on History
from the Dawn of Classical Warfare
to the End of the Second World War

DA CAPO PRESS • NEW YORK

To
COLONEL L. A. CODD
who suggested this book

Library of Congress Cataloging-in-Publication Data

Fuller, J. F. C. (John Frederick Charles), 1878–1966.
Armament and history: a study of the influence of armament on history
from the dawn of classical warfare to the Second World War / J. F. C.
Fuller.—1st Da Capo Press ed.
    p.   cm.
Originally published: New York: C. Scribner's Sons, 1945.
Includes index.
ISBN 0-306-80859-5 (alk. paper)
    1. Military weapons—History. 2. Military art and science—History. I.
Title.
U800.F85   1998
355.8—dc21   98-7689
                                                                  CIP

First Da Capo Press edition 1998

This Da Capo Press paperback edition of *Armament and History* is an
unabridged republication of the edition published in London in 1946.
It is reprinted by arrangement with the Estate of J. F. C. Fuller.

Published by Da Capo Press, Inc.
A Subsidiary of Plenum Publishing Corporation
233 Spring Street, New York, N.Y. 10013

Manufactured in the United States of America

PREFACE

THIS study, as mentioned in the Dedication, was suggested to me by my friend Colonel L. A. Codd, Executive Vice-President and Secretary of the Army Ordnance Association of the United States, as a subject worth enquiring into. Gladly falling in with his idea, its first seven chapters were published in *Army Ordnance* between July 1944 and July 1945, after which they were set together to appear in book form both in America and in this country [Great Britain].

Though in a work of this description it would clearly have been preferable before writing it to have waited until the war was over, in the circumstances this was not practicable. And when early in March 1945 I posted the seventh chapter to Colonel Codd, little did I dream that within five months a new weapon of such tremendous power would appear as to force the surrender of Japan within a week of its first use. At once my problem became one of procedure. Except for the insertion of a footnote, the American edition was too advanced to be amended; but, thanks to shortage of paper, the publication of the English edition was delayed until 1946. The question I had to answer was: should I rewrite certain parts of the book or merely add to it an eighth chapter?

On re-reading the MS. I decided on the latter course and for the following reasons: (1) The arrival of the atomic bomb did not seem in any radical way to change my argument. (2) Rather it went far to confirm several of my leading statements, such as: "Tools, or weapons, if only the right ones can be discovered, form ninety-nine per cent. of victory" (Chapter I), and that the hidden impulse in the technological epoch of war is "the elimination of the human element both physically and morally, intellect alone remaining" (Chapter IV). (3) As at present the future of the bomb is so little predictable, instead of changing or modifying certain statements better to fit its spectacular powers, it appeared to me to be both wiser and more honest to leave it for the future to decide whether the appearance of this master weapon—no new thing in history—would undermine the main buttress supporting my theory of weapon development—namely, the "Constant Tactical Factor," as discussed in Chapter I. I have, therefore, left the first seven chapters as they were originally written, and such amendments that I might have made in them I will note in Chapter VIII, which should be looked upon rather as a provisional appendix than the final chapter of the book.

Though I am well aware that in so small a work as this it is impossible to give more than a bird's-eye view of so vast a subject as the influence of armament upon history, I hope that my readers will find sufficient of importance in it to awaken their interest. Not only do I believe that this essay is the first of its kind, but that an appreciation of the influence of armament on civilization is not the least of the several steps that must be taken to restrict the ravages of war.

My indebtedness, as is patent to all historical writing, is to my predecessors and contemporaries. Among the latter, particularly I wish to acknowledge my debt to Lewis Mumford and his *Technics and Civilization*; Sir Charles Oman and his histories on Medieval and Sixteenth-Century Warfare; Edward Mead Earle and the other writers of *Makers of Modern Strategy*; Quincy Wright and his *A Study of War*, and Alfred Vagts and his *A History of Militarism*. Without the assistance of the first of the above books I much doubt whether this essay would ever have been written.

J. F. C. F.

November 6, 1945

CONTENTS

INTRODUCTION

In the year 595, when the Dark Ages had engulfed the Western World, Gregory the Great wrote to the Patriarch at Constantinople saying:

"It is the last hour. Pestilence and sword are raging in the world. Nation is rising against nation, the whole fabric of things is being shaken."

Yet in that anarchic age the destruction wrought was insignificant when compared with what we see to-day, and at times even the most barbarous of warriors hesitated to dishonour their names by acts which are now commonplace. For instance, when, in the year 546, Totila, King of the Ostrogoths, entered Rome and for military reasons was about to burn that city and " turn it into a sheep-run," Belisarius addressed to him the following letter:

"Fair cities are the glory of the great men who have been their founders, and surely no wise man would wish to be remembered as the destroyer of any of them. But of all cities under the sun Rome is confessed to be the greatest and the most glorious. No one man, no single century reared her greatness. A long line of kings and emperors, the united efforts of some of the noblest men, a vast interval of time, a lavish expenditure of wealth, the most costly materials and the most skilful craftsmen of the world have all united to make Rome. Slowly and gradually has each succeeding age there reared its monuments. Any act, therefore, of wanton outrage against that city will be resented as an injustice by all men of all ages: by those who have gone before us, because it effaces the memorials of their greatness; by those who shall come after, since the most wonderful sight in the world will be no longer theirs to look upon. Remember, too, that this war must end either in the Emperor's victory or your own. If you should prove to be the conqueror, how great will be your delight in having preserved the most precious jewel in your crown. If yours should turn out to be the

losing side, great will be the thanks due from the conqueror
for your preservation of Rome, while its destruction would
make every plea for mercy and humanity on your behalf
inadmissible. And last of all comes the question what shall
be your own eternal record in history, whether you will be
remembered as the preserver or the destroyer of the greatest
city in the world."

Compared with these latter days, the remarkable thing is
that, to his own disadvantage, the savage Goth heeded these
words and left Rome undamaged. How many of the leaders
of the nations in the present war have sought to spare London
or Berlin ? Not one !

Indeed, the Dark Ages are beginning to shed their gloom,
now that we can strike a comparison. Here is another
example: In 503, when Clovis, King of the Franks, the
complete barbarian, having defeated the Alamanni, threatened to blot their name from the earth, Theodoric the
Ostrogoth, the semi-barbarian, wrote to him as follows:

"Hear the advice of one who has had much experience in
matters of this nature. Those wars of mine have had a successful issue, over the ending of which moderation has
presided."

How many of the statesmen of to-day believe in moderation? Not one!

Again, in 544, in which year the garrison and inhabitants
of Tivoli were massacred in unusually atrocious circumstances, we find Procopius writing: "The Goths killed all the
inhabitants with the priest of the place, in a manner which I
shall not describe, although I know it, that I may not leave
memorials of inhumanity to a later age." What journalist
to-day would be so squeamish? Who, among the legion of
war correspondents, would not have "scooped" the massacre
and embellished it, in order to squeeze the last sadistic thrill
out of his readers?

And so, throughout all subsequent history, the barbarism
of any period pales before the barbarism of to-day. In
1631, during the ferocious Thirty Years' War, Magdeburg
was stormed by Tilly and its 30,000 inhabitants were

massacred. In 1943 Hamburg was bombed into ruins, and its inhabitants were also massacred, for we read: "The heart of Hamburg was old; it comprised narrow streets and buildings ill-fitted to stand up to our 'block-busters' and incendiaries. During one of our heavy concentrated attacks, about one square mile of the centre of the town was ablaze. Eye-witnesses described how the holocaust was so terrible that the air was sucked into it from outside the perimeter of the fire. Many were suffocated or shrivelled up by the intense heat. Others were drowned on throwing themselves into the canals that run through the city. Days later, when nearby cellars were opened, thousands were found to have perished as though cooked in an oven."

The one great difference between these two atrocities is that, in 1631, the massacre of Magdeburg sent a thrill of horror throughout Christendom, whereas, in 1943, the massacre of Hamburg was received with acclamations in England, as had been the massacre of Coventry in 1940 in Germany.

In the Thirty Years' War, when it was suggested to Gustavus Adolphus that he should demolish the Ducal palace in Munich, not only did he reject the advice with indignation, but he took particular care to preserve it. To-day that palace is a rubble heap.

Why have I set down these several things in the introduction to a book on armament? Because, when we think it out, it is the inventive genius of man which has obliterated his sense of moral values. From the javelin and the arrow to the super-fortress and the rocket-bomb, the very power to destroy, first slowly and then at terrific speed, has intoxicated man.

From out the first flint axe and bended bow has at length emerged a Frankenstein monster—the inventiveness of to-day—that is destroying man's own work, his own culture, his own civilization, his past, his present and his future.

The machine sprung from out the intelligence of man has, through man's worship of it, turned man himself into a piece of machinery. Machines flood in upon us, and nearly every machine is a potential weapon of war. We are entranced by their cunning, their power and precision, also by the things they give us and the profits we reap by means of them. Yet, how they influence us, as living creatures, is left uncalculated. Truly it has been said that "we have got into a maze of machinery," and that in it "we have lost the vision of man's place in the universe."

In this book my aim is not to solve this tremendous problem—the de-mechanization of man—but solely to examine things, the things man fights with, and how throughout the ages these things have influenced history.

Rightly or wrongly, I do not believe that war can be eliminated, because it is part and parcel of life; for life in its broadest meaning is the shifting outcome of destructive and constructive propensities. Therefore I do not believe that man's inventiveness can be restricted, and, in consequence, that all bans on weapon development will prove futile. What I do believe is that war can be restricted, because history clearly shows that normally it has been. Yet also I believe that man is so blind to his own interests that he never restricts war until disaster is so overwhelming that, unless he does restrict it, he and all his will inevitably be destroyed.

During the last 2,000 years four very different systems of restricting war have been tested out, and in each case with considerable success. First, there was the *Pax Romana*, which established a common culture through the Latin world. Its principle was integration, based on a common army, a common language, common citizenship, common laws, common coinage, common weights and measures, etc., and last but not least a magnificent system of roads. Though civil wars were frequent, they were almost entirely restricted to conflicts between actual or would-be Cæsars, in which the people of the Empire took little or no part. Secondly, there was the Medieval or Christian system, which struggled out of the Dark Ages. Its principle was the limitation of war, based on religious sanctions and feudal privileges. Though private wars were frequent, great wars were the exception and not the rule. Thirdly, there was the Royal or eighteenth-century system, which emerged from out the horrors of the Thirty Years' War. Its principle was behaviour, based on rules, customs and laws of war. Though great wars abounded, devastation and unnecessary bloodshed were largely kept in check. Fourth and lastly, there was the *Pax Britannica*. Its leading principle was the balance of power, based on naval supremacy, and in its heyday—the nineteenth century—it localized wars and therefore prevented them assuming continental or world-wide dimensions.

Since the *Pax Britannica* foundered there has been no restrictive system, and it is no coincidence that, because of this, the world has witnessed the two most devastating wars in its history.

It would seem that the next restriction will be sought in the creation of some kind of international or supranational police power. If so, I am of opinion that it will fail, because the inevitable result will be that the policemen will first quarrel and then fight among themselves. Be it noted that a firing squad cannot solve the problem, because the firing squad mentality is at the bottom of the whole trouble.

What, then, is the solution? I suggest that, as the age in which we live is pre-eminently a scientific one, war should be examined scientifically, which means that its causes must be discovered before cures are suggested. In fact, the problem is not a political, a legal or a military one at all; instead it is a pathological one, like that of any ordinary disease.

Because war is the effect of a diseased state of peacefulness, how is police power going to eliminate or restrict the disease? Clearly it cannot, for all it can do is to bind up the peace poison in the war wounds, which automatically makes a third world war inevitable. In which case it is certain that the scientific development of armaments will make that war several times as destructive as the present one.

Already war has very nearly become a thing in itself—that is, an activity divorced from the very idea of peace—

with destruction as its sole aim. To-day this is becoming more and more apparent, because every type of atrocity is excused on military grounds, as if military reasons were the sole, let alone the highest values in war. They certainly are not, because war can only be considered sane when it is looked upon as a political instrument, an instrument subservient to policy, which, to be curative, must be based on moral principles. If it is, then policy demands that the peace aimed at should be a better peace than the one the war has broken; for, should it be a worse peace, then, morally, the war will be lost, however decisively the enemy may have been beaten. Let us, therefore, ever bear in mind the words engraved on the plinth of General Sherman's statue in Washington: "The legitimate object of war is a more perfect peace."

While I write, I read that, for military reasons, it was necessary to destroy Dresden, one of the great cultural centres not only in Germany but in the world. This being so, then it logically follows that for military necessity anything and everything, irrespective of its intrinsic value, either to the immediate peace or the future of mankind, may rightly be destroyed in war-time. Such logic is Juggernaut gone mad, for in the name of war it justifies and condones every atrocity and abomination. In its insanity it is total. Already, several of the belligerent powers have sunk to such depths of infamy that at times they refuse quarter to their adversaries, and resort to the torturing of prisoners in order to extract military information.

What, then, is the final consequence which military necessity will demand? The wholesale massacre of nations! And what will future generations think of the perpetration of these horrors? What past generations thought of the Huns, the Vandals, the Goths, the Lombards, the Seljuks and the Mongols.

It is in this appalling dissolution of morality that armaments have played so great a part. Though man fashions them, it is they which endow him with power to destroy, and to-day it is they which have got their maker by the throat.

Therefore, should I be right in my belief that the restriction of war is a pathological problem, to such as are interested in the future peace of the world this brief essay on the influence of armament upon history should prove of some interest, and, possibly also, of some value.

CHAPTER I
ARMAMENT AND HISTORY

"War in its literal meaning," wrote Clausewitz, "is fighting. . . . The necessity of fighting very soon led men to special inventions to turn the advantage in it in their own favour: in consequence of these the mode of fighting has undergone great alterations; but in whatever way it is conducted its conception remains unaltered, and fighting is that which constitutes War. . . . Fighting has determined everything appertaining to arms and equipment, and these in turn modify the mode of fighting; there is, therefore, a reciprocity of action between the two."[1]

Herein is included the whole technique of war: on the one hand the instruments, and on the other their use. The first embrace weapons and their organizations; the second, operations and policies. Quincy Wright defines the technique of war as "the art of preparing military instruments for mastering, with the least cost, all possible enemies and of utilizing available military instruments in the most efficient combination against an actual enemy." To which he adds: "From the standpoint of preparation, technique is a problem of weapon type, material, and organization. From the standpoint of utilization it is a problem of mobilization, strategy, and tactics."[2]

Though, in its fullest meaning, the word "armament" includes the whole paraphernalia of war—the sea, land, and air forces of a nation—in this study I intend to adhere to its more restricted sense—namely, the weapons and ancillary means by which battles are fought and wars waged. "A military instrument," Quincy Wright defines, "is a material or social entity used by a government to destroy or to control by threats or violence another government or to ward off such destruction or control."[3] And Rear-Admiral Bradley A. Fiske has written: "If used to guard or attack, an implement becomes a weapon—a weapon is merely a tool

15

for a warlike purpose."[4] Personally, I prefer an even more restricted definition—namely, that of an instrument with striking power. Thus a shield or helmet is not a weapon, instead it is a means of protection; nor is a ship, a tank, or an airplane a weapon, for they are no more than vessels or vehicles to carry weapons in. Nevertheless, the dividing lines between hitting, guarding, and moving are fine, and, as the mechanization of weapon power proceeds, are daily growing finer.

In order to trace armament development clearly, the simplest way is to begin at the beginning, the fight between two unarmed men—that is, between fighters whose sole weapons are their hands, feet, and teeth. At once it will be seen that to guard, to strike, to hold and to move are its tactical elements. To these may be added the moral elements of will, tenacity and terror, and later on, when the fighters take to throwing stones, the economic element of supply: first, supply of missiles (munitions), then of men, and lastly of food.

In their turn, these elements can be endowed with "striking power"; for the will of an enemy can be attacked by yells, invocations, and acts of calculated cruelty, and his stomach by pillage, devastation, and blockade.

With reference to this, it is of interest to note that, during the eleventh century, anathema, excommunication, and interdict—all moral weapons—were in "striking power" far more formidable than weapons of the commoner sort, and that, in the War of 1914-1918, the Allied blockade was of all the "weapons" employed the most powerful in effecting the collapse of the Central Powers.

Tactically, unarmed man is less well endowed than many of the animals, whether herbivorous or carnivorous. He has not the strength of the bull, the hide of the rhinoceros, nor the teeth and claws of the tiger. Yet, because he is more intelligent than they, he has conquered them. As his struggle with the animal world has shown, once he took to making weapons, his cunning overcame even the most savage of beasts; in the end to leave the prolific—the rabbit, rat, mosquito, and bacillus—rather than the powerful as his most formidable enemies. Even to-day the science which is his is still at grips with them. Thus, in its way, reproduction is also a weapon, and, of all, the one which possesses the most potent survival value.

Whether we accept the Biblical account or the Darwinian theory of man's origin makes no great difference, for so long as Adam inhabited Eden or ape-man the jungle—that is, in either case in an unarmed state—without his superior intelligence—his supreme weapon—man could not have survived. In its turn, his tactical weakness must have stimulated his cunning, forcing it to develop until from the defensive existence of the hunted he was able to assume the offensive life of the hunter. As Thomas Carlyle has written: "Savage Animalism is nothing, inventive Spiritualism is all."[5] Therefore, I think, Bergson is right in ascribing the appearance of man—the human being—"to the period when the first weapons, the first tools, were made." And Carlyle is of the same opinion when in *Sartor Resartus* he makes his imaginary professor say: "Man is a Tool-using Animal . . . feeblest of bipeds! Three quintals are a crushing load for him; the Steer of the meadow tosses him aloft, like a waste rag. Nevertheless he can use Tools, can devise Tools: with these the granite mountain melts into light dust before him; he kneads glowing iron, as if it were soft paste; seas are his smooth highway, winds and fire his unwearying steeds. Nowhere do you find him without Tools; without Tools he is nothing, with Tools he is all."[6]

What, then, was his first tool and weapon?—for in the beginning industry and war were one, as, to-day, they are once again verging towards unity. With Lewis Mumford, many suppose "the first efficient tool . . . to have been a stone held in the human hand as a hammer."[7] Yet there is a possible alternative. Did the discovery of making fire precede that of the stone hand-hammer? Or again, did Thor and Prometheus descend from heaven arm in arm?—for to strike certain stones together is the simplest way of producing a spark. As Dr. Nicolai writes: "Not domestic animals but fire it is which makes man lord of the world. When man

first caused the solar energy stored up in plants to explode
and catch fire, he opened up for himself a novel source of
power, and this lent such an extraordinary impetus to the
conversion of energy that we are quite entitled to speak of
things in general having taken a new turn, and to date the
mastery of Nature from the kindling of the first fire."[8]
Mumford writes much the same: "Prometheus, the fire-
bringer, stands at the beginning of man's conquest: for fire
not merely made possible the easier digestion of foods, but
its flames kept off predatory animals, and around the warmth
of it, during the colder seasons of the year, an active social
life became possible, beyond the mere huddle and vacuity
of the winter's sleep."[9]

There is yet a third alternative. For tens of thousands of
years jungle-man must have watched burrowing animals,
such as rabbits, emerging from and seeking shelter in their
holes. His more likely way of killing them would be to seize
them as they crept out. This may have led to his digging
holes with his hands or with sea shells, stones and bits of
bone or of broken wood in order to trap his prey.

Thus we have three possible tool or weapon origins—
the hammer, fire and the spade. Which can claim priority
we cannot say, yet all three—to strike, to burn and to
snare—have since their beginnings been steadily and progressively developed in war.

Once tools and weapons came into being, it is not possible
to imagine any tribe or race of men remaining for long
unarmed, for without weapons its members would have been
rapidly exterminated. This means that to be armed was to be
endowed with a survival value, a condition which still holds
good, and which, as we shall see, has profoundly influenced
history.

Further, once tribes were armed—that is, tooled—law
and order within them could be enforced. As Machiavelli
wrote: "There cannot be good laws where there are not
good arms, and where there are good arms there must be
good laws."[10] In other words, the weapon was the originator
of police power, and to prevent the policeman revolting

against the order he protected, the laws upon which it was based had to be acceptable to him. Thus, by means of weapon power rather than through agriculture, we find man stepping on to the road to civilization—towards the establishment of a law-abiding and not merely a food-producing society.

For ages on end agricultural implements and weapons of war must have remained identical. Nor was this identity confined to the most primitive conditions of culture, for in the Book of Samuel we read: "Now there was no smith found throughout all the land of Israel: for the Philistines said, Lest the Hebrews make them swords or spears: but all the Israelites went down to the Philistines, to sharpen every man his share, and his coulter, and his axe, and his mattock."[11] Thus was the army of Saul and of Jonathan armed.

Many parallels to this are to be found up to the present day, for in 1940, when the great invasion scare swept England, in its earlier stage farm labourers and others armed themselves with pitchfork, axe and bill-hook to settle with German paratroops should they descend.

A typical example of the arming of a popular rising is that of the short-lived yet highly dramatic rebellion of Masaniello against the Government of Naples in 1647. Of it we read: "The soldiers march'd with their drawn swords, their muskets and arquebuses cock'd, and arm'd likewise with lances and targets . . . the country people thronged into the town in great multitudes . . . armed with plough-shares, pitchforks, spades, pikes and other implements. . . . Nor were the women . . . backward in their zeal: for they assembled in great numbers, furnished with fire shovels, iron tongs, spits, and other family-instruments. . . . Even the very children were seen with canes and sticks in their hands, threatening the nobility, and urging their fathers to battle."[12]

From this it will be seen that the number of potential weapons is incalculable, for anything which can be brandished or thrown can be used in a fight. Notwithstanding, for practical purposes the bulk of all weapons may be grouped into two primary classes—namely, shock and missile (including their projectors), the former being used for in- and the latter for out-fighting. Of the first, the more common are the club, mace, spear, lance, sword, axe, pike and bayonet, and of the second—the pebble, javelin, arrow, bolt, ball, bullet, bomb and shell. The one may be called individual or single weapons, weapons the force of whose striking power is derived from human muscle; the other, dual weapons, weapons which are propelled by mechanical or chemical energy—tension, torsion and explosion. Though there are certain weapons which fit into neither of these classes, such as the lasso, bolas and blowpipe, the two main secondary groups are: (1) fire, asphyxiants and poisons, and (2) traps, snares, nets and mines. Roughly, the one may be called "chemical weapons" and the other "weapons of stratagem."

The powers and limitations of the majority of these instruments of war, and more particularly of the single and dual weapons, may be classified under the following headings: (1) Range of Action; (2) Striking Power; (3) Accuracy of Aim; (4) Volume of Fire, and (5) Portability.[13] These may be defined as follows:

(1) *Range of Action:* The greater the reach or range of a weapon, the more speedily can striking power be brought into play.

(2) *Striking Power:* The greater the striking power of a weapon, the more effective will be the blow struck.

(3) *Accuracy of Aim:* The more accurately a weapon can be aimed—that is, thrown or projected—the more likely is it that the target will be hit.

(4) *Volume of Fire:* The more the number of blows dealt or missiles thrown or projected in a given time, the greater the effect is likely to be.

(5) *Portability:* The more easily a weapon can be carried, hauled or moved, handled or wielded, the more rapidly will it be brought into use.*

---

* A friendly writer has suggested to me that these definitions elucidate the obvious. The points are not, alas, obvious to all soldiers, as the history of armaments clearly proves. For example: when I joined the army in 1898 the Maxim gun was in the tenth year of its adoption. Its range was

Of these, the first may be called the dominant characteristic—that is, the characteristic which dominates the fight. Therefore the parts played by all other weapons should be related to the dominant one. Otherwise put, the weapon of superior reach or range should be looked upon as the fulcrum of combined tactics. Thus, should a group of fighters be armed with bows, spears and swords, it is around the arrow that tactics should be shaped: if with cannon, muskets and pikes, then around the cannon; and if with aircraft, artillery and rifles, then around the airplane.

The dominant weapon is not necessarily the more powerful, the more accurate, the more blow-dealing, or the more portable; it is the weapon which, on account of its superior range, can be brought into action first, and under the protective cover of which all other weapons, according to their respective powers and limitations, can be brought into play. Further, the higher its striking power, accuracy of aim, volume of fire and portability are, the more dominant will the weapon be. Thus, to-day, because of all weapons the air-carried bomb possesses the superior range, and because

equal to that of the Lee-Metford rifle, its striking power equal, its accuracy equal, its volume of fire thirty times as great. In every respect it was superior except in portability (Axiom 5). So what did the soldier do—what was self-evident to him? A gun-carriage weighing 4 cwts. (448 lbs.!) with wheels 4 ft. 8 in. in diameter! At Paardeberg we got three gun teams wiped out in ten minutes, and all because the soldier during the past ten years could not see a self-evident truth—an axiom.

In 1867 the Ordnance Committee suddenly woke up and invented a new cannon. It was a small piece, and how did they mount it (portability)? They strapped it broadside on the back of a horse, and then tested their invention. The horse was tied to a post, the committee standing on one side. The fuse was lit, whereupon the horse, somewhat startled, turned round, pointing the muzzle at the heads of the interested spectators. Thus, writes Sir John Adye: "Not a moment was to be lost; down went the chairman and members, lying flat and low on their stomachs. The gun went off, the shot passed over the town of Woolwich, and fell in the Dockyard; the horse was found lying on its back several yards away. The committee were fortunately unhurt, and gradually recovered their equilibrium, but reported unanimously against any further trial."

Now, in 1900, had we had the horse to strap our Maxim on, and in 1867 had the Ordnance Committee had our 448-lb. gun carriage, the axiom, so self-evident to any sane man, would have been self-evident to two generations of soldiers; but it wasn't, hence my Borax-like definitions.

its striking power is enormous and its portability easy, it is the dominant weapon. Set against these powers are the following limitations: the low accuracy of aim and low volume of fire of the airplane as a projector. The second of these is due to the limit of the bomb load, because the airplane, once its bombs have been "fired," has to return to its base to reload. Could these limitations be surmounted, then the airplane would become what may be called "a master weapon"—that is, a weapon which monopolizes fighting power. From time to time such weapons have appeared, but their effective reign has been generally short. Thus we shall see that Greek Fire, the cannon, the ironclad ship and the rifle have, in certain circumstances, either attained or closely approached this ideal.

These characteristics of weapon power should be borne in mind when tactics are considered—that is, the combined use of weapons. This use introduces the problem of protection, of holding—ability to stand firm or to halt—and of movement.

Being hairless and virtually hideless, of all animals man is the least well protected, and as for a vastly longer period of time he was the hunted and not the hunter, his protective problem must for long have predated the invention of weapons.

By making himself invisible, by seeking his food at night time, by living in caves and trees, by developing his voice, using yells and then words as moral weapons, and by clothing himself in skins, suggest themselves as his first protective means.

As his condition was one of perpetual wardom he had to be in a constant state of readiness to fight and, therefore, to live in a permanently protected order. His first village was, therefore, a fort built in a swamp, on an island, on the margin of a lake, or on a hill-top. Later he banked his settlements in, built castles, fortresses, Great Walls of China and Maginot Lines. He did these things so that he might stand firm and thereby hold off his enemy until his food was exhausted or until he himself was ready to fight. Thus, the inaccessible village, the moated settlement, the walled city and eventually the fortified country became not only his bases of war but also centres of his civilization.

This protective idea is also carried into the field: first, no doubt, in the form of a stick or branch or raw hide, used to ward off blows, and later, when implements appear, in the fashioning of shields, helmets and ultimately body armour, until we arrive at the medieval man-at-arms armoured *cap-à-pie*—the human armadillo or lobster—and later on the tank.

It needs no argument to prove that, should other things be equal, a man armed with a sword alone is no match for an opponent armed with sword and shield. This simply means that protected offensive power is superior to unprotected offensive power. It is only necessary to carry this truism a step further, in order to appreciate that, when a body of men replaces the individual fighter, should it be organized into two groups, the one offensive and the other defensive, the latter may be formed into a protected base for the former to operate from—that is, a harbour to set out from and to return to. Thus is established the primary tactical division between the fighters: they are divided into those who can better deliver blows and those who can better withstand them. The one hits, the other holds; the one moves, the other stands firm.

As reach or range is the dominant characteristic of an offensive weapon, speed and mobility in attack are the dominant characteristics of the offensive itself. Thus, to quote General Lloyd:

"The first problem in tactics should be this: how a given number of men ought to be ranged so that they may move and act with the greatest velocity; for in this chiefly depends the success of all military operations.

"An army superior in activity can always anticipate the motions of a less rapid enemy, and bring more men into action than they can at any given point, though inferior in number. This must generally prove decisive and ensure success."[14]

The first radical change in mobility came with the taming of the horse, and its use in war either to haul chariots and supply vehicles or to carry a rider. As we shall see, this innovation revolutionized warfare, for it placed in the hands of the war chief two different forces of fighters, a mobile force wherewith to exert pressure and a stable force wherewith to resist it. From this development eventually sprang another; the mobile force was divided into two bodies, a finding and a shock group, and the stable also into two bodies, a holding and a protective group. Until recently these groups were represented by light cavalry, heavy cavalry, infantry and artillery; to-day by aircraft, tanks, infantry and artillery, including flying artillery—bombers.

Movement has been called "the soul of war," which is true, for movement is to organization what range is to weapon power—it is the governing element. Thus, when the energy from which military movements were derived was generated by muscle power, because the muscular energy of the horse was greater than that of man, tactical organization was built around that animal. This remained true so long as the range and volume of fire of missile weapons were limited, and it was not until the introduction of the rifled musket that the holding power of infantry became so great that cavalry movements were immobilized. When this occurred, as it did during the nineteenth century, tactical organization became decadent. It was based not on power to move but on ability to hit; therefore volume of fire became the be-all and end-all of the military organizer.

The advent of the internal combustion engine introduced a new source of energy, many times superior to that of man or horse. And, from a military point of view, what was equally important was the invention of the endless chain track, for it enabled the internal-combustion-engine-driven vehicle to move in all directions over a comparatively smooth earth surface. Coupled with the ability to carry armour, a bullet-proof horse, called a tank, was created, and as its power of movement was greater than that of the foot soldier, the whole of existing military organization should have been modelled around it. Thus, had the military organizer followed this pivotal idea, long before the Second World War was unleashed he would have designed not only tanks—combat bullet-proof cross-country vehicles—but also cross-country supply vehicles. He would not merely have thought of hauling artillery by means of tractors, armoured or unarmoured; but, instead, he would have mounted his guns on bullet-proof tracked vehicles. Further, he would have moved his infantry in somewhat similar vehicles. In short, he would have fashioned his new model army round the internal combustion engine, armour and the caterpillar track, as armies of the muscle age of war had been fashioned round the horse, armour and the wheel.

As we shall see, this was not done, because it was not realized that movement is the master element in organization.

Such, in brief, are the ingredients of armament—the power and limitations of weapons and the organizations in which they are expressed. Therefore from them I will now turn to the general influence of armament on history.

In this problem the first point to appreciate is that civilizations are cyclical and repetitive. Though each possesses an individuality of its own, each passes through similar phases of birth, growth, decay and disintegration, in each of which war plays a dominant part.[15] As Quincy Wright has pointed out: "While animal war has required hundreds of thousands of years to register important evolutionary changes, civilized war has produced marked changes in the course of centuries —changes which have been registered in the stages of the civilization. These changes caused by war have reciprocally influenced the character of war. Thus civilized war has been correlated primarily with the stages of the civilization in which it takes place. All civilizations have indulged in similar types of war when young, when middle-aged, and when old. The primary function of war has apparently been to assure these successions in the life of a civilization."[16]

First, war unifies a people, lastly it disintegrates them. So long as it is the instrument of change, like a plough it tears up the social soil and thereby creates a more fertile field for change to germinate in. Consequently, the longer and more destructive a war is, the greater are the changes which follow it. But when each change is succeeded by a greater war, finally a state of wardom is established in which the military mind dominates. Then policy becomes the instrument of war, for as Mumford points out: "In the act of making himself a master, the soldier helps create a race of slaves."[17] Change—that is, growth—is at an end, decay sets in, to be followed by disintegration. Such is the warp upon which armaments are woven.

From the cycles of civilization I will turn to history, a continuous and endless story in which these cycles are but chapters, and by examining it I will attempt to show the influence played by armament throughout its course.

In perusing history as a whole, or any historical period, the first thing noticeable is that events are woven on a dual theme—peace and war. Further, that, with few exceptions, peace is little more than a period of incubation and preparation for war. This has been noticed by many historians and philosophers, and notably so by William James. "Every up-to-date dictionary," he writes, "should say that 'peace' and 'war' mean the same thing, now *in posse*, now *in actu*. It may even reasonably be said that the intensely sharp competitive *preparation* for war by the nation *is the real war*, permanent, unceasing; and that battles are only a sort of public verification of mastery gained during the 'peace' intervals."[18]

The second thing which strikes us is that the character of war changes with civil progress and beliefs, as they develop from out of the central idea in each cultural cycle. Thus, during medieval times war was circumscribed by religion, the central fact in which was the spiritual world, whereas to-day it is circumscribed by science, the central fact in which is the material world.

The third thing which strikes us, though at first not so obviously, is that as war is changed by civil progress, so also is civil progress changed by war—there is a reciprocal action between them. Further, that war is the one permanent factor in its changings, for whether the period under examination be predominantly religious, commercial or industrial, and whatever its political and social systems may be, war is never absent. It is possible to have all manner of societies—theocratic, atheistic, plutocratic, communistic, democratic, autocratic, etc., but so far it has not been found possible to have a warless society. Again, whereas religious, political, economic and moral systems not only change, but at times vanish in their entirety, though military systems also change, war is never annihilated. Except for brief periods of lassitude, the evolution of the weapons and means of war has been continuous and progressive. Further, the inventiveness which has always been stimulated by war has gone far to foster culture. On this point Mumford says: "How far shall we go back in demonstrating the fact that war has been the chief propagator of the machine?"[19]

As we glance over the records of man's activities, periods of peace and war follow one another in rapid and regular succession. Normally they represent but the roughs and smooths on the surface of the social ocean, yet, now and again, a sudden tornado of conflict is met with: a world crisis, revolutionary in its results. These world storms are not only due to the birth of some new religious, economic or social idea, but at times also to some fresh acquisition in the munitions of war. Thus, according to Peake and Fleure, in all probability the great crisis in Europe which occurred between the fifteenth and thirteenth centuries B.C. was due to the arrival from Central Asia of the horse and the sword.

According to these two historians, at the beginning of the second millennium B.C., the copper dagger in use in the Ægean region gave birth to the dirk, a longer weapon, and from the Ægean it spread throughout Central Europe. "The dirk was of obvious value to the pedestrian, but on horseback a slashing weapon would be more useful, and we think that it was somewhere among the horse-riding men of the later Bronze Age that the dirk gave birth to the sword."[20]

What caused the great outpouring of warriors from the

steppe-lands into India, Europe, Mesopotamia, Egypt, and probably also into China is not known. One hypothesis is that it was due to climatic changes, and another that these warriors "had acquired the use of the horse and that, when they had combined this with a knowledge of metal, their power of conquering and organizing settled cultivators was immensely increased. . . . In support of the second suggestion there is the evidence of the spread of the horse into India, Mesopotamia, Egypt and Europe. . . .

"The advent of the horse into Egypt seems to be associated with a change in the character of that country from that of a self-contained economy to that of the widespread empire, with strong military and commercial activities, that developed under Hatshepsut and Thutmose. The consequent exchanges of thought led on, apparently, to the famous attempt of Ikhn-aton to found a universal religion. . . .

"The rise of the mounted spearmen and swordsmen in Central Europe led to the supersession of the hammer or battle-axe, which had been the typical weapon of the steppe-landers who had dominated a mining area in Slovakia for a considerable time. The new weapons used by horsemen seem to have opened up larger possibilities of conquest and organization, and the Hungarian basin of the Danube became a veritable melting-pot of cultures. . . ."[21]

Though much of this, largely based as it is on archæological discoveries, is conjectural, when compared to analogous world crises it carries with it conviction. Thus, as we shall see, it was the armament of the Macedonians coupled with the genius of Alexander the Great which, by overthrowing the Persian Empire in the fourth century B.C., led to the emergence of the Hellenistic cultural period, which, when Rome conquered what to-day is represented by the Middle East, profoundly influenced her destiny. Again, as we shall see five centuries later, it was the armament of the Goths which was one of the main factors in the extinction of the Western Empire. Later still, that it was the armament of the Eastern (Byzantine) Empire which secured its existence until 1453, when yet a new weapon not only proclaimed its end, but also the end of medieval civilization throughout Europe. Finally, when we step into the present century, we shall see that, once again, it was a change in armament which radically revolutionized the art of war, and at this moment is creating social, political and economic problems which seem likely to transform the whole of existing civilization.

If war, then, which at bottom is a question of armaments, has been the grand catalytic in history, well may it be asked, are there such things as laws, principles or general rules which govern the development of weapon power? This question I will now examine.

Because weapons are material things, their development is at bottom an industrial and scientific problem, a problem both of quantity and of quality. Thus, should two opposing forces be armed with identical weapons, then, other things being equal, the more numerous will overwhelm the less numerous. This mathematical principle, we shall see, fitted the democratic age—the century following the French Revolution—and was the main factor in the growth of mass armies. It has been expressed by Mr. Lanchester in his " N-Square Law." "The fighting strengths of two forces," he writes, "are equal when the square of the numerical strength multiplied by the fighting value of the individual units are equal." Therefore, " . . . the fighting strength of a force may be broadly defined as proportional to the square of its numerical strength multiplied by the fighting value of its individual units. . . ."

"As an example of the above," he writes, "let us assume an army of 50,000 giving battle in turn to two armies of 40,000 and 30,000 respectively, equally well armed; then the strengths are equal, since $(50,000)^2 = (40,000)^2 + (30,000)^2$. If, on the other hand, the two smaller armies are given time to effect a junction, then the army of 50,000 will be overwhelmed, for the fighting strength of the opposing force, 70,000, is no longer equal, but is, in fact, nearly twice as great—namely, in the relation of 39 to 25."[22]

The second part of the problem it would appear was first

clearly expressed by Friedrich Engels, and, in spite of his
Socialism, its character is aristocratic; for, according to
him, quality beats quantity and not merely a greater quantity
a lesser, therefore it fits well into an autocratic age. He set out
to show "that force is no mere act of will but calls for very
real conditions before it starts to work, in particular tools, of
which the perfect one overcomes the imperfect one; that
furthermore these tools must be produced, which means at
the same time that the producer of more perfect tools,
vulgo arms, beats the producer of more imperfect ones."[23]

This truism draws directly from the five weapon characteristics listed earlier in this study; yet, so far as I am aware,
Engels is the first to set it down as the fundamental principle
in weapon production. Though, obviously, since weapons
were first used, it was realized that a good weapon is to be
preferred to a bad, before his day, weapon progress largely
depended on accident or individual genius—civil more so
than military—far more so than on corporative scientific
study. "It should seem," writes Lord Bacon, "that hitherto
men are rather beholden to a wild goat for surgery, or to a
nightingale for music, or to the ibis for some part of physic,
or to the pot-lid that flew open for artillery, or generally to
chance, or anything else, than to logic for the invention of
the Arts and Sciences."

Were it not for man's unprogressiveness, it would be
inexplicable that, though so important a military invention
as the bridle bit dates from the early Bronze Age, if not still
farther back, saddles were unknown in Europe until the
fourth century A.D., and then remained without stirrups
until the reign of the Emperor Maurice (A.D. 582-602).

Generally speaking, it is only during war-time that a
difficulty, which could well have been foreseen, awakens the
soldier's inventive genius. And then, as often as not, once
the danger has passed the invention is forgotten. Thus, as
an example: In 54 B.C. the Britons used hot clay balls to
fire Cæsar's camp:[24] in A.D. 69 igneous missiles were employed in the attack on Placentia;[25] in the year 630, when
Mahomet lay siege to Tayif, the defenders had recourse to

burning arrows;
greek fire

heated projectiles;[26] in 1579 Stephen Bathory, King of Poland, introduced red-hot cannon shot,[27] and in 1782 d'Arcon's floating batteries and a great part of the Spanish fleet were destroyed by red-hot shot fired from the batteries of Gibraltar. Nevertheless, so far as I am aware, incendiary projectiles were not recognized as a permanent weapon of war until the advent of aircraft.

During the First World War this haphazard and unforeseeing procedure struck me so forcibly that I set down my views on weapon development in an official paper entitled *The Secret of Victory*.[28] In it I wrote:

"Tools, or weapons, if only the right ones can be discovered, form 99 per cent. of victory. . . . Strategy, command, leadership, courage, discipline, supply, organization and all the moral and physical paraphernalia of war are nothing to a high superiority of weapons—at most they go to form the one per cent. which makes the whole possible. . . .

"In war, especially in modern wars, wars in which weapons change rapidly, one thing is certain: no army of 50 years before any date selected would stand 'a dog's chance' against the army existing at that date. . . . Consider the following examples:

"(1) Napoleon was an infinitely greater General than Lord Raglan; yet Lord Raglan would, in 1855, have beaten any army Napoleon could have led against him, because Lord Raglan's men were armed with the Minié rifle.

"(2) Eleven years after Inkerman, Moltke would have beaten Lord Raglan's army hollow, not because he was a greater soldier than Lord Raglan, but because his men were armed with the needle gun.

.   .   .   .

"During the present war we have had a series of vivid pictures thrust under our noses in such rapid succession and so close to our eyes that it is extremely doubtful whether many of us have read aright what they portend—namely, that it is machine-power and not man-power which wins in war . . . that war is primarily a matter of weapons, and that the side which can improve its weapons the more rapidly is the side which is going to win."

In spite of this truism, so unscientifically minded were the English and French that, between the years 1919-1939, little attempt was made to mould their respective armies round it. In 1940 the result was Dunkirk and the collapse of France.

Even had the British alone possessed a small quality army of but a third the size of the quantity army they sent to France, the probabilities are that there would have been no Dunkirk, and the possibilities are there might well have been a German Sedan. But had the British had a quantity army several times larger than the one they landed, though the *débâcle* of France might have been delayed, it is highly unlikely that it would have been altogether prevented.[29]

The reason for this lack of foresight was that, between the two wars, the development of French and British military power was unscientific: (1) Because it was not appreciated that war is endemic in Western civilization, and (2) that, apparently, the French and English General Staffs were oblivious of the fact that throughout history the evolution of weapons has been governed by a law which I will call the law of military development.

It is common knowledge that man is influenced by his surroundings, and that should he consciously fail to adapt himself to them, unconsciously he will be adapted by them. This knowledge is generalized in the law of evolution, which simply means that those who adapt themselves the more rapidly and perfectly to material, intellectual, moral and physical changes, more readily survive. In the life history of military organizations, which are corporate entities, it is the same: civilization is environment, and armies must adapt themselves to its changing phases in order to remain fitted for war.[30]

When civilization depended upon brigandage more so than on trade, as it did in early medieval times, and when roads were few and generally unfit for wheeled traffic, military power was founded on mounted troops. When this epoch was succeeded by a more stable agricultural one, infantry became the dominant arm. Lastly, after the industrial revolution set in, as manufacture grew and grew, and because it is based on science and inventions, it was a foregone conclusion that, to survive in war, armies would have to follow suit and become more and more mechanized. That they did not was due to lethargy and routine.

From this law may be deduced a principle I will call the Constant Tactical Factor, which is: every improvement in weapon-power has aimed at lessening the danger on one side by increasing it on the other. Therefore every improvement in weapons has eventually been met by a counter-improvement which has rendered the improvement obsolete: the evolutionary pendulum of weapon-power, slowly or rapidly, swinging from the offensive to the protective and back again in harmony with the pace of civil progress; each swing in a measurable degree eliminating danger. Thus, in the days of the stone age, when progress stood all but at a standstill, weapon development was proportionately slow, and may be said to have been always up to date. To-day, conditions are diametrically reversed, for civil progress is so intense that there is not only a danger but a certainty that no army in peace-time can in the full sense be kept up to date. This means that in war-time evolution will be extremely rapid, and, therefore, that the army which is mentally the better prepared to meet tactical changes will possess an enormous advantage over all others.

As an example of this, it is only necessary to quote the astonishing German campaigns which preceded the invasion of Russia in 1941. They were not won by mass armies, but instead by, comparatively speaking, small forces of highly offensive troops. Thus, in the most decisive of them—namely, that against France—the Germans would appear to have employed no more than ten armoured divisions, and there can be no question that they were the main cause of the French collapse. This in part is corroborated by the insignificance of the German casualties, which were reported to be 27,074 killed, 111,034 wounded and 18,384 missing:

a total of 156,492, or less by over two-thirds those sustained by the British during the battle of the Somme in 1916.

From the offensive to the defensive and then back again to the offensive is the normal rhythm in tactical development, and it is this rhythm which has always had the profoundest influence in shaping history. As Quincy Wright and others have pointed out, superiority of attack over defence has favoured political unification, whereas superiority of defence over offence has led to political disintegration. Further, by prolonging a war the defensive has increased destructiveness, not only physical but also moral. And finally, "the importance of success in war in the survival of states has tended to spread military discipline and organization by conquest and imitation throughout the civilization,"[31] until eventually a condition of international wardom is established, in which the staple industry is the production of arms. When this finality is reached, war from a means to an end becomes the end itself. Its survival value passes into a death value, and, morally and politically, victor and vanquished immolate each other on the selfsame altar invoking the selfsame god.

REFERENCES

1. *On War*, Carl von Clausewitz (English Translation, 1908), vol. i, pp. 84, 85.

2. *A Study of War*, Quincy Wright (1942), vol. i, p. 501.

3. *Ibid.*, vol. i, p. 291.

4. *The Art of Fighting* (1920), p. 12.

5. *Sartor Resartus*, chap. viii.

6. *Ibid.*, chap. v.

7. *Technics and Civilization* (English Edition, 1934), p. 65. He adds: "The German word for fist is *die Faust*, and to this day the miner's hammer is called *ein Faüstel.*"

8. *The Biology of War*, Dr. G. F. Nicolai (1919) pp. 52-53.

9. *Technics and Civilization*, Lewis Mumford, p. 37.

10. *The Prince*, Niccolo Machiavelli, chap. xii.

11. 1 Samuel xiii, 19-20.

12. *The History of the Surprising Rise and Sudden Fall of Masaniello the Fisherman of Naples* (n.d., seventeenth century), p. 38.

13. So far as I am aware, Lord Bacon is the first to consider weapon power scientifically. In his essay "Of Vicissitude o Things," he writes: "The conditions of weapons and their improvements are, first, the fetching

afar off; for that outruns the danger, as it is seen in ordnance and musketry. Secondly, the strength of the percussion. . . . The third is, the commodious use of them, as, that they may serve in all weathers, that the carriage may be light and manageable, and the like."

14. *History of the Late War in Germany*, General Henry Lloyd (1790), part ii, p. 2.

15. See in particular Oswald Spengler's *Decline of the West*, and Professor Arnold J. Toynbee's *A Study of History*.

16. *A Study of War*, Quincy Wright, vol. i, p. 126.

17. *Technics and Civilization*, Lewis Mumford, p. 95.

18. *Memories and Studies*, William James (1911) p. 273.

19. *Technics and Civilization*, Lewis Mumford, p. 86.

20. *The Horse and the Sword*, Harold Peake and Herbert John Fleure (1933), p. 86. (See also the *Cambridge Ancient History*, vol. i, pp. 107-109, vol. ii, p. 227.)

21. *Ibid.*, pp. 143-145.

22. *Aircraft in Warfare: The Dawn of the Fourth Arm*, Frederick William Lanchester (1916), pp. 28, 36.

23. Quoted by Alfred Vagts, *A History of Militarism* (1938), p. 227.

24. *De Bello Gallico*, Caius Julius Cæsar, book v, 43.

25. *The History*, Tacitus, book ii, 21.

26. *Life of Mahomet*, Sir William Muir (1858), p. 432.

27. *The Origin of Artillery*, Lieut.-Colonel Henry W. L. Hime (1915), p. 173.

28. *Weekly Tank Notes*, January 25, 1919. (See also *On Future Warfare*, J. F. C. Fuller, 1928, chap vii.)

29. I have been criticized because before the war I advocated a small army in place of the mass armies of 1914-1918. Certainly I did, but not a small army only, instead a small *mechanized* army, which makes all the difference. When a soldier sets out to propose the type of army required for the next war, rightly he considers the opening phase of that war, and not those which, because of the non-acceptance of his ideas, follow it.

30. As Spengler points out: ". . . in every Culture, the technique of war hesitatingly followed the advance of craftsmanship, until at the beginning of the Civilization it suddenly takes the lead, presses all mechanical possibilities of the time relentlessly into its purpose, and under pressure of military necessity even opens up new domains hitherto unexploited . . ." (*The Decline of the West*, English Edition, 1928, vol. ii, p. 420). N.B.—According to Spengler, civilization is the last phase of a culture.

31. *A Study of War*, Quincy Wright, vol. i, p. 129.

CHAPTER II

THE AGE OF VALOUR

WHEN we look back upon Western warfare as it was before
the introduction of firearms, of the differences we see, the
one which most boldly stands out is the precedence of
valour over cunning. It is out of valour that European
history rises: the spear and sword, and not, as in Asia, the
bow and arrow, are its symbols.

The bravest and not the most crafty are the leaders of
men, and it is their example rather than their skill which
dominates battle. Fighting is a contest between man and
man more so than between brain and brain. The spearman
Achilles, and not Paris the archer, is the typical hero. Psychologically the *arme blanche* dominates the missile, and, as
generations pass along their way, out of this dominance
emerges Western idealism and finally realism, when Paris
comes into his own.

On the one hand we have the religion of the sword, and on
the other the politics of the bow: aristocracy and democracy;
quality and quantity; castle and city; warrior and merchant;
soldier and artisan; priest and politician, and many other
antagonistic associations related to these two weapons
through the moral values they instil.

Here, however, I intend to restrict myself to the influence
of armament during the first half of this romantic age—that
is, from the dawn of Classical warfare to the sunset of the
Western Roman Empire. And, in so long a period, I can do
no more than touch upon the salient influences of weapons
and military organization upon history.

It opens with the palisaded village, which, growing into
the walled city, established an agricultural city state. Wars
between these city communities were frequent, and as the
cities, because of their walls, were all but invulnerable,
warfare in this age centred in the attack and defence of their
food supplies. In fact, whichever side won literally garnered

the harvest; therefore warfare was restricted to a few months each year, winter operations being unknown.

In this warfare armies were citizen levies, and as training had to be of the simplest, therefore also tactics; and the simplest of tactical formations is the hoplite phalanx, a deep line of armoured heavy infantry armed with shield and spear. In one compact body this line marched straight forward to engage. The attack was, therefore, in parallel order, and was a test of endurance rather than of skill. Thus Greek fought Greek up to the battle of Marathon in 490 B.C., after which some semblance of tactics was developed.

This type of warfare was brought to its highest perfection by the Spartans, who established their state on a military footing. By law the citizen soldier was required "to conquer or die."[1] To him war was a festival, and battle a competition of courage. The place of honour was in the front rank, as Tyrtæus acclaims in one of his war songs:

"Glorious indeed is death in the front rank of the combat, when the brave man falls fighting for his country."[2]

Each Spartan soldier was accompanied by a shield bearer, for his equipment weighed some 72 lbs. At the battle of Platæa, in 479 B.C., the hoplite had seven helots, or serfs, who formed the rear ranks, making the depths of the phalanx eight in all. These men clubbed to death the enemy wounded,[3] and attended to their masters should they be injured. In order to maintain line of battle, the hoplites kept step to the music of flute-players.[4]

In these ceremonial battles, tactics were concentrated in push of pikes, and remained so until light troops were added to the phalanx. And had it not been for the religion of valour, there can be little doubt that this would have been done from the start. Yet, even so late as the Peloponnesian War (431-404 B.C.), except among the northern semi-Greek tribes, light troops were held in disdain.[5] Nevertheless, in 426 B.C. the Athenians under Demosthenes were severely defeated by Ætolian javelin men who, refusing to close, destroyed the phalanx from a distance.[6]

Through force of circumstances this change was, however,

imminent, for early in the fourth century B.C. the Athenian General Iphicrates raised a true body of light infantry called peltasts, and trained them for rapid movements. They wore a quilted or leather jerkin and carried shield, javelins and sword. In 390 B.C. he proved their worth by all but annihilating a Spartan *mora* (battalion).[7]

It is strange that the Athenians, a mercantile people, should have been so slow in creating this essential arm, for their cunning equalled their valour. Also for long past they had maintained a highly efficient body of naval bowmen,[8] recruited from the second richest class, those not wealthy enough to keep a horse. During the Peloponnesian War these archers were so successfully employed in sea raids on Sparta that, according to Thucydides,[9] the Spartans, in order to meet them, "took the unusual step of raising four hundred horse and a force of archers."

When, during the first two decades of the fifth century B.C., the Persian invasions of Greece were launched, first by Darius Hystaspes and secondly by Xerxes, the sole true cavalry soldiers in Greece were the Thessalian. They played no part in these wars, for they were completely outclassed by the Persian cavalry.[10]

In spite of the mountainous nature of their country, it is strange that the Greeks should have been so backward in this arm; for twenty years earlier, in 511 B.C., the Spartans had experienced its value and to their cost, for they had been defeated by Thessalian horsemen not far from Athens.[11] According to Delbrück, "the whole course of the Persian Wars was determined by the Greek fear of Persian horsemen."[12]

The point to note in this brief summary of Greek warfare is that changes in armament are due solely to compulsion, because, throughout, valour looked with disdain upon inventiveness. Only in siege operations, which during the earlier half of the Classical Age improved little on what is recorded in the Book of Ezekiel,[13] do we find play given to imagination. Thus, at the siege of Platæa, in 429 B.C., the Platæans used fire arrows to burn the besiegers' engines;[14]

at the siege of Delium a gas attack with sulphur fumes was made;[15] and, in 413 B.C., it would appear that the Syracusans defended their walls with liquid fire.[16]

Had the intelligence of the soldier not been so completely exorcised by valour, through a rational development of weapons and tactical organization Sparta might have changed the course of history.[17] Instead, this task was left to a small, obscure and semi-barbaric people under two kings of supreme intelligence and valour. They were Philip II of Macedon and his son Alexander the Great.

Though it would appear that Dionysius I (430-367 B.C.), tyrant of Sicily, was the first among the Greeks to organize a combined fighting force, it was not until his contemporary, Philip II of Macedonia (382-336 B.C.), a man of incomparably greater genius, set out to do the same that the first scientifically organized army appeared on the continent of Europe.

That he accomplished what he did is an outstanding example that history, as Carlyle says, "is at bottom the History of the Great Men": for Macedonia, a poor country, was mainly peopled by peasants and shepherds, and its wealthy class was too small to furnish many hoplites.

Denied quantity of suitable man power, Philip aimed at quality instead. His first step was to create a small *standing* army recruited from his own subjects. With it he was able to break away from the summer rule, and so, chronologically at least, make war total by waging it all the year round. Also, this army was a totally new instrument, for though its arms differed little from those in common use, Philip scientifically arranged them into a combined fighting force.

He placed the phalanx on a new tactical footing. From a shock arm he converted it into a holding force, and in part or whole armed its hoplites with the *sarissa*, a pike probably 13 feet in length,[18] and therefore nearly twice as long as the heavy infantry spear. This not only gave the phalanx greater reach, but multiplied the "volume" of spear heads it could bring to bear to its front. Therefore it vastly increased its power to resist and to press, though it made it less mobile, which, however, was of small account, seeing that it was not asked to charge at the run.

The principles upon which the traditional phalanx was based were: (1) depth to give it weight, and (2) length to enable it to overlap its enemy, and so outflank him. The second of these principles Philip scrapped, as he clearly recognized the weaknesses in the phalangial order. These were: The difficulty of keeping in line on the move, and that confusion is the deadliest enemy of the phalanx.[19] The impossibility of rapidly forming front to a flank, or to pursue in line.[20] The vulnerability of the flanks to attack, more especially by cavalry.

To remedy these weaknesses, Philip hinged his heavy cavalry on to the right of the phalanx, making it his offensive or shock wing. The bulk of his auxiliary cavalry he linked to the left of the pahalanx as a defensive wing. In between the heavy cavalry and the right of the phalanx he interposed a new body of troops, the hypaspists, to protect the left flank of the heavy cavalry when it advanced, and for a similar purpose he drew up his light troops on the right of the cavalry. The whole order was, therefore, both defensive and offensive. Whereas the wings were highly mobile, the centre was as firm as a rock.

His heavy cavalry, the Companion or *Hetairai* (followers), were recruited from the Macedonian aristocracy and armed with the sword and *xyston*, a short cavalry spear used both for hurling and thrusting. The troopers carried a shield and wore heavy armour. They were the first real heavy cavalry in Europe. Also Philip raised a body of lancers (*Sarissaphori*), armed with a light *sarissa*. They were the forerunners of the cataphract cavalry of a later age, and the distant parent of the medieval knights. His auxiliary cavalry was mainly recruited in Thessaly, and was armed and equipped like the Companion Cavalry.

The hypaspists—named after *aspis*, the great shield they carried—formed a standing corps of household infantry guards. They were equipped much like the old hoplites and trained for close combat. They were particularly useful in mountain warfare, forcing a river passage and supporting cavalry.

The light troops were slingers, archers and javelin men. Besides, Philip formed a fully organized siege train of arrow-firing catapults, stone throwers and battering rams—an essential instrument in an age of walled cities.

Looked upon as a whole, Philip's army was a moving fortress. The purpose of the phalanx was to form an impenetrable defensive front until the heavy cavalry issued forth. Also, their purpose was, by shock action, to disrupt the enemy's line, and, normally, not to attack cavalry. This was the duty of the auxiliary horse, as well as to attack the enemy in flank.

Such was the formidable instrument of war his son Alexander (356-323 B.C.) inherited, and with it he conquered the known world of his day, and thereby changed the course of history.

With consummate genius Alexander carried out this task in twelve crowded years. As a statesman and a general he towered above his age, and still to-day stands in a unique position. He won every battle he fought, and took every city he besieged. Both in summer and winter he marched in whatever direction he desired, whether over plains, mountains or deserts. He knew how to exploit victory politically and strategically, and how to combine strategy and policy. He was on the whole a chivalrous combatant and to his men the prince of valour and a master of craft. Yet, without the army he inherited, he could have accomplished nothing. For the first time in history a superb armament was mated to a supreme genius, and together they surmounted every obstacle. Droysen called his army "the first strategic unit known," and he adds, "it carried in itself the certainty of victory,"[21] and because of Alexander.

In the spring of 334 B.C., at the head of 30,000 foot soldiers and 5,000 cavalry,[22] he invaded Asia, and thence onwards to the defeat of Darius at Gaugamela, in 331 B.C., from right to left his normal order of battle was as follows: Light Infantry (javelin men, slingers and bowmen); Com-

panion Cavalry; Hypaspists; Phalanx; Confederate Cavalry
and Thessalian Cavalry.

Cavalry was his dominant arm, and in battle he invariably
led his Companions in person. Of the twenty-two battles he
fought, Denison[23] has estimated that fifteen were decided by
cavalry. And, as a cavalry general, Dodge has written of him:
"Had Alexander not been one of the world's great captains,
he would have been the typical *beau sabreur* of the world's
history."[24]

Second only to his cavalry came the hypaspists and light
troops. As regards the latter, Professor Tarn points out,
before his day they had never been used seriously, and after
it "we seldom hear of their doing anything particular in
battle."[25] Among them the Cretan archers were held in
highest esteem.

In battle, Alexander's phalanx, sixteen ranks deep, played
a subordinate yet important part. Its mission was to maintain the cohesion of the army as a whole, and for its own
defence it relied on the Thessalian and Confederate Cavalry.
By lengthening the line it protected the rear of the right
wing against attack, and its holding power enabled that wing
to operate with calm and assurance. As Rüstow and Köchly
point out: "Alexander would never have dreamed of fighting
with the phalanx only . . . it is the shade in the picture
of a battle fought by Alexander and the right wing in the
light."[26]

Though the catapult was essentially a siege piece, on
several occasions Alexander used it as field artillery. Thus,
in his early Illyrian campaign, he covered the retreat of his
men over a river by " all sorts of projectiles from his
engines."[27] At the crossing of the river Jaxartes (Syr Daria)
he reversed this procedure,[28] and when storming Aornus
(Pir-Sar), he employed his catapults as mountain artillery.[29]
In sieges his engines were used with great effect, notably
so at Tyre, one of the most remarkable sieges in history.
Further, when in India, he organized a pontoon train.[30]

Once he had defeated Darius, faced as he then was by a
different tactical problem—a national uprising instead of

organized resistance—he broke his army up into a number of self-contained columns, and largely increased his light cavalry, light infantry and archers. His small wars against Scythians and hill tribes were as masterly as had been his great battles. He never failed to fit his instrument to the material it had to work on and to the conditions which it had to face.

His system of war was novel because it was common sense. He, it would appear, first discovered the principle "March divided and fight united." Also, he was the first general in Western history to press the pursuit after a great battle, and when occasion demanded he moved with an astonishing speed. Thus, in his pursuit of Darius, he marched 400 miles at an average of 36 miles the day including halts, and in the relief of Maracanda (Samarcand) his column advanced 135 miles in little over 72 hours. To defeat his enemy's army and not merely his cavalry, as later became customary, was always his aim. Once he decided to attack, he never abandoned the offensive until his enemy was routed or destroyed. His campaigns were *blitzkriegs*.

Though the army he bequeathed to his successors, the Diadochi,[31] was organized to police his empire, in their hands it was employed to disrupt it. Wars were no longer fought against undisciplined barbarians, but between similarly organized armies under equal leadership. Though technical improvements were introduced, tactics and morale degenerated. More and more was reliance placed in mercenaries who could be bought and sold; therefore gold began to become a decisive tactical factor. The *sarissa* was considerably lengthened, and the light armed troops were cut down, with the result that when, in 280 B.C., the Gauls inundated Thrace and Macedonia, the Greeks were unable to face them. Further, an increasing reliance was placed on cavalry, but as often as not unrelated to the other arms. Field fortifications crept on to the battlefields; but the greatest innovation of all was the employment of elephants as a shock arm.

This animal, it may be said, established the tactical

problem of the age; but how elephants were combined with infantry and cavalry is not known.

Alexander, for the first time, faced the war-elephant at the battle of Gaugamela, and then again on the Hydaspes (Jhelum) in 327 B.C. Fearing that his horses would not face them, he decided to turn Porus's right flank by crossing the river.[32] It would appear that he judged them at their doubtful worth, for he never employed them in war. Not so his Successors, who used them extensively. So important were they considered to be by Seleucus that he ceded the eastern provinces of Alexander's empire to Chandragupta for a herd of 500, and with them won the decisive battle of Ipsus in 302 B.C.[33]

Generally speaking, their terrors were soon overcome by experienced troops, but frequently, when used for the first time, their moral effect was deadly. For instance, it was with his elephants that Antiochus I first checked the Gauls. This saying of his has been recorded: "I am ashamed to think that we owe our safety to these sixteen animals."[34] At the battle of Raphia, in 217 B.C., Antiochus III's Indian elephants were matched against Ptolemy IV's African, and beat them.[35] Their last serious employment[36] was at Magnesia in 190 B.C., where Antiochus's elephants, becoming unmanageable, threw his army into such confusion as to lead to his defeat. Much the same had happened to Hannibal at Zama in 202 B.C.

Anti-elephant tactics were also developed. Instruments were invented to injure their feet. The most extraordinary device was adopted by the Megareans. They drove against Antigonus's elephants, pigs smeared with pitch and set alight. In order to counteract this, Antigonus ordered his Indian mahouts always to keep swine among the elephants so as to accustom them to this "device."[37]

As in field warfare tactics declined, so also in siege, and in spite of technical improvements. It was lack of siegecraft which mainly accounted for this. Among the Successors, Demetrius alone acquired the reputation of a city taker; yet, in 305 B.C., tactically, he failed in his greatest siege—namely, that of Rhodes.[38] During it the Rhodians fired off 800 flame carriers which burnt Demetrius's armoured towers. At the siege of Thebes, the tower which Demetrius built was so heavy that it took two months to move it two furlongs.[39]

Listening devices for detecting mining and counter-mining had been used as early as the fourth century B.C.[40] Polybius describes one employed by the Ætolians at the siege of Ambracia in 189 B.C. It consisted in a row of thin metal vessels sensitive to the slightest vibration.[41]

The wars of this period had a remarkable influence on history. The vast hoards of gold and silver seized by Alexander in Persia were, in the wars of the Diadochi, set in circulation to fertilize a new civilization, known as the Hellenistic, the intellectual and commercial centre of which was Alexandria. Gold-power was transformed through leisure into brain-power, and, as wars were unceasing, brain-power turned towards military mechanization.

So it came about that, in the century following the death of Alexander, the progress in mechanics was unrivalled for close on 2,000 years. We still have accounts of the engines invented by Heron, 284-221 B.C., Philo, about 200 B.C., and Agesistratus, of the same date. The last mentioned informs us that the artillery of his day could fire missiles up to a range of 800 yards. Dionysius, an Alexandrian engineer, invented a *polybolos*, a machine gun which enabled a succession of arrows to be fired from a magazine.[42] And Ctesibius, another engineer of the same city, discovered a means of gearing to the bow arms of catapults pistons working in "carefully wrought cylinders" which were filled with compressed air.[43] At the battle of Mantinea, 207 B.C., Machanidas, the tyrant of Sparta, advanced with a large number of "carts carrying quantities of field artillery and bolts for the catapults";[44] but Philopœmen, the Achæan general, seeing that the enemy's plan was "by pouring volleys from the catapults into his flanks, to throw the ranks into confusion," brought forward his cavalry and charged the engines.

Thus valour was supplemented by technique, when a people arose in the West who knew better than the Hellenistic Greeks how to combine the two. This people emerged from out of the city of Rome to reap in full the cultural crop sown by Alexander and his Successors.

The Romans were a highly patriotic people, eager to subordinate themselves to the State. Those who belonged to one of the original family clans were burgesses of Rome, and their most important duty was military service, for they alone had the right to bear arms. They formed the "spear-armed body of warriors upon whom the blessing of Mars was invoked." And as service in war was the sole road to civic honours, these men of valour, as a military caste, shaped the character of the Roman people. Of them Livy wrote: "Such is the temper of the Roman nation that it knows not how to remain at peace, vanquished though it be." To this war-loving people, life was battle, and heroism —religion.

In the Roman army the military unit was the legion or "gathering of the clans"; originally it was a phalanx armed in the old Doric style. At an early date it consisted of 4,200 men in eight ranks. The first six were hoplites and the last two *velites*—the light armed. On its flanks stood two squadrons of cavalry, each 150 strong. Like the Greek phalanx its tactical principle was shock. It had no reserves and pursuit was difficult.

This primitive organization was completely revolutionized in the fourth century B.C. by, as some suppose, Marcus Furius Camillus, the most celebrated Roman General of the Gallic Wars (391-360 B.C.). This seems probable, for in these wars the Romans were faced by a new type of army, the Celtic sword phalanx.

The phalangial legion was now divided into three separate divisions ordered in depth. These divisions were known as *hastati*, *principes* and *triarii*. Their men were paid soldiers and allotted to their divisions according to service, the *hastati* being the youngest soldiers and the *triarii* veterans. All these divisions were organized in companies (*manipuli*), the first two of 120 men each and the third of 60. A cohort consisted of one maniple of each class as well as 120 *velites* and a squadron (*turma*) of cavalry, 30 strong: in all 450 soldiers. Ten cohorts made up a legion. In battle order the maniples were drawn up checkerwise, so that those of the second division covered the intervals in the front of the first and the third those of the second. The cavalry, ten *turmæ*, formed a wing (*ala*).

The armament of the legion is fully described by Polybius in sections 22-25 of his Second Book. The *velites* carried a sword, spear and a target (*parma*) three feet in diameter. The spear was for throwing, and had so slender a point that, once cast, it bent and became useless in the hands of the enemy.

The *hastati* carried a large shield (*scutum*) semi-cylindrical in shape. It was two feet six inches wide and four feet long, and was made of two layers of wood glued together, covered with hide and bound with iron. These soldiers were armed with a short thrusting sword (*gladius*) and two javelins (*pila*) and wore a brass helmet and greaves as well as a brass breastplate on their breasts (*pectorale*), or if they could afford it a cuirass (*lorica*). The *principes* and *triarii* were armed and armoured in like manner, except that instead of *pila* they carried long spears (*hastæ*).

The cavalry, it would seem, were completely neglected, for even at the opening of the Punic Wars they had no armour: their shields were of leather and their swords and lances indifferent. Normally, they preferred to fight on foot.

Collective fighting was discouraged in favour of single combats. The one great shock of the phalanx gave way to a series of shocks in rapid succession. The entrenching of camps was also introduced, even when a halt was made for a single night. The old discipline, always severe, was unaltered, and drill and training were prolonged.

Looking back on the whole picture, Vegetius wrote in the fourth century A.D.: "We see that the Roman people have conquered the world by nothing other than drill in arms,"[45] and Josephus describes the Roman drills as bloodless battles, and their battles as bloody drills.

Tactically, these changes were radical. Close and distant

fighting were combined; a reserve came into being, and the offensive and defensive were closely knit together. Considering the manipular legion Mommsen writes:

"The Roman combination of the heavy javelin with the sword produced results similar . . . to those attained in modern warfare by the introduction of bayonet and muskets; the volley of javelins prepared the way for the sword encounters, exactly in the same way as a volley of musketry now precedes a charge with the bayonet. Lastly, the thorough system of encampment allowed the Romans to combine the advantages of defensive and offensive war and to decline or give battle according to circumstances, and in the latter case to fight under the ramparts of their camp just as under the walls of a fortress—the Roman, says a Roman proverb, conquers by sitting still."[46]

With this formidable fighting machine Rome set out to conquer first Italy, secondly Carthage and thirdly Macedonia. The first she accomplished in the three Samnite Wars (343-290 B.C.) and the war with Pyrrhus, King of Epirus (280-275 B.C.); the second in the first two Punic Wars (264-241 and 218-201 B.C.); and the third in the three Macedonian Wars (214-168 B.C.), after which she utterly destroyed Carthage in 146 B.C.

In the war against Pyrrhus, for the first time the legion met the Greek phalanx and in the end it beat it. Yet, as Professor Tarn points out: "Given its own conditions—a formal battle on level ground, with an Alexander or a Pyrrhus to guard its flanks—the later phalanx would have defeated the legions or anything else, but a formation which can only fight under special conditions had ceased to be of much use."[47]

The Carthaginian army was also based on the phalangial order, and once the Romans had, during the First Punic War, gained command of the sea—an amazing effort—in the Second they were called upon to face this army under Hannibal.

That this Great Captain accomplished what he did is in itself remarkable, seeing that his army was mainly composed of mercenaries drawn from many races, all armed with their own weapons—swords, spears, flails, bows, etc.—combined in no scientific arrangement. His most useful infantry were the Balearic slingers, who carried two slings, one for long range and the other for short range fire. His decisive arm was, however, his cavalry, to which, more so than to any other arm, he owed his great victory of Cannæ in 216 B.C.

After this battle Hannibal sought to entice the Romans to fight in open country where he could employ his cavalry to advantage. But they had learned their lesson, and kept to the hills. With discernment Polybius remarks: "I think the reason of the strategy adopted by the two sides respectively was that they both had seen that Hannibal's cavalry was the main cause of the Carthaginian victory and Roman defeat."[48]

The Carthaginian order of battle was normally as follows: In the centre the heavy infantry—Carthaginian, Liby-Phœnician, Spanish or Gallic—with the Balearic slingers and sometimes elephants in front. On its flanks were posted heavy cavalry and swarms of Numidian horsemen. It was only when commanded by a genius, such as Hamilcar or Hannibal, that so heterogeneous a gathering could be forged into a reliable instrument.

For sixteen years the Romans fought this motley army, and though their valour was unexcelled and their staunchness unequalled, it was not until Scipio Africanus raised and armed a body of cavalry worthy of the legion that he finally defeated Hannibal at Zama in 202 B.C. This defeat broke the Carthaginian power and reduced Carthage to a defenceless mercantile town.

The words both of Livy and Polybius have for all time summed up the influence and results of this decisive battle. The first, as he set forth to describe it, wrote: "Before tomorrow night they would know whether Rome or Carthage should give laws to the world; and that neither Africa, nor Italy, but the whole world, would be the prize of victory."[49] And the second: "To the Carthaginians it was a struggle for their own lives and the sovereignty of Libya; to the Romans for universal dominion and supremacy."[50]

Power, as always, soon corrupted the Romans, and as wealth increased the old burgess army rapidly changed into a long-service professional one recruited from the poorer classes and from the provinces. The ancient love of country rapidly declined, and in its place crept in a spirit of avariciousness. Conquests were no longer made for the security and glory of Rome, but instead to enrich the plutocrats and increase the pay of the soldiers.

About 104 B.C., Marius (157-86 B.C.) abolished the property qualification for recruiting, when the legions became wholly proletarian and professional. Further, in order to lessen the danger inherent in the many intervals in the front of the manipular system, he reorganized the legion in three lines of cohorts, each cohort consisting of five maniples. The tactical unit was thus increased from 120 to 600 soldiers, and as there were ten cohorts in the legion, normally four in the first line, three in the second and three in the third, the strength of the legion was raised from 4,200 to 6,000. The legionary cavalry were abolished, their place being taken by foreign cavalry (*auxilia*). By degrees the intervals between the cohorts were diminished, until, to all intents and purposes, the phalangial order was reintroduced.

As the class of soldier deteriorated, pay was increased. Avarice replaced honour. Armies more and more belonged to the chiefs who paid them; yet as the rank and file degenerated the urge towards good leadership increased.

Thus, the old militia system gave way to the professional army, and, as we shall shortly see, to a highly mechanized force, engineering, the art of fortification and siegecraft developing by leaps and bounds.

Such armies demanded highly educated and skilful generals, and, when these were forthcoming, success was assured. Of Julius Cæsar's army Mommsen says: "Perhaps there never was an army which was more perfectly what an army ought to be." Nevertheless, it carried within it the seeds of its own ruin, and with it the ruin of the Empire to which it belonged.

The exact structure of the legion in Cæsar's days is

unknown, but probably it was much as Marius had left it. Its arms and armour would appear to have been little changed, except that light troops, slingers and bowmen were increased.

The most remarkable innovations were the increase in cavalry, artillery and engineers. The first was largely brought about by contact with the Numidians and other mounted foreigners; and the second and third were due to wars with the Greeks and Carthaginians, as well as contact with the engineers of Alexandria.

Here, I can only give a few examples of this radical change towards machine fighting, yet they are sufficient to show what was taking place.

In 53 B.C., during the siege of Avaricum (Bourges), Cæsar apparently made use of some form of quick-firing engine.[51] In his campaign against the Bellovaci (a tribe round Beauvais), in 51 B.C., we find him using veritable bombardments of projectiles in the open field. Having built a bridge over a morass he "led his army across, and soon reached the plain on the top of the hill, which was fortified on either side by a steep ascent." From this position: "Having there drawn up his army in order of battle he marched to the furthest hill, from which he could, with his engines, shower darts upon the thickest of the enemy."[52]

We read of a similar operation when he attempted to hem in Pompey at Dyrrachium (Durazzo); for his ninth legion, having gained a hill, began to fortify it. Whereupon Pompey seized a neighbouring hill and brought such concentrated artillery fire to bear on these men that they had to abandon the work and withdraw.[53]

We know that Antony, in his expedition against the Parthians, had a siege train of three hundred wagons.[54] The smaller field-pieces were transported in carriages called carrobalistæ, some of which may be seen among the sculptures on Trajan's Column, erected in Rome between A.D. 105-113. This field artillery was probably in use a hundred years earlier. Mules were harnessed to these vehicles, and the pieces carried on them could be discharged over the heads of the animals. According to Vegetius,[55] every cohort was equipped with one catapult, and every century with one *carrobalista*: eleven soldiers were required to work this engine. Therefore the legion possessed an artillery train of 60 *carrobalistæ* and 10 catapults—that is, 60 field guns and 10 howitzers. This corresponds closely to the number of guns in a modern infantry division. But as the legion was seldom more than 6,000 strong, frequently less, whereas in a modern division the number of guns to infantry is about six per thousand, in the legion it was approximately double that number.

Hand in hand with mechanization went progress in fortification and siege work, and in these branches of the art of war Cæsar is without a rival. For instance, in 52 B.C., at the siege of Alesia (Auxois) it has been calculated that his men shifted 2,000,000 cubic metres of earth from the trenches they dug,[56] and four years later, at the siege of Dyrrachium, it must have been much the same. At the siege of Massilia (Marseilles), in 49 B.C., all manner of engines were employed, and the largest trench of this period was the one Crassus dug from sea to sea across the toe of Italy. It was 15 feet deep, 15 feet broad and 34 miles long.[57]

With reference to engineering, it should never be overlooked that the Romans of Cæsar's day owed as much if not more to their entrenched camps and roads as to their legions. Their camps rendered them all but unattackable, and their roads enabled them to swoop down on an enemy at unexpected speed.

Nevertheless, though mechanization of war saved lives and made soldiering easier, it cramped initiative and exorcised valour. Two consequences arose from this. The first was the imperative necessity for high-grade generalship, and the second was the barbarization of war.

Cæsar was a genius, therefore he could handle his fighting machine superbly well. His conduct of war was scientific: he always aimed at the decisive point; he turned his entrenched camps into mobile fortresses; he struck at his enemy's line of communications; and his plans were so subtle that he unfailingly kept his antagonists guessing. Yet he was inordinately brutal: his campaigns were largely massacres and his battles ferocious killings.

The age of valour and with it chivalry was withering. Polybius noticed this, for in his day, with reference to the destruction of cities and wasting of the lands, he pointed out that, in the century following Alexander, Greek warfare was far more humane than under the Romans. Further, he comments, and with no uncommon vision: "To destroy that for which a war is undertaken seems an act of madness, and madness of a very violent sort."[58]

Once the destructive civil wars which heralded the final destruction of the Roman Republic had spent themselves, Augustus (63 B.C.–A.D. 14), the first of the Emperors, reorganized the army in three classes: legions, *auxilia* and Prætorian Guard. The first were recruited from Roman citizens, though by now millions of them were foreigners; the second were composed of enlisted non-citizens, and in the main were bowmen and cavalry; and the third were a body of household troops, in all ten cohorts, each 1,000 strong. After A.D. 70 recruiting in Italy practically ceased, nevertheless service in the legions was still confined to citizen rank.

In short, what Augustus established was a military state with himself as Commander-in-Chief. Then onwards the soldier's oath of loyalty was to the Emperor, and not to his General.

The problem which faced Augustus and his successors until the year 250 was imperial security. Therefore powerful field armies were no longer required, but instead frontier garrisons. To meet this change he placed the army on a footing of twenty-five legions and, probably, an equal if not superior number of *auxilia*: in all some 380,000 troops. These he distributed in twenty-five frontier groups, each of which was based on a strong military centre called a *castellum*. Further, the frontiers were fortified and these centres linked up by roads. As the aim of the legions was now to maintain peace and not make war, the old Roman valour, whether based on patriotism or plunder, deteriorated rapidly.

This change in moral values had two effects. The first was to breed pacifism through loss of fear, and the second to establish a most pernicious form of militarism through the dependence of the Emperor on the army.

The social conditions which the first led to are well described by Petronius Arbiter, a writer of the Neronian age, in his *Satyricon*, of which the following extract is a sample:

"Greed of money . . . has produced this revolution. . . . We, engrossed in wine and women, have not the courage to master the arts already discovered; depreciators of antiquity, vice is the only thing we learn and teach. . . . Do not wonder then if painting is decayed, since in all eyes, both gods' and men's, a lump of gold is a more beautiful thing than ever was produced by those crazy Greeks, Apelles and Phidias."[59]

By 175 the dry rot of peace had so eaten into Roman valour that the Greek sophist, Ælius Aristides, with approbation described the conditions of his day as follows:

"Now the whole world keeps holiday and laying aside its ancient dress of steel has turned in freedom to adornment and all delights. The cities have abandoned their old quarrels, and are occupied by a single rivalry, each ambitious to be more pleasant and beautiful. Everywhere are playgrounds, fountains, arcades, temples, workshops, schools. To use a metaphor from medicine, the world, sick from creation, has recovered its health. . . . To be safe, it is enough to be a Roman. . . ."[60]

The direct effect of this pacifism on the legions, and more particularly on the Prætorian Guard, was that, as fewer and fewer citizens would enlist, more and more had barbarians outside the Empire to be recruited, and they were not men of peace but men of war. Their wholesale enlistment rendered the army un-Roman, yet it was they who made and unmade Emperors. Thus it came about that pacifism bred militarism and the old Roman discipline disappeared.

As this degeneration was advancing, in 250 the Allemani (All-men) and Franks broke into Gaul. Thus were initiated the barbaric invasions. As the frontier defences and garrisons (250,000 infantry and 110,000 cavalry) could no longer be relied on, Diocletian (264-305) created a field army of 150,000 foot and 46,000 horse as a central reserve. Apparently for the sake of mobility the legion was reduced to a unit 1,000 strong, and archers, slingers and war engines were multiplied.

Nevertheless, the Germanic tribes continued to pour in. For a space they were held back by Valentinian (364-375), who shortly after he was elected Emperor appointed his brother Valens as co-Emperor to rule the eastern provinces, and by doing so unwittingly opened the Danubian door to the great Gothic invasion.

When Valens was informed that the Goths had asked to be allowed to cross the Danube, he gave them permission to do so, for in them he saw a splendid recruiting ground for his army. But, once over the river, they were so badly treated that they rose in revolt and devastated Thrace.

Professor Oman describes the armament of the Germanic tribes as follows:

"The rank and file bore iron-bound bucklers, pikes, the short stabbing sword (*scramasax*), as well as the long cutting sword (*spatha*), and among some races the deadly *francisca*, or battle-axe, which whether thrown or wielded would penetrate Roman armour and split the Roman shield."[61]

The Gothic method of fighting, like that of the Huns, and later on of Zisca in the fifteenth century and the Boers in the nineteenth, was founded on their wagon-forts or laagers. Equally important, their main arm was a formidable body of shock cavalry. Lacking siege engines, they could not storm walled cities; therefore decisive victories were hard to win.

When Thrace was ravaged, Valens was at Antioch. At once he hastened back to Constantinople and appointed Sebastianus, an able soldier, to command against Fridigern and his Goths. Zosimus tells us that "observing the indolence and effeminacy both of the tribunes and soldiers," Sebastianus picked out 2,000 of the best of them, for "he knew well the difficulty of commanding a multitude of ill-disciplined, dissolute men, and that a small number might more easily be reclaimed from their effeminacy."[62] Having trained them he harried his enemy.

From Constantinople Valens at the head of a large army moved to Adrianople, and was advised by Sebastianus to remain there under shelter of its walls. This advice he set aside, and moving on, towards noon on August 9, 378, he came in sight of the Gothic laager.

While attacking it his army was charged by Fridigern's horse, under Alatheus and Saphrax, who descended on it "from the mountains like a thunderbolt."[63] Driven into an unmanageable mass, it was utterly destroyed: 40,000 men are said to have perished.

Never before had the Romans suffered so decisive a defeat, not even at Cannæ, for then and long after their valour was indestructible. "The Empire rocked on its foundations," writes Professor Martin Bang. "Sheer panic fell upon all that bore the name of Rome. The power and glory of the Empire seemed stamped into the dust by the barbaric hordes. . . . The battle of Hadrianople introduces the last act of the great drama, the most pregnant with consequences which the history of the world has ever seen."[64]

This great battle clearly showed: (1) that valour remained the first requisite in shock warfare, and that a return to barbaric vigour was inevitable unless a new moral inspiration could be discovered; and (2) that the old tactics of phalanx and legion had exhausted their virility, therefore a new technique was required.

Hitherto, under the Romans, infantry had dominated, and when they relied upon shock weapons, they had little to fear from cavalry, so long as they maintained their order. The increasing use of missiles, however, carried with it an unavoidable loosening and disordering of the ranks. The old shield-wall began to be replaced by a firing line, and as archers and slingers cannot easily combine shield with bow or sling, and as the range of these weapons is strictly limited, and as the bow is at a discount in wet weather, opportunity for the cavalry charge steadily increased. Therefore the problem was how to combine fire power with security against cavalry. As we shall see in another chapter, this problem was not solved until the mid-nineteenth century.

When, thirty-two years after this decisive battle, Alaric and his Goths sacked Rome, St. Augustine was at Hippo (Regius) in Numidia, and, overwhelmed by the news, "inflamed with zeal for the Lord's house," as he says, he wrote his greatest work—*The City of God*. Such was the new inspiration which, through long years of turmoil and chaos, was to rejuvenate valour in the Age of Chivalry.

REFERENCES

1. *Herodotus*, vii, 104.
2. Quoted from *Geschichte des Griechischen Kriegswesen*, etc., Rüstow and Köchly (1852), book i, p. 49.
3. Pausanias, iv, 8, 7.
4. Thucydides, v, 70.
5. *Ibid.*, iii, 94.
6. *Ibid.*, iii, 98. Xenophon (444-355 B.C.) clearly appreciated the value of light troops. In the *Cyropædia* he makes Cyrus say: "I will post the javelin men behind the cuirassiers, and the archers behind them: it would be absurd to place in the van troops who admit that they are not made for hand-to-hand fighting; but with the cuirassiers thrown in front of them they will stand firm enough, and harass the enemy over the heads of our own men with their arrows and their darts" (*Cyropædia*, vi, 3, 24).
7. Xenophon, *The Hellenics*, iv. 5, 14-16.
8. Polyænus, vi, 46.
9. Thucydides, iv, 55.
10. Herodotus, vii, 196.
11. Herodotus, v, 63.
12. *Geschichte der Kriegskunst*, Hans Delbrück (1900), part iii, p. 92.
13. Ezekiel iv, 1-2.   Born about 622 B.C.
14. Thucydides, ii, 75.
15. *Ibid.*, iv, 100. At the siege of Ambracia, in 189 B.C., the Ætolians smoked out the besieging Romans by burning feathers in their counter-mines. An interesting description of the instrument used is given by Polybius, xxi, 28.
16. Thucydides, vii, 43. A very old device pictured in Assyrian bas-reliefs in the British Museum.
17. According to Plutarch, Lycurgus (ninth century B.C.)—the reputed founder of the Spartan constitution—"was rigid and aristocratical, banishing all the base and mechanic arts to the company of servants and strangers,

and allowing the true citizens no implements but the spear and shield, the trade of war only, and the service of Mars. . . . Every sort of money-making was forbad them as freemen; and to make them thoroughly so and keep them so their whole lives, every conceivable concern with money was handed over, with the cooking and the waiting at table, to slaves and helots" (Plutarch's *Lycurgus*).

18. This is W. W. Tarn's reckoning, see *Hellenistic Military and Naval Developments* (1930), pp. 14-16. Delbrück (part i, p. 143) is of opinion "that the front of the two advanced ranks of the phalanx carried, as usual, the handy 'hoplite' spear, and that the rear ranks only were provided with the long spear."

19. As Delbrück points out, the same applied to eighteenth-century armies. In 1757 the Emperor Francis I wrote on the Prussian method of warfare: "It was but seldom that they secured important advantages as the result of a victory. The reason was that they feared nothing so much as to throw their ranks into confusion, for which reason they avoided a hasty pursuit" (part i, p. 31).

20. Thucydides, v, 73.

21. *Geschichte Alexanders des Grossen*, Joh. Gust. Droysen (1833), p. 93.

22. Arrian's *Anabasis of Alexander*, i, xi.

23. *History of Cavalry* (1877), p. 33.

24. *Alexander* (1890), vol. ii, p. 661.

25. *Hellenistic Military and Naval Developments*, p. 19.

26. *Geschichte des Griechischen Kriegswesen*, etc., book iv, p. 268.

27. Arrian, I, vi.

28. *Ibid.*, IV, iv.

29. *Ibid.*, IV, xxx.

30. Diodorus, xvii, 86, 3. See also Arrian, V, vii.

31. Antigonus and his son Demetrius Poliocetes, Antipater and his son Cassander, Seleucus, Ptolemy, Eumenes and Lysimachus.

32. Arrian, V, x.

33. See Plutarch's *Demetrius*.

34. Quoted by Delbrück, p. 202.

35. Polybius, v, 85-86.

36. The last recorded employment was at Thapsus in 46 B.C.

37. Polyænus, iv, 3, 6.

38. Plutarch's *Demetrius* and Diodorus, xx, 91.

39. Plutarch's *Demetrius*.

40. Æneas Tacticus, 37.

41. Polybius, xxi, 28.

42. *Mathematici Veteres*, Melchisedech Thévenot (1693), pp. 73-74.

43. Philo, iv, 78, 33.

44. Polybius, xi, 11.

45. Vegetius i, 1.

46. *The History of Rome*, Theodor Mommsen (Everyman's Edition, 1911), vol. i, p. 436.

47. *Hellenistic Military and Naval Developments*, W. W. Tarn, p, 29.

48. Polybius, ix. 3.

49. Livy, xxx, 32.

50. Polybius, xv, 9.
51. Cæsar, *De Bello Gallico*, vii, 25.
52. *Ibid.*, viii, 14.
53. Cæsar, *The Civil War*, iii, 45.
54. Plutarch's *Antony*.
55. Vegetius, ii, 25.
56. *Revue des Deux Mondes*, May 1, 1858, p. 113.
57. Plutarch's *Crassus*.
58. Polybius, xviii, 3.
59. *Satyricon* (Bohn's Edition, 1854), chap. ii, pp. 287-288. On May 26, 1944, when a question on preventing the U.S.A. buying up British art treasures was raised in the House of Commons, Mr. Maclaren stated: "So disposed was the mentality of the nation in recent years that the people did not care a damn for art. They preferred to go twice a night to see muck from Hollywood."
60. Aristides, *Panegyric of Rome* (tr. R. W. Livingstone).
61. *A History of the Art of War* (1898), p. 12.
62. Zosimus, iv.
63. Ammianus Marcellinus, XXXI, xii, 13.
64. *The Cambridge Medieval History*, vol. i, p. 217.

CHAPTER III

THE AGE OF CHIVALRY

THE barbarian invasions of the Roman world as profoundly influenced the course of history as did the differences between Latin and Greek civilization. Whereas in the Western Empire those incursions led to the disappearance of the Roman legion and with it of the Pagan Order it sustained, and in consequence compelled the Latin Church to build upon barbarism; in the Eastern Empire, because there was no permanent military collapse, the Pagan Order lived on to become christianized. In the one, military organization disappearing, valour in its most primitive form possessed the soldier. In the other, military organization being vastly improved, the soldier's intelligence was appealed to. The result was that, whilst in the West tactics and armament deteriorated, in the East they were improved, until a perfection was reached not again to be approached until the nineteenth century.

In the West the barbarian invasions, by forcing the Romans to adopt a mobile defensive policy, compelled the substitution of cavalry for infantry. By the middle of the fifth century, the legion vanishing, the horse soldier was left as the one operative arm. Thus it came about that the sword and *pilum* gave way to the lance and bow. At the battle of Châlons, fought in 451 between the Romans and Visigoths under Aëtius and Theodoric and Attila's horde of Huns, lancer and horse-archer met horse-archer and lancer, the infantry playing the part of onlookers. Except as foragers, pillagers and light troops for forest and mountain fighting, infantry were useless. Armour was little worn, partly because of its cost, partly on account of deterioration in the armourer's art, but mainly because it impeded mobility. When it reappeared, as it did in the sixth century, it was in the form of the mail shirt (byrnie), which was more pliant and comfortable than ill-fitting plate.

In the West, at this date, as Lecky points out, "It would be difficult to conceive a more frightful picture of society than is presented by the history of Gregory of Tours (538-594): but that long series of atrocious crimes, narrated with an almost appalling tranquillity, is continually interspersed with accounts of kings, queens, or prelates, who, in the midst of the disorganized society, made the relief of the poor the main object of their lives."[1]

It is in this contradictory compatibility—the essence of practical Christianity—that a new epoch took root, to sprout into two complementary yet antagonistic stems. The first was the Church of Christ, in which the people, now sunk in abject fear, and helpless without an ideal to lean upon, discovered a new moral purpose in their lives. The second was the new social order created by Feudalism, which provided the security in which this purpose could fructify. But as the Church was the Ministry of the Eternal, whereas the State represented no more than the temporal, it followed that complete religious dominance could only become possible when war, as much so as peace, was conducted according to the rulings of the Church.

Out of this search for dominance emerged the medieval conception of war as a trial by battle, in which the Church refereed for God. War was not prohibited, nor were attempts made to abolish it, because it was recognized as part of man's very nature, the fruit of original sin, which was the fulcrum of the Church's power. Therefore, war could only be restricted and mitigated by christianizing—ennobling—the warrior and by limiting its duration.

As war teaches men how to die bravely, war is the school of heroism: such was the Pagan ideal. But as death is the portal of the life eternal, war must also be the school of righteousness, otherwise death can lead only to eternal damnation: such is the Christian outlook. Thus the Classical soldier is transformed into the idealized Christian Knight of Chivalry, "uniting all the force and fire of the ancient warrior with something of the tenderness and humility of the Christian saint . . . and although this ideal, like all others, was a creation of the imagination not often perfectly realized in life, yet it remained the type and model of warlike excellence to which many generations aspired; and its softening influence may even now be largely traced in the character of the modern gentleman."[2]

Having ennobled the fighter, the next task was to restrict his activities by sanctions and rules. The first step taken towards this end was the establishment of "The Peace of God" (*Pax Dei*), which is first heard of in the year 990. Its aim was to protect ecclesiastical buildings, clerics, pilgrims, women and peasants from the ravages of war; also cattle and agricultural instruments. The second step was "The Truce of God" (*Treva Dei*), initiated by the Synod of Elne in 1027. According to it all warfare was suspended from noon on Saturday until dawn on Monday. Later, this truce was extended from Wednesday evening to Monday morning. Later still, on 1095, at the Council of Clermont, Pope Urban II—the initiator of the Crusades—"proclaimed a weekly truce for all Christendom, adding a guarantee of safety to all who might take refuge at a wayside cross or at the plough."[3]

The means of enforcing this truce were religious sanctions —excommunication and interdict—and though the results were meagre, these sanctions did effect something, for in the eyes of Christendom they branded the aggressor as the culprit.

A collateral restriction arose out of the Feudal System. It also took two forms. The first was that war was restricted to the nobility, and hedged in by codes of honour, and the second was the introduction of ransom; the price at which a prisoner redeemed his life or freedom, a city secured immunity from sack and a ship was repurchased from her captors. The right of ransom was recognized by law. Not only did it diminish the ferocity of war, but it grew into a veritable trade, until in fifteenth-century Italy the hope of gaining ransom all but reduced fighting to a farce.

These various restrictions, as well as the economic conditions of the period, limited the ravages of war. So much so that, in the present age of unlimited destruction, the following ordinances of Henry V of England—not exactly a mild warrior—sound foreign to our ears:

"That no manner of man be so hardy as to go into any chamber or lodging where any woman lieth in childbed, in order to rob her, or pillage any goods belonging to her refreshing, nor make any affray whereby she or her child be in any disease or danger."

"That no manner of man be so hardy to take from no man going to the plough and harrow, cart, horse, nor ox, nor none other beast belonging to labour without payment and agreement."

"That no manner of man beat down housing to burn, nor no apple trees, pear trees, nuts, nor no other trees bearing fruit."[4]

Such ordinances were generally observed until the breakdown of Papal authority during the Wars of Religion, which culminated in the ferocious Thirty Years' War (1618-1648).

The ennoblement of war carried with it two further restrictions. The first was, that as only men of wealth and position could afford armour, war was placed on an aristocratic footing. And as the wearing of armour led to infighting, missile warfare was restricted, and in consequence casualties were vastly reduced. Many of the battles of this period were no more than shock skirmishes between small bodies of armoured knights, in which individual combats were sought, to prove rather the worth of the fighter than his destructive capabilities. The object was to unhorse one's opponent rather than to slay him. In short, battles were frequently little more than sharp-weapon tourneys.

The second was an attempt on the part of the Church to limit the use of missile weapons which were likely to proletarianize war, such as the arbalest or cross-bow. Though the origins of this weapon are unknown, it would appear to have come into use at the beginning of the eleventh century. It was the most deadly missile thrower before the introduction of the longbow. In 1139 the Second Lateran Council forbade its use—except against infidels—under penalty of anathema "as a weapon hateful to God and unfit for

Christians." The employment of foreign cross-bowmen was also prohibited by *Magna Carta*.[5] As a weapon of war it was much admired by Richard I (Cœur-de-Lion), and when he went on his Crusade to Palestine he took 1,000 cross-bowmen with him.[6] Yet, in spite of anathema its adoption was fairly general, except in England.[7]

It is essential to bear these restrictions in mind when considering the warcraft of this period, for though, as Oman points out, the accession of Charles the Great in 768 marks the birth of a new epoch in the art of war,[8] that epoch was essentially a romantic one. "The hero of the imagination of Europe," as Lecky writes, "was no longer a hermit, but a king, a warrior, a knight. . . ." The age of the ascetic and of martyrdom was fast withering and the age of the crusader and of chivalry blossoming forth.[9]

This romanticism was thrilled into life by the conquests of Charles, who to consolidate his empire began to give shape to such elements of feudalism as already existed,[10] and which during his reign and the succeeding century were further bound together by the incursions of the Vikings and Magyars.

To hold his vast empire, which stretched from the Elbe to the Pyrenees and from the English Channel to south of Rome, Charles made a systematic use of fortified posts. Each district was, so to say, picketed by a number of palisaded "burgs," which could be used as pivots of manœuvre by his mobile forces, which were placed on a quality rather than a quantity footing. In the main they consisted of armoured cavalry, consequently the poorer classes were relieved from the burden of war. Such foot soldiers as Charles raised were not, as had hitherto been the case, a rabble carrying clubs and agricultural implements, but instead a well-equipped force with sword, spear and bow. Further, each Count was compelled to provide his horsemen with shield, lance, sword, dagger and bow.

Realizing that no army could really be mobile so long as it relied on foraging and was unable to storm walled cities and fortified posts, Charles organized two separate trains, one for siege and the other for supply, the latter carrying rations for three months and clothing for six. It is of interest to note that each was provided with bundles of iron-shod stakes as a protection against cavalry attack.

It was, however, to armour that Charles paid the greatest attention. Not only did he establish a census of the armour in his realm, so that none should be hoarded,[11] but by law he prohibited its export.

The importance he placed on armour may be gauged from the somewhat dramatized picture of his army left to us by Monachus Sangallensis:[12]

"Then appeared the iron king, crowned with his iron helm, with sleeves of iron mail on his arms, his broad breast protected by an iron byrnie, an iron lance in his left hand, his right free to grasp his unconquered sword. His thighs were guarded with iron mail, though other men are wont to leave them unprotected that they may spring the more lightly on their steeds. And his legs, like those of his host, were protected by iron greaves. His shield was of plain iron, without device or colour. And round him and before him and behind him rode all his men, as nearly like him as they could fashion themselves; so iron filled the fields and the ways, and the sun's rays were in every quarter reflected from iron. 'Iron, iron everywhere,' cried in their dismay the terrified citizens of Pavia."

The first Viking raids occurred soon after Charles ascended the Frankish throne, but it was not until after his death, in 814, that they grew formidable. In 850 the whole manhood of Scandinavia took to the sea, and the half-century which followed was one of the darkest periods in European history.

> And as the foeman's ships drew near,
> The dreadful din you well might hear;
> Savage berserker roaring mad,
> And champions fierce in wolf-skins clad,
> Howling like wolves; and clanking jar
> Of many a mail-clad man of war.[13]

These ferocious incursions vastly stimulated the military organization initiated by Charles. As the ill-armed local levies were useless, professional soldiers became essential. And as mounted men could alone keep pace with the raiders, more and more did military power pass into the hands of the nobility. Castles arose, strongholds were built, towns palisaded and fortified bridges thrown over the rivers, either to block the path of the raiders or to form refuges for the peasantry.

Thus, out of those troubled times, to be followed by the Magyar incursions of the tenth century, emerged a completely militarized society based on the stockaded stronghold and the mounted knight, which, as time passed on, was modelled into the Feudal Order.

In England other means were adopted by King Alfred (848-900). Though he also relied on fortifications, instead of raising cavalry he built a fleet, and beat the Vikings in their own element. This led to the English continuing to rely on infantry, whereas on the Continent cavalry became the dominant arm.

Of these many raids, the most important in future events was that of Rolf, Rollo, or Rou. Of him we read in the *Heimskringla Saga:* "Gange-Rolf went afterward over sea to the West to the Hebrides, or Sudroyar (Soder); and at last farther west to Valland (Brittany), where he plundered and subdued for himself a great earldom, which he peopled with Northmen, from which that land is called Normandy."[14] Little is known of his activities until 911. That year he took possession of Rouen, and became vassal of Charles the Simple of France, as Duke of Normandy.

When we come to his three times great grandson, William the Conqueror, and his victory over Harold of England at Hastings on October 14, 1066, there is presented to us one of the clearest examples of the influence of armament upon history.

In this famous battle, which decided the destinies of England, two very different armies met. The English was composed solely of infantry armed with sword, axe, club and spear. The house-carls—Harold's bodyguard—wore helmets, byrnies, and carried kite-shaped shields. The axe was the dominant weapon.

The Norman consisted of three distinct bodies of men: knights who fought mounted, men-at-arms who fought on foot and archers. The first and second were mail-clad and carried kite-shields; the three main weapons were lance, sword and bow.

It would seem evident from the start that William recognized his armament superiority, for in his address to his troops he said: "Is it not shameful, then, that a people accustomed to be conquered, a people ignorant of the art of war, a people not even in possession of arrows, should make a show of being arrayed in order of battle against you?"[15]

From these weapons were developed two very different tactical formations. Harold's was that of the normal " shield wall "—a hedge of shields: "Shield to shield, and shoulder to shoulder," as Æthelred I describes it at the battle of Ashdown in 871.

In his turn William divided his army into three divisions—left, centre and right—each formed into three brigades, archers in front, then men-at-arms, and lastly mounted knights.

The battle opened at 9 a.m. and passed through four phases:

(1) Under cover of a flight of arrows, William's knights charged the shield-wall and were repulsed. Other ineffective charges followed, and William's left retiring in disorder, Harold advanced only to be driven back again.

(2) A second general assault was delivered; yet the shield-wall held firm.

(3) William next made a feint withdrawal, whereupon Harold again advanced, but to no purpose. Both sides were now dead beat.

(4) As a further direct assault was not likely to succeed, William "commanded his bowmen not to aim their arrows directly at their enemy, but to shoot them in the air, that their cloud might spread darkness over the enemy's ranks."[16]

The effect was immediate and fearful, as Freeman writes: "Helmets were pierced; eyes were put out; men strove to guard their heads with their shields, and, in so

doing, they were of course less able to wield their axes."[17]
Thus, at length, was the shield-wall disarrayed; whereupon a crowd of horsemen burst through and the battle
was won.

From an armament point of view, the facts to note are
these: Though good cavalry could not break good infantry,
and good infantry could not attack good cavalry, when fire
and shock are combined, infantry relying on weapons for
close fighting are impotent. Further, had the archers been
unsupported by the knights, they could easily have been
driven off the field by Harold's infantry. Little realized at
the time, except perhaps by William in the West, as for long
had been accepted in the East, the bow had proved itself to be
the dominant weapon.

Why this was not grasped earlier, and why after William's
victory it took nearly three centuries before the English
revolutionized tactics with the bow, and why even then
Western Chivalry failed to adopt it, can only be satisfac-
torily explained by the hypothesis that missile fighting was as
abhorrent to Western military ideals as gas warfare is to-day.

In the Eastern or Byzantine Empire no such antipathy
existed. This may be clearly seen in Justinian's army commanded by Belisarius (505-565). That great general said:
"I found that the chief difference between them [the Goths]
and us was that our Roman horse and our Hunnish Fœderati
are all capital horse-bowmen, while the enemy has hardly
any knowledge whatever of archery. For the Gothic knights
use lance and sword alone, while their bowmen on foot are
always drawn up to the rear under cover of the heavy
squadrons. So their horsemen are no good till the battle
comes to close quarters, and can easily be shot down while
standing in battle array before the moment of contact arrives.
Their foot-archers, on the other hand, will never dare to
advance against cavalry, and so keep too far back."[18]

The battle of Taginæ, won in 552 by the eunuch Narses
over the Gothic king Baduila (Totila), is an exact forerunner
of Crécy. Drawing up some 10,000 dismounted knights,
Narses flanked them by two advanced wings of 4,000 archers,

each in crescent formation, and in rear of the centre he held in reserve a body of mounted knights. Baduila's army, advancing against the dismounted knights, was decimated by the archers, and when exhausted was charged and routed by Narses' mounted reserve. "So ended in complete success," writes Oman, "the first experiment in the combination of pike and bow which modern history shows."[19]

Why, in spite of its internal rottenness, the Eastern Empire endured for a thousand years, whereas the kingdoms of Western Europe were in a state of anarchy, was due not to valour but to military organization. The wealth of the Empire, the incomparable strength of Constantinople as a fortress, and the codification of the art of war by the Emperors Maurice (562-602) and Leo the Wise (886-911) in their manuals the *Strategicon* and *Tactica* gave the armies of the Empire a stability utterly unknown in the West. War was looked upon from a practical and not an heroic point of view. Battles were avoided rather than sought, and to sacrifice lives in attempting to achieve by valour what could be gained by cunning was considered the worst of bad generalship.

The combatant forces of the Empire were divided into cavalry, infantry and artillery. The first wore steel caps and mail shirts, carried circular shields and were armed with bow, lance, sword, axe or mace. The infantry, organized in sections, companies and battalions, were divided into heavy and light. The first were clothed in mail and carried shield, lance, sword or axe. The second consisted entirely of archers equipped with a bow, a quiver of forty arrows and an axe. The artillerymen worked the mangonels—a generic name for any engine which projected stones, arrows or fire-balls. There were three distinct types—the catapult, balista and trebuchet.[20]

Besides these weapons, the Byzantines possessed one which was unique, and which Colonel Hime rightly calls "the palladium of the Empire."[21] It was "sea-fire," also called "Greek fire," an inflammable mixture which ignited on contact with water.

According to the *Chronography* of Theophanes,[22] written

between 811-815, in 673 an architect by name Kallinikos fled from Syria to Constantinople, and there compounded a "sea-fire" which enabled the Byzantines to destroy the Moslem fleet during the first Moslem siege of that city.

Its composition is unknown, but apparently it was an oleaginous substance discharged by means of a siphon, which Hime clearly proves was "a *fire-engine*, or *water-engine*, or *squirt*."[23] These engines were known to have been used as early as the first century A.D., and are described by Heron of Alexandria.[24] Hime writes: "The lump of inflammable matter was projected, and at the same time ignited, by applying the hose of a water-engine to the breach of the tube [wood lined with copper], which thus became an integral part of the apparatus. . . ."[25]

According to the *Alexiad*[26]: "In the bow of each ship he (the Admiral) put the heads of lions and other land animals, made of bronze and iron, gilt, so as to be (quite) frightful to look at; and he arranged that from their mouths, which were (wide) open, should issue the fire to be delivered by the soldiers by means of (or through) the 'flexible' apparatus."[27]

At close quarters in a sea fight the effect of this fire was deadly, because it was impossible to extinguish it. Therefore, as a projectile, sea-fire may be classed among the few master weapons known. In the second siege of Constantinople (717-718) it proved catastrophic to the Moslem fleet, and in 941 and 1043 two Russian fleets were destroyed by it.

It is not to be confounded with "wild-fire," various mixtures of sulphur, naphtha, pitch, petroleum, etc.,[28] which for ages had been known throughout the East. Hime points out that the only passage he can recall among the old writers in which the two fires are discriminated and correctly named occurs in the metrical romance *Richard Cœur-de-Lion* (*temp.* Edward I, 1272-1307):

> Kyng Richard, oute of hys galye,
> Caste wylde-fyr into the skye
> And fyr Gregeys into the see.
> . . . .
> The sea brent all off fyr Gregys.[29]

Wild-fire, frequently called " Greek fire," was used by Edward I in 1304, during the siege of Stirling Castle, and on many subsequent occasions.[30] To-day it is represented by the flame-projector or *flammenwerfer*.[31]

As regards sea-fire, its composition was kept so close a secret that, after the conquest of Constantinople in 1204 by the Crusaders, it would seem to have been lost. Probably they were too ignorant and disdainful to show interest in such low cunning.

The first decisive disaster suffered by the Byzantine Empire was at Manzikert in 1071, a defeat due almost entirely to the Emperor Romanus Diogenes neglecting to follow the tactics of Maurice and Leo. So catastrophic were the results of this battle that, in order to secure Europe against a Seljuk invasion, in 1095 Pope Urban II called Christendom to arms and proclaimed the First Crusade.

The war he preached was far more a miraculous than a military adventure; for all men were offered alliance with the supernatural, remission of their sins and life eternal under the invincible banner of their General—Jesus. In idea and intent it was the apotheosis of chivalry.

As in all ideological wars, strategy was smothered by propaganda. Destruction rather than victory was its aim.[32] In it, as through a fog, the weaknesses in the feudal system were exaggerated. Though there were innumerable leaders, there was no single chief. Though in the armies of this period infantry had lost all tactical worth, tens of thousands of foot soldiers followed the knights, not to form line of battle, but to save their souls; for poor and rich were, spiritually, equal.

Passing through the Byzantine Empire, the Crusaders learnt nothing from its many wars. Ignorantly they struggled on into Asia Minor to discover in the Turkish horse-archers as deadly an enemy as Crassus had in the Parthian;.for in spite of their arrows having little effect on mail armour, the horses suffered terribly.

At the battle of Dorylæum (1097), the first of any size fought, the impetuosity of the knights, not forgetting a stroke of good luck, won through, but at so heavy a cost that the following year, at the battle of Antioch, they began to change their tactics. The infantry were divided into companies under competent leaders and in part, at least, armed with bow and cross-bow. These companies were deployed into line in front of the knights, a distribution which proved so successful that both sides were filled with wonder, the Moslems attributing their defeat to the inscrutable will of Allah, and the Christians their victory to the Holy Lance which had been borne before them. Nevertheless, little by little it dawned upon the Crusaders, and in spite of their superstitions, that when they combined mailed cavalry with organized bodies of foot archers and fought on ground which was unfavourable to their enemy's Parthian tactics, they generally won, and when they did not—they lost. As Professor Oman comments: "The one all-important canon which had to be observed was that there must be infantry on the field to serve as a support and rallying point for the cavalry. If the foot-soldiery seldom won the battle, they always made the winning of it by the knights possible."[33]

Of all the Christian leaders, Richard Cœur-de-Lion showed the highest tactical grasp. In 1192, having raised the siege of Acre, he lay encamped near that town, when, on August 5, he learnt that 7,000 Mamelukes were rapidly advancing on him. Though he had but 55 knights and 2,000 infantry, mainly cross-bowmen, he deployed them as follows: In front, a line of infantry spearmen kneeling. Immediately in rear, a line of cross-bowmen covering the intervals between the spearmen, and behind each cross-bowman a cross-bow loader, so that fire might be continuous. This combination of pike and bolt not only kept the Mamelukes at bay, but killed 700 of them and 1,500 of their horses. When at length they broke back, Richard, at the head of no more than fifteen knights, hewed his way through his demoralized enemy, and then cut his way back again. In this astonishing battle his losses were two men.

Strange to say, field tactics of this excellence were completely lost on Western Europe. There, militarily, little was learnt from the Crusades. Though they called forth the heroic and for a hundred and fifty years inspired Western Europe with a unity it has never since known and has never quite forgotten, so far as the art of field warfare and armament are concerned, they might never have been fought.

The two main reasons were that war had been monopolized by the nobility and that military thought was defensive. Only contests between nobles ranked as war; consequently thought was concentrated on improving armour and building castles.

Towards the end of the twelfth century plate armour was introduced, which, until the armourer's art was sufficiently advanced, led to the wearing of double armour—that is, plate over mail. Together, they became so heavy that, at the battle of Tagliacozza in 1268, Charles of Anjou's knights rolled the exhausted Ghibellines out of their saddles by seizing hold of their shoulders. In the fourteenth century plate armour reached its full development and double armour was virtually abandoned. As plate armour made the long kite shield less necessary, its size was considerably reduced.

As the weight of armour increased, until the barded warhorse had to carry between 350 and 400 lbs., when ground was unsuitable for charging or their horses were exhausted, knights took to fighting on foot. Not as infantry, but as dismounted cavalry, because their armour impeded the free movement true infantry require in order to wield their arms. The battles of Tenchebrai (1106), Bremûle (1119), of the Standard (1138) and Lincoln (1146) were all dismounted cavalry contests. In the first, which was fought between Henry I of England and his brother Robert, whereas Robert dismounted all his knights, Henry kept a small mounted force in hand. This body decided the battle, and so well were men armoured that not a single knight on Henry's side was slain. At Bremûle Henry dismounted 400 of his 500 knights, whereas Louis VI of France dismounted none and was beaten. Again, the battle was all but a bloodless one: 140 French knights were captured, and only three killed. As Oderic said: "For they were clothed from head to foot in mail, and because of the fear of God and the fact that they were known to each other as old comrades, there was no slaughter."[34]

Whereas the English and the Flemings never quite abandoned the infantry idea, amongst other peoples battles between dismounted knights were exceptional. Most encounters were clashes between horse and horse, in which infantry took little or no part, and frequently were altogether absent. Nevertheless, on account of the increasing wealth of the towns, due in no small measure to the loans raised by them to finance the Crusades, we find, first, a steady increase in mercenaries, and secondly, the appearance of well-equipped city militias.

Mercenaries, who had for long existed, seem to have been considerably increased after the introduction of the cross-bow, for simultaneously with its advent came into use the term *solidarii* (soldiers)—hired fighters. Thence onwards the mercenary bands grew in importance, and became essential in all other than purely local wars. In the thirteenth century they evolved into the Condottiere system, which was the very opposite of the Feudal, because it relied on professional soldiers who sold their services to the highest bidder, and, therefore, served no permanent master, nor were they bound by any code of honour.

The second—militias—are mainly connected with the Netherlands, which, never having been conquered, had throughout maintained considerable infantry forces along-side their feudal cavalry. In the twelfth century, these militias, generally called Brabançons, were armed with pike, mail shirt and steel cap; later on the pike was replaced by the cross-bow. Thousands of Brabançons were present at the battle of Bouvines in 1214; but they did not distinguish themselves greatly until Courtrai in 1302. There they won the day, utterly routing the French under Robert of Artois. As Villani wrote, it was something new and marvellous for a feudal army of 50,000 men, including 7,500 cavalry and 10,000 cross-bowmen, to be beaten by 20,000 burghers.[35]

However, the tide in favour of infantry had not yet turned. Two years later a much larger army of Flemish burghers was no match for the well-handled feudal army at Mons-en-Pevèle; again this was confirmed at Cassel in 1328, and at Roosebecke in 1382.

Though without armour there could have been no feudal overlord, for not only did it give its wearer personal security, but it differentiated him from all unarmoured men, without the castle there could have been no Feudal system, for it was the castle which gave permanence to the knightly caste. This was the greatest military contribution of the Crusades. They put Western chivalry in touch with the superb castles and fortified cities of the Eastern Empire. There, the most perfect example was Constantinople itself, a city surrounded by a single sea-wall nine miles in length and a triple wall on its landward side. The latter had been built by Theodosius II in the fifth century. It was four miles long and the inner wall was forty feet high and provided with a hundred and twelve sixty-foot towers.

One of the most renowned of the crusading castle builders was Richard Cœur-de-Lion; his masterpiece was Château Gaillard. In Palestine many of the Crusaders' castles were of enormous strength, notably Kerak-in-Moab and Krak des Chevaliers. These strongholds, if adequately garrisoned, were impregnable except by means of starvation or through treachery.

Though in the eleventh century castles of masonry were both few and crude, in the fourteenth they dominated every district and county. As Oman points out: "The methods of attack made no corresponding advance, and by 1300 the defensive obtained an almost complete mastery over the offensive, so that famine was the only certain weapon in siegecraft."[36]

The effect of this was the infrequency of great battles and the frequency of sieges, the weaker side finding it more profitable to seek shelter than to take the field. As the knights would not dig, hew, mine and batter, infantry became essential in the form of pioneers as well as of castle garrisons. Further, it was the defence and attack of castles, more so than field battles, which encouraged the growth of the cross-bow. Siege engines, however, remained much as they had been, with the single exception of the trebuchet, an engine supposed to have been introduced during the twelfth century. Its "projectile force . . . was obtained from the gravitation of a heavy weight, and not from twisted cordage as in the catapult and balista. . . . Provided the engine was of sufficient strength and could be manipulated, there was scarcely any limit to its power."[37] We read of a machine which cast a stone projectile weighing twelve hundredweights.[38]

As the castle was the mainstay of the Crusaders against the Moslems, also, as I have mentioned, it was the mainstay of the Feudal system. On account of the primitive commissariat of field armies in those days, which limited the duration of their campaigns, a people could not be conquered so long as their castles and walled cities held out. Further, as a hundred reliable men could hold a strong castle against thousands, the castle dominated war.

The results were not only the long survival of the Eastern Empire and of many of the smaller states, but also the prolonged resistance Feudalism put up against centralized authority. As in Classical Greece civilization was built around the city state, in Feudal Europe it was built around the castle until the introduction of the cannon.

Nevertheless, for a full century and a half before the bombards of Mohammed II thundered against the walls of Constantinople, missile power in the form of the English longbow was preparing the way, for by placing a dominant weapon in the hands of the common soldier, psychologically as well as tactically, it heralded the downfall of Feudalism.

This weapon was of elm, six feet in length, from which a three-foot arrow was propelled. It was a far more powerful weapon than the short Norman bow.[39] It was adopted from the South Welsh by Edward I (1272-1307), who in his wars in Wales had learnt its value when combined with armoured cavalry.

In 1298, at Falkirk, he put this weapon to the test against the Scots under Wallace. Wallace drew up his spearmen in four schiltrons or phalanxes, with archers on either flank and a reserve of 1,000 cavalry in rear. Edward formed his army into three battles—right, left and main—the third was under his own command. The right and left battles charged the Scots, and dispersed their archers, nevertheless the schiltrons held firm. Edward then brought up his bowmen and ordered them to concentrate their arrows on selected points in the enemy's front. This they did with terrific effect. Thereupon Edward charged at the breaches in the Scottish line, and a general massacre followed.

Strange to say, in 1314, though Edward II (1307-1327) had 30,000 bowmen at Bannockburn, he placed them behind his cavalry and made such poor use of them that he was decisively defeated. Thus the lesson of the longbow had to be relearnt, as it was, in 1332, at Dupplin Muir.

This battle—one of the most astonishing in medieval warfare—was fought between the "Disinherited"—Edward Baliol, Henry of Beaumont and others—and Donald Earl of Mar, the Scottish regent. The former had 500 knights and men-at-arms and between 1,000 and 2,000 archers. The latter commanded 2,000 men-at-arms and 20,000 foot.

Fully aware of the desperate odds against them, the "Disinherited" first attacked Mar by night. But when dawn broke and they discovered their enemy advancing in battle array they took up position on the slope of a hill. Dismounting all but 40 of their cavalry, they formed them up in phalangial order, with archers thrown forward on their flanks. Thus their order of battle assumed a crescent formation.

Paying no attention to the archers, Mar charged down on Baliol's centre and drove it in. Thereupon the flanking archers wheeled inwards, and opened so devastating a fire that the Scots were driven into a confused mass and all but exterminated. At once Henry of Beaumont and some of his followers mounted their horses and chased the fugitives off the field.

In 1333, Edward III (1327-1377) may be said to have patented these tactics at the battle of Halidon Hill; for thence onwards for a hundred years they remained the English sealed pattern, the most notable example of which is the battle of Crécy, fought on August 26, 1346.

The two armies which faced each other on this famous field were very different both in armament and outlook. The French, under Philip of Valois, was purely feudal; the English, under Edward III, semi-national.[40] The one not only despised infantry, but regarded their appearance on the field as an insult. The other was largely composed of infantry. To the French, to be differently armed was unchivalrous,[41] nor was it knightly to rely on missiles as decisive weapons. To the English, all this was absurd.

The French army consisted of 12,000 men-at-arms, of whom two-thirds were "*gentile gens*,"[42] and some 50,000 foot, including 6,000 Genoese cross-bowmen. The English, of 3,900 men-at-arms, of whom a quarter were knights, 11,000 archers and some 5,000 Welsh infantry. Many of the archers were mounted.[43]

Edward divided his army into the customary three battles, two forward and one in rear. In the interval between the forward he drew up a wedge of archers, its apex facing the French, and on the outer flank of the two battles he posted wings of archers as at Dupplin.

The attack was opened by an advance of the Genoese, who, outranged and decimated by the English arrows, broke back. Thereupon the French knights, suspecting treason, cut their way through them and charged, to be decimated in turn. These reckless charges were repeated again and again until the battle ended in a catastrophic defeat for Philip.

Of Philip's army 1,542 lords and knights fell and an unknown number of foot. Edward lost two knights, one squire, forty men-at-arms and archers and a few dozen Welsh.

Thus, once again, the bow linked to a defensive base proved triumphant against shock alone. Yet the French refused to acknowledge this, and though in subsequent battles—notably at Poitiers in 1356—they so far copied the

English as to dismount their men-at-arms, it would seem that their abhorrence of the bow, more so than the difficulty of raising archers, was the cause of its non-adoption. In brief, this weapon did not fit their code of war. The sword knew where it struck, the arrow did not, therefore it was a scoundrel's weapon.

From now onwards Feudalism rapidly lost ground, not only because the bow had become the dominant weapon, but because the idea it gave expression to was the need of a professional, national army. Already during the previous two centuries the national armed gatherings of the Albigenses had for long proved invincible, as later did the Hussite armies in the fifteenth century. Foremost in this democratization of war were the Swiss, for their peasant armies of halberdiers and pikemen taught the Austrian knights a lesson equal to the bow. At Morgarten (1315), at Laupen (1339) and at Sempach (1386) the Swiss were invincible, and as Colonel Lloyd remarks: "After this achievement . . . it was idle to say that the wearing of armour and the use of weapons was reserved by God and nature for persons of quality."[44]

The growth of national militias and the corruption of the Condottiere system,[45] as much so as the pike and the longbow, brought the Age of Chivalry to a close. Feudalism had not only outgrown its usefulness but also its ideals. Beaten as the armoured knight now was in the field, all that was lacking to accomplish his final doom was a weapon which would batter down his castle. Thus we pass to the Age of Gunpowder and its weapons of cunning.

REFERENCES

1. *History of European Morals*, William Edward Hartpole Lecky (1902), vol. ii, p. 95.
2. *Ibid.*, vol. ii, pp. 259-260.
3. *Encyclopædia Britannica* (Eleventh Edition), vol. 27, p. 321.
4. *Agincourt*, H. Nicolas (1833), Appendix 31.
5. *Magna Carta*, clause li. The word used is "*balistarios.*"
6. *The British Army*, Sir Sibbald Scott (1868-80), vol. ii, p. 78. The standard work on this weapon is *The Crossbow, Medieval and Modern*,

Military and Sporting, Sir Ralph Payne-Gallewey, Bt. It is of interest to note that the cross-bow "was considerably used by the Chinese in the China-Japan war of 1894-95" (*The Art of Attack*, H. S. Cowper, 1906, p. 266).

7. New inventions have always shocked the conventionally religious mind. As Spengler says: "Ever and ever again, true belief regarded the machine as of the Devil" (*The Decline of the West*, vol. ii, p. 502). Until recent times Aryan peoples have generally preferred clean fighting to crooked in order to maintain the supremacy of the valiant. Thus, in the Code of Manu, vii, 90, we read: "The king shall not slay his enemies in battle with deceitful or barbed or poisoned weapons, nor with any having a blade made hot by fire, or tipped with burning materials." For a like reason the "insidious bow" was proscribed in the wars of the early Teutons, whose valour was outstanding.

8. *A History of the Art of War*, Charles Oman (1898), p. 75.

9. *History of European Morals*, vol. ii, p. 272.

10. The germ of feudalism is to be seen in Tacitus's description of the German tribes: "In the field of battle, it is disgraceful for the chief to be surpassed in valour; it is disgraceful for the companions not to equal their chief. . . . To aid and protect him; to place their own gallant actions to the account of his glory, is their first and most sacred engagement. The chiefs fight for victory, the companions for their chief. . . . The companion required from the liberality of his chief, the warlike steed, the bloody and conquering spear; and in place of pay, he expects to be supplied with a table, homely indeed, but plentiful" (*Germania*, Bohn's edition, 1854, section 14). A note on the above reads: "Hence Montesquieu (*Spirit of Laws*, xxx, 3) justly derives the origin of vassalage. At first, the prince gave to his nobles arms and provision; as avarice advanced, money, and then lands, were required, which from benefices became at length hereditary possessions, and were called fiefs. Hence the establishment of the feudal system."

11. See *A History of the Art of War*, Charles Oman, p. 80.

12. Quoted *Ibid.*, p. 86.

13. See *Heimskringla, the Norse King Sagas*, Snorre Sturlason (Everyman's Library), chap. iii, p. 64.

14. *Ibid.*, p. 68. Valler or inhabitants of Wales and Cornwales (Cornwall). Welsh is the same as Valskr.

15. *The Chronicles of Henry of Huntington* (Bohn's Edition), p. 211. It is strange that the English never took to the bow. Most naval peoples used it—the Athenians, Vikings, and Genoese.

16. Henry of Huntington, p. 212.

17. *The Norman Conquest*, Edward A. Freeman (1869), vol. iii, p. 497.

18. Procopius, *The Gothic Wars* (Loeb's Edition), vol. iii, p. 261.

19. *A History of the Art of War*, Charles Oman, p. 35.

20. For a full description of the organization and tactics of the Byzantine Army, see Oman's *A History of the Art of War*, pp. 169-226. (Also, for a brief account, my *Decisive Battles*, chap. ix.) For a description of these engines, see *The Projectile-Throwing Engines of the Ancients*, Sir Ralph Payne-Gallewey (1907). Also, *Mathematici Veteres*, Thévenot (1693).

21. *The Origin of Artillery*, Lieut.-Colonel Henry W. L. Hime (1915), p. 44.

22. *Ibid.*, p. 27.

23. *Ibid.*, p. 37.

24. See *Mathematici Veteres*, Thévenot, p. 180.

25. *The Origin of Artillery*, Lieut.-Colonel Henry W. L. Hime, p. 38.

26. A Byzantine History, written by Anna Comnena, covering the years 1081-1118.

27. Quoted by Hime, *The Origin of Artillery*, p. 39.

28. For these, see *ibid.*, Table II, p. 28.

29. *Ibid.*, p. 40.

30. *Ibid.*, pp. 41-42.

31. "Dans une expérience faite au Havre, 1758, avec une pompe à huile de napthe, dont le jet était enflammé par une mèche allumée, en brûla même une chaloupe" (Berthelot, *Revue des Deux Mondes*, August 15, 1891, p. 800). At the siege of Charleston, 1863, not only was solidified Greek fire in tin tubes employed (*History of the War of Rebellion*, Ser. 1, vol. xxviii, pt. 1, p. 33), but coal naphtha placed in shells or pumped through a hose. Suggestions for its use were again made in 1870.

32. Quincy Wright points out: "But when war is for an idea . . . the necessary limits to destructiveness have not been evident. If one fights for democracy, it may be appropriate to destroy all the states and most of the individuals that a clear field will remain in which democracy can grow. If it is Christianity against Islam, each may be prepared to destroy all the adversaries if only a few of its side can remain to perpetuate the true faith" (*A Study of War*, vol. i, p. 160).

33. *A History of the Art of War*, Charles Oman, p.294. At the Horns of Hattin, in 1187, they failed to do so and suffered their most decisive defeat. For this battle see chapter x of my *Decisive Battles*.

34. *A History of the Art of War*, Charles Oman, p. 384.

35. See *A Review of the History of Infantry*, Colonel E. M. Lloyd (1908), p. 53.

36. *A History of the Art of War*, Charles Oman, p. 356.

37. *Projectile-Throwing Engines*, Sir Ralph Payne-Gallewey, pp. 27-28.

38. "These siege engines throw other missiles besides stones and javelins. They throw millstones, flaming projectiles, putrid corpses and live men. A dead horse in the last stage of decomposition, bundled up and shot by a trebuchet into a town of which the defenders were half dead with starvation, started a pestilence. Froissart tells us that John Duke of Normandy infected a town in the low countries thus, and made it capitulate. Manure and offal, and even the bodies of dead soldiers were used in the same way. William of Malmesbury describes the Turks at Antioch throwing from their petraries (catapults) the heads of townsmen into the Frankish camp. Worse than all, an envoy or messenger was sometimes tied up alive and cast back into the town. . . . Froissart actually describes such an act at the siege of Auberoche . . . for most of these pretty jobs the trebuchet was the engine" (Cowper's *The Art of Attack*, p. 274).

"Varillas writes that 'at his ineffectual siege of Carolstein in 1422, Coribut caused the bodies of his soldiers whom the besieged had killed to be thrown into the town in addition to 2,000 cartloads of manure. A great number of the inhabitants fell victim to the fever which resulted from the stench, and the remainder were only saved from death by the skill of a rich apothecary who circulated in Carolstein remedies against the poison which infected the town" (Payne-Gallewey, *Projectile-Throwing Engines*, p. 39).

39. As a national sport, archery was encouraged in England after the Conquest. In 1252, according to Henry III's Assize of Arms, all forty shillings freeholders were required to possess a bow and arrows. The long-bow arrow penetrated two layers of mail. In a trial made before Edward VI in 1550, arrows were shot through a one-inch board of well-seasoned timber (*Archery*, Badminton Library, C. J. Longman and others, 1894, p. 431). The range of the longbow was about 250 yards. Shakespeare mentions as a notable feat 280 to 290 yards (*King Henry IV*, Second Part, Act III, Scene 2). In 1798, 1856, 1881, 1891 and 1897 longbow arrows were shot at the following ranges: 340, 308, 286, 290 and 310 yards.

40. By 1350 feudalism in England was practically extinct, as the King had ceased to summon the feudal host.

41. "In olden times he received great praise and honour who let his enemy have equal arms. Challenges went out in good order to those who were good knightly people. Now no one is a good captain who cannot beat his handicapped enemy. Now he is praised and extolled in war, who is able and knows how to cheat his enemy" (Max Jähns, *Geschichte der Kriegswissenschaften*, 1889, p. 335; quoted by Vagts in *A History of Militarism*, 1938, p. 43).

42. *Chandos Herald* (1883), p. 310.

43. *English Historical Review*, vol. xiv, p. 767.

44. *A Review of the History of Infantry*, p. 82.

45. The corruption of the Condottieri had become so great as to neutralize their use. "Machiavelli explained that the Condottieri and their troops fought so badly because their interest in the war was purely mercenary. 'They have no love or other motive to keep them in the field beyond a trifling wage, which is not enough to make them ready to die for you.' . . . Since soldiers were the working capital of the Condottiere, he did not want to waste them. He shunned battles and preferred a war of manœuvre. If a battle, however, could not be avoided, he tried to keep the losses down. This was a period of bloodless battles [Zagonara, 1423, and Mollinella, 1467]. On the other hand, short wars were not in the interest of the Condottieri; they did not want to lose their employment" (*Makers of Modern Strategy*, edited by Edward Mead Earle, 1942, pp. 12, 13).

CHAPTER IV

THE AGE OF GUNPOWDER

WITH the discovery of gunpowder, a substance unknown to the ancients, we pass into the technological epoch of war, the hidden impulse of which is the elimination of the human element both physically and morally, intellect alone remaining. As Lecky points out,[1] hence onwards it is the great inventions more so than the great men which disturb and accelerate the process of society.

Valour gives way to mechanical art: he who wields the superior weapon is the more formidable foe, irrespective of his social status or his courage. For as Carlyle has said, the genuine use of gunpowder is "that it makes all men alike tall."[2] In short, it democratizes fighting.

Thus, by changing the character of war, gunpowder changed the Medieval (Christian) way of life. The search after the perfecting of weapons and of defences against them gave birth to a spirit of enquiry which soon embraced all things in general. It was gunpowder, more so than contact with Islam during the Crusades (1095-1444) or the fall of Constantinople in 1453, which gave life to the Renaissance, because it shattered the Medieval Order both physically and morally.

The idea that war is a trial of moral values by battle in which the Church referees for God is replaced by a new certainty: that war is a means towards a political end, in which the deciding factor is power. As war was secularized, peace followed suit, idealism giving way to realism. For instance, by the end of the fifteenth century, we find such noted soldiers as the Condottieri Gian Paolo Vitelli and Prospero Colonna declaring that "wars are won rather by industry and cunning than by the actual clash of arms."[3]

Not only, as we shall see, did gunpowder blast the feudal strongholds, but also the ideals of their owners. As portable firearms were multiplied, the medieval contempt for unmounted troops was undermined, until in tactical importance foot soldiers were raised to the level of the mounted men-at-arms. Thus it came about that, whereas among the feudal knights, ruses of war, surprisals, pursuits and even the exploitation of the enemy's defeat were considered dishonourable and unchivalrous, they now become customary, until Machiavelli (1469-1527) says: "Although in all other affairs it is hateful to use fraud, in the operations of war it is praiseworthy and glorious."[4] This moral *débâcle*—the antithesis of all the Crusades had stood for—reached its zenith in the sixteenth century when Francis I (1515-1547) and Henry II (1547-1559) of France, in order to further their aims against the Emperor Charles V, went into alliance with the Turks, the common enemy of Christendom.[5]

Such were the results of the discovery of gunpowder by Roger Bacon (1214-1292) in his half-magical laboratory. Anyhow, he it was who, in his *Epistolæ de Secretis Operibus Artus et Naturæ et de Nullitate Magiæ*, written before the year 1249, has left to us its earliest formula. And because, as Colonel Hime points out, without saltpetre there can be no gunpowder, and as no mention of saltpetre is made anywhere before the thirteenth century, the probability is that Bacon was the discoverer of gunpowder. His formula was hidden away in the following cryptogram: "Sed tamen salis petre LURU VOPO VIR CAN UTRIET sulphuris." Rearranging the letters of these strange words we get: RVII PARTVNOUCORULVET; and combining them into groups: R.VII. PART V. NOU CORUL. V. ET. This makes the sentence read: "Sed tamen salis petre recipe VII partes, V. novelle coruli, V et sulphuris," or—" but take 7 parts of saltpetre, 5 of young hazelwood (charcoal) and 5 of sulphur."[6] Though Bacon suggests that by means of this explosive mixture an enemy's army "might be either blown up bodily or put to flight by the terror caused by the explosion," there is nothing in his writings to lead us to suppose that he ever contemplated using it as it is in firearms. Who first thought of propelling a ball through a metal tube by exploding gunpowder is unknown; anyhow, it certainly was not monk Berthold Schwartz.[7]

Apparently the earliest extant document mentioning cannon is one in Arabic; it is dated 1304.[8] Of others, two belong to the city of Ghent, dating 1313 and 1314 respectively; also in an illuminated MS. of 1326, now in Christ Church, Oxford, there is a picture of the earliest form of cannon, a " dart-throwing vase," or as it was also called a "pot-de-fer." This primitive weapon appears to have been used as early as the siege of Metz in 1324,[9] and by Edward III in Scotland in 1327.[10]

According to Sir Charles Oman,[11] in 1339 the first mention is made of another firearm, called *ribauld* or *ribauldequin*, a primitive mitrailleuse which consisted of several small iron tubes so arranged that they could be fired simultaneously. This weapon was used by Edward III in his war with France, and in 1387 one of 144 barrels was built, the barrels being grouped in batteries of twelve apiece, allowing twelve salvos of twelve balls each to be fired.[12] Volume fire was clearly its aim.

Considering the crudeness of fourteenth-century mechanics as well as the religious restrictions of the age, progress in firearms was rapid. In 1340 we hear of powder mills in Augsburg, and if, in 1346, Edward III did not make use of cannon at Crécy, as some doubt, that year they are known to have been used at the siege of Calais.

> Gonners to schew their art
> Into the town in many a parte
>   Schot many a fulle great stone.
> Thanked be God and Mary mild,
> They hurt neyther man, woman, nor child;
>   To the houses, though, they did harm.[13]

By 1391 iron shot are met with; for that year mention is made of 928 stored in the arsenal of Bologna. Before the century was out progress had so far advanced that it was possible to build bombards of a calibre of twenty-five inches, such as the still existing *Dulle Griete* of Ghent. About this time the hand-gun, first heard of in 1364, was more generally adopted. It resembled a small cannon on a straight stock which could be carried and fired by a single man. It weighed about ten pounds, was fired by applying a match to its touch-hole, and its bullet was of lead. Normally it was used from behind defences, indifferent infantry being armed with it.

Towards the end of the fifteenth century the hand-gun gave way to the match-lock, an iron barrel mounted on a stock which fitted against the chest. It was provided with a cock to hold the match and a trigger to bring it down on to a pan containing the priming. This weapon appears to have been a German invention. It was called "hakenbüsche," in France "arquebus," and in England sometimes "caliver." It was the first true infantry firearm.

So far as armament is concerned, the fifteenth and six-teenth centuries were marked by inventiveness. Setting aside speculative inventions, such as Leonardo da Vinci's (1452-1519) airplane, tank and submarine, all of which were impossible until the mechanical sciences and arts had advanced, the following incomplete list will give some idea of the progress made:

Hand-grenades, 1382; smoke-balls, 1405; time match, 1405; case shot, 1410; corned gunpowder, 1429; fire balls, 1400-1450; match-lock or arquebus, 1450; bronze explo-sive shell, 1463; explosive bombs, 1470; wheeled gun carriage, about 1470; pistol, 1483; incendiary shell, 1487; rifling, 1520; wheel-lock and Spanish musket, 1521; improved hand grenades, 1536; wheel-lock pistol, 1543; paper cartridges, 1560; a type of shrapnel shell, 1573; hot shot, 1575; common shell, 1588; fixed cartridges (powder and ball in one), 1590; rifled pistols, about 1592; and per-cussion fuze, 1596.

During the first half of this period, the principal work of artillery was to batter down city and castle walls, the main exceptions being the Hussite Wars (1420-1434), and the battle of Formigny, which virtually closed the Hundred Years' War. The first are marked by a tactical development of a highly ingenious kind, which went far to undermine the prestige of feudal chivalry.

Faced by the full strength of the Empire, the Czechs, whose army consisted mainly of undisciplined and badly armed peasants, seemed to be in a hopeless position. Nevertheless, John Zisca, a man of tactical genius, led them from victory to victory. Realizing that his army was offensively useless as a defence against cavalry, he adopted the Russian and Tartar wagon laager, turning it into a movable fortress—the Wagenburg—and defending it by means of hand gunners. He was the first general who specialized in this arm, his tactics consisting in letting his enemy attack his mobile castle, and then when he was exhausted to issue forth and counter-attack him. By means of these defensive tactics the Czechs won battle after battle, their most notable victories being those of Deutschbrod, 1422; Aussig, 1426, and Tachau, 1427.

At the battle of Formigny, fought in 1450, tactics were the reverse, for it was the gun coupled with the offensive which won. The English, some 4,500 strong, under Sir Matthew Gough and Sir Thomas Kyriel, were faced by an equal number of Frenchmen commanded by the Count of Clermont. As was normal throughout the Hundred Years' War, the English, covered by their archers, awaited attack. Thereupon, after some initial skirmishing, Clermont ordered Giraud, Master of the Royal Ordnance, to bring up two culverins and enfilade the English archers. The effect of their fire was so galling that part of Gough's and Kyriel's army rushed forward and captured them; but unsupported they were driven back. Whereupon the French men-at-arms attacked the now disorganized English, burst through their ranks and all but annihilated them, leaving no less than 3,774 dead on the field.

It was, however, at the siege of Constantinople in 1453 that the cannon proved itself to be the dominant arm. On April 5, Mohammed II, the first great gunner in history, at the head of an immense army, appeared before the city and planted his cannon opposite its triple land wall. There, on the 12th, amidst the beating of drums and the shouting of thousands of excited men, the first of the great historical bombardments opened. Of it Mijatovich says: "Since the creation of the world, nothing like it had been heard on the shores of the Bosphorus."[14] Yet it was a slow affair, for as it took two hours to load them, the great cannon could fire but seven times a day.

Mohammed's most formidable pieces were bombards cast for him by a Hungarian or Wallachian cannon-founder named Urban. They threw stone shot thirty inches in diameter, weighing from 1,200 to 1,500 lbs.[15] These clumsy pieces required sixty oxen to drag them, 200 men to march alongside and keep them in position, and 200 more to level the road.[16] In all Mohammed had fourteen batteries, consisting of thirteen great bombards and fifty-six smaller cannon of various kinds.

On Tuesday, May 29, after a breach had been made, Constantinople was carried by storm. Thus ended the Eastern Roman Empire, and thus was finally established Turkey in Europe.

In the West, as in the East, and in spite of its crudeness, the cannon was forcing decisions still unequalled in the days of its perfection. Like Mohammed, Charles VII of France, relying on artillery, raised a siege train, and with it he reduced the English strongholds in an incredibly short space of time. As Sir Charles Oman points out: "In the re-conquest of Normandy in 1449-50, the French conducted sixty successful siege-operations in a year and four months."[17]

Also Sir Charles writes: "The same complete mastery of modern cannon over old fortifications was seen in England during the Wars of the Roses" (1455-1487).[18] These wars not only placed Henry Tudor on the throne, but resulted in so deep-rooted a dislike for the professional soldier that for a hundred and fifty years England was left without an army, and precisely during those years when technical military organization on the Continent was becoming a science.

This work of castle battering reached its zenith under Charles VIII of France (1483-1498), who, by invading Italy in 1494, started the long Valois-Hapsburg struggle, which with few breaks lasted until the peace of Cateau-Cambrésis in 1559.

Charles's strength lay in his artillery, which during his reign was revolutionized. Gun-carriages were adopted; sighting was greatly improved; schools were established for gunners; iron cannon were replaced by bronze and lead shot by iron cannon balls.

As Taylor writes: Against this organized artillery "citadels which had previously held out for months fell in a few hours."[19] And so startling were the successes gained that a general belief arose in the futility of fortifications. As we shall see, this belief was dictated by fright rather than by reason.

It was not, however, until the bloody battle of Ravenna, won in 1512 by Gaston de Foix over the Army of the Holy League, that artillery first played a decisive part in the open field. Both sides brought their guns into action at the outset, a mutual bombardment following. As this was in progress, and whilst the guns on the French right were enfilading the Spanish left, the Duke of Ferrara manœuvred his batteries round the Spanish right, and so galled his enemy that he forced him to abandon his entrenchments and come into the open. There the Spaniards were charged by Gaston de Foix; yet not until their rear was attacked did they give way, retiring under cover of the fire of their arquebusiers.[20]

In order to neutralize the power of artillery, battle-fields became more and more entrenched, as was notably the case at Bicocca in 1522, and at Pavia three years later. Further, no sooner had Charles VIII's cannon reduced the Italian castles to rubble or terrified their garrisons into surrender, than a system of fortifications was introduced which defeated the gun. Moats, walls and towers were replaced by wet ditches, ramparts and bastions, the last two covered by earthwork, and mounting heavy guns. In 1509, at the siege of Padua, the Emperor Maximilian's artillery was completely nonplussed, and in spite of the fact that his siege train was many times more powerful than the one brought into Italy by Charles VIII. It is remarkable that, whereas in 1494-1495 Charles, as Machiavelli wrote, "seized Italy with chalk in hand"[21]—that is, his artillery took him to whatever spot he chose to chalk on the map—from 1521 onwards successful sieges became a rarity.[22]

This return to the defensive, coupled with the decline of cavalry and the progress in firearms, more and more brought infantry to the fore, and as the Swiss were already in the field, pikemen were multiplied. To meet them, Gonzalo de Corduba, the Great Captain, reverted to the tactics of the Roman legion. Arming his infantry with sword and buckler, in 1502, at Barletta, he defeated the Swiss in the same way as Flamininus and Æmilius Paulus had defeated the Macedonian phalanx at Cynocephalæ and Pydna.

Though the sword could master the pike, it was a poor weapon against cavalry. Therefore it fell out of use, and the problem became one of how best to combine pikes and firearms, for the battle of Marignano, in 1515, had conclusively proved that the arquebus had challenged the supremacy of the pike.

It was solved by the introduction of the musket by the Spaniards, who first used it at the siege of Parma in 1521. It was an arquebus six feet in length, weighed fifteen pounds and was fired from a fork-shaped rest. Its range was 240 yards and its killing power considerably higher than the older arquebus.

The tactics of this improved match-lock were rapidly developed by the Marquis of Pescara, who has every right to be called the father of modern infantry. In 1522, at the battle of Bicocca, he demonstrated on a large scale the value of musketeers holding a defensive position. In this battle the Imperial Army was protected by a sunken road, behind which Pescara drew up his musketeers in four ranks, massing his pikemen in rear of them. The former were instructed to hold their fire until the Swiss of the French Army came within close range, when each rank was to fire in turn. This was done with complete success, and the Swiss were decimated and forced to retire.

At Sesia, in 1524, he manœuvred his musketeers inde-

pendently in the open, and for the first time pikemen became
no more than their auxiliaries. The year following, at Pavia,
the steady shooting and manœuvring of Pescara's musketeers
won for the Imperialists the most decisive battle of that
generation: a battle which founded modern infantry fire
tactics.

Thence onwards, until the introduction of the bayonet,
the musket and the pike remained the dominant arms.
Artillery opened the way; the pike protected the musket,
and the musket cleared the road for the advance of the pike,
and frequently also for the cavalry sword and lance. Thus
for over a hundred years were tactics set.

This change from the medieval way of fighting to the
modern was remarkably rapid, which may be seen in the
change of the composition of armies. Whereas in 1494 two-
thirds of the French army were cavalry, in 1528 no more than
one-eleventh was. In the Spanish Army it was much the
same. In 1503 cavalry numbered one-fifth of the total, and
in 1525 one-twelfth.[23] So completely had the shock value of
cavalry declined, that some time before 1521—the year of
his death—Giovanni de' Medici (Pope Leo X) defined the
duties of cavalry as follows: to protect, to forage, to observe,
to collect intelligence and to keep the enemy in suspense.[24]
No mention is made of charging.

These changes were not introduced without opposition.
For instance, Gian Paolo Vitelli, who died in 1499, was in
the habit of blinding and cutting the hands off arquebusiers,
whilst Bayard—"Chevalier sans peur et sans reproche"—
the last great representative of medieval chivalry, shot them
when captured. Ironically enough he was himself killed in
the battle of Sesia by a ball fired from an arquebus.

Blaise de Monluc (1502-1577), Marshal of France, though
he in no way despised the new firearms, said of the arquebus
that it was "the Devil's invention to make us murther one
another." In this there was a certain amount of truth, for
it did place an easy means of killing into the hands of the
common people. Cervantes (1547-1616) was not far wrong
when he wrote: "The devilish invention of artillery" enables

a "base cowardly hand to take the life of the bravest gentleman. . . . A chance bullet, coming nobody knows how or
from whence, fired perchance by one that fled affrighted at
the very flash of his villainous piece, may in a moment put a
period to the vastest designs. . . ."[25]

Ariosto (1474-1533) was even more outspoken:

> O! curs'd device! base implement of death!
> Fram'd in the black Tartarean realms beneath!
> By Beelzebub's malicious art design'd
> To ruin all the race of human kind.[26]

Milton also assigned the invention of artillery to the
Devil, and Shakespeare made Hotspur say:

> That villainous saltpetre should be digg'd
> Out of the bowels of the harmless earth,
> Which many a good tall fellow had destroy'd
> So cowardly. . . .[27]

Though Thomas Fuller (1608-1661), divine and historian,
in his *Worthies of England* considered that firearms had
reduced casualties on the battlefield, and, over two centuries
later, Lecky was of opinion that "gunpowder and military
machinery have rendered the triumph of barbarism impossible," could they have witnessed the holocausts of the
twentieth century they might have changed their views to
those held by Ariosto, Milton and Cervantes.

Technical opposition was also forthcoming, and mainly in
England, militarily the most conservative of all countries.
There, so late as 1590, Sir John Smyth, in his *Certain
Discourses Concerning the Formes and Effects of Diuers Sorts
of Weapons*, etc., still championed the longbow, and was
challenged by Humphrey Barwyck, who pointed out that,
when in the service of the King of France he had com-
mended that weapon, the answer he received was: "Non,
non, Anglois, vostre cause est bien salle, car dieu nous a
donnés moyen de vous encountrer après un autre sorte
que en temps passé. . . ."[28] Really there was no more to
be said, and by an order of the Privy Council the longbow
was finally abolished in 1595.

As has so frequently been the case throughout history,

instead of impeding its development, opposition to a new invention has hastened it. If artillery were of the Devil, then it was his Satanic Majesty who suffered more so than the cannon, and should an older weapon possess certain uses beyond the powers of the new to attain, then the arguments for its retention only speeded up the improvement of its rival.

Thus also with war itself, as it is a human activity, by ousting an old system of warfare, gunpowder created a new system of peace. So it came about that in the sixteenth century it revolutionized not only the method of fighting, but also the way of living, and in consequence civilization itself. In fact, it established an outlook on things in general as different from the outlook of the Medieval Age as its outlook differed from that of the Classical. Therefore, with the advent of firearms we do not merely turn over another page in human history, instead we open a new volume, the title of which is *The Will to Power*.

In it the first notable development is the centralization of power in the hands of the King. In feudal times, as we have seen, power was distributed among the nobles; now it becomes concentrated in the monarchy. The cost of artillery and the expenses entailed in equipping large numbers of arquebusiers were too great to be borne by any individual, and in consequence were met by the State. Further, this concentration of power in secular hands raised the monarchy above the Church; for war, becoming a political instrument, ceased to be a moral trial.

It is during the sixteenth century that we see the rise of standing armies, the development of competitive armaments and the introduction of the balance of power as a policy. Military service ceased to be the perquisite of a class and became a State profession. The development of mass fighting, if not of mass armies, was a characteristic of this age. If Machiavelli was not the first in modern times to suggest conscription, he, nevertheless, "composed the decisive memoranda on the basis of which was promulgated the Ordinanza (1506)—*i.e.*, the law which established obligatory military service [in Tuscany] for all men between 18 and 30."[29]

Upon England's development as a naval power the influence of gunpowder was decisive. As the Wars of the Roses had eliminated the little of feudalism that still remained within her borders long before it had been swept away on the Continent, she was better placed than any of her greater neighbours to forestall the approaching armament revolution, as later on, in the eighteenth century, she forestalled the industrial revolution. Her rise as a naval power was due as much to gunpowder as her rise in the nineteenth century to world economic dominion was due to coal.

This portentous event, which for 350 years was to make her the dominant sea power in the world, is traceable first to Henry VII's (1485-1509) interest in his new ships the *Regent* and the *Sovereign*, and secondly to his son, Henry VIII (1509-1547), who was the first prince to grasp that in the rough northern waters oars must give way to sails and boarding to broadside fire. Thus it came about that, between 1520 and 1530, gun foundries in England were placed on a permanent footing, in order to provide cannon for his great ships, such as the *Great Harry* and the *Henry Grace à Dieu*. Financially he was well placed to meet the cost, for the plunder of the Church enabled him to spend on a scale which had been impossible for his predecessors, as it was for his successors, without aid of grants from Parliament.

The *Great Harry* carried four "great cannon," 60-pounders, and a number of "demi-cannon," 32-pounders, as well as smaller pieces. The tendency was more and more to make the "great ship" an off-fighting instead of a boarding vessel. "This idea," writes Sir Charles Oman, "of making the warship a machine destined to operate by force of gunnery, rather than a fort with a garrison of soldiers who were to board the enemy in close combat, was a cardinal change in naval psychology."[30]

This idea, under Henry's daughter, Queen Elizabeth, was destined to wrest the sceptre of the seas from Spain. In the hands of the Elizabethan seamen the cannon became the chief instrument of battle. "The gun was the weapon on which the English seamen had learnt to rely. It was the gun, plied with rapidity, just out of pistol-shot of his lofty ships, which in the year 1588 harassed and put to confusion the Spaniard, the haughty fighter who still maintained a quixotic contempt for the use of cannon and esteemed artillery 'an ignoble arm.' "[31]

Describing the action against the Spanish Armada on July 23, Lord Howard of Effingham wrote: "This fight was very nobly continued from morning until evening, the Lord Admiral [himself] being always in the hottest of the encounter . . . there was never seen a more terrible value of great shot . . . for although the musketeers and harquebusiers of crock [swivel] were then infinite, yet could they not be discerned nor heard, for the great ordnance came so thick that a man would have judged it to have been a hot skirmish of small shot, being all the fight long within half musket shot of the enemy."[32]

These tactics are so well described by Sir Walter Raleigh (1552-1618) that they are worth quoting in full:

"Certainly, he that will happily perform a fight at sea must believe that there is more belonging to a good man of war upon the waters than great daring, and must know that there is a great deal of difference between fighting loose or at large and grappling. To clap ships together without consideration belongs rather to a madman than to a man of war; for by such an ignorant bravery was Peter Strossi lost at the Azores, when he fought against the Marquis of Santa Cruz [battle of Terceira, 1583]. In the like sort had the Lord Charles Howard, Admiral of England, been lost in the year 1588, if he had not been better advised than a great many malignant fools were, that found fault with his demeanour. The Spaniards had an army aboard them and he had none; they had more ships than he had, and of higher building and charging; so that, had he entangled himself with those great and powerful vessels, he had greatly endangered this Kingdom of England. For twenty men upon the defences are equal to a hundred that board and enter; whereas then, contrariwise, the Spaniards had a hundred for twenty of ours, to defend themselves without. But our admiral knew his advantage and held it; which had he not done, he had not been worthy to have held his head."[33]

That he was worthy led to astonishing results, for the defeat of the Spanish Armada opened North America to English colonization, which, in its turn, founded the United States.

Changing the secular world, gunpowder also changed the religious, and by enabling Christendom to spread its faith, it revived the spirit of the Crusades and led to Imperialism. Before its discovery, writes Max Jähns in his *Geschichte der Kriegswissenschaften*, "both the Indies were in the jaws of hellish Satan and in the very darkest obscurity, more like cattle or wild beasts in custom and belief than like reasonable creatures of the Great God. Gunnery has been the only means by which the command of Christ could be performed (Luke xiv, 23: 'compel them to come in, that my house may be filled')."[34]

Gunpowder and the horse enabled the Conquistadores, notably Cortés and Pizzaro, not only to conquer the Americas as if by magic, but to change the whole trend of aboriginal civilization. Greater distances could be travelled; tribal habitats were revolutionized; tribal equilibrium was upset, and tribal warfare became constant and more destructive. Much the same would seem to have taken place on the introduction of the horse and sword into Europe during the second millennium B.C.[35]

Yet another change must be mentioned, and possibly the most important of all—the influence of cannon on industry.

First, it increased the consumption of iron, which stimulated mining. Secondly, it increased cost, compelling the rulers of Europe to have recourse to the financiers, such as the Fuggers, and so fostered Capitalism. On this question Lewis Mumford writes: "As security for the loan, the lender took over the royal mines. The development of the mines themselves then became a respectable avenue of financial enterprise, with returns that compared favourably with the usurious and generally unpayable interest. Spurred by the unpaid notes, the rulers were in turn driven to new conquests or to the exploitation of remote territories: and so the cycle began over again."[36]

In England, in Sussex and Kent, cannon foundries sprang up all over the Wealden country, and so depleted the forests of wood that in Elizabeth's reign legislation was required to prevent the charcoal-burners from robbing the shipwright of his timber. Further, the export of English cannon became an exceedingly lucrative trade.

As Mumford points out, "the gun was the starting point of a new type of power machine: it was, mechanically speaking, a one-cylinder internal combustion engine. . . ." Because of it heavy fortifications were developed and road-building, canal-building and bridge-building became necessary adjuncts of warfare. "War established a new type of industrial director who was not a mason or a smith or a master craftsman—the military engineer. . . . It was to the Italian military engineers from the fifteenth century on that the machine owed a debt quite as high as it did to the ingenious British inventors of James Watt's period."[37]

These many changes, stimulated as they were by the influx of bullion from the New World which gunpowder was then conquering, were rapidly establishing a new social myth, neither religious nor military, instead economic. Luther (1483-1546) inveighed against the monopolists and usurers as much so as against the Pope; whereas Calvin (1509-1564) accepted both. In fact the whole Western World was at quarrel within itself. The Devil had been unchained, and his agents were legion, for the disbandment of Henry II's army after the Peace of Cateau Cambrésis had thrown tens of thousands of soldiers out of employment. These men were ready at hand for the religious war which broke out in France in 1562. Thus a new period of conflict opened which, with a few breaks, was to last until the Peace of Westphalia in 1648.

Ideologically it was a period of total war unequalled in atrocities since the days of the Arian Schism.[38]

Politically, much may be learnt from this long conflict, above all that when ideas instead of things are fought for, each party ascribes *all* virtue to itself and imputes *all* guilt to its adversary. In the end this means that ideological wars are largely fought in vain, because ideas cannot be killed by bullets, or even changed if fervently held. Militarily, little is to be learnt from the French Wars of Religion (1562-1598). And not much either from the revolt of the Netherlands (1568-1607), except that, during the struggle with Spain, Maurice of Nassau (1567-1625) proved himself to be a master of siegecraft and a military organizer of vision. It is not until we come to the Thirty Years' War (1618-1648) that, in the technique and tactics of Gustavus Adolphus (1594-1632), we find a noticeable advance in armament and fire power.

Reviewing military organization as it then was, Gustavus saw that the day of the national army was dawning and that the dominant weapon was the musket. Therefore he decreased the number of pikemen, shortened their pikes from sixteen to eleven feet, lightened their armour and combined them with the musketeers in companies six files deep. The musket he lightened in order to dispense with the crutch or rest, reduced its calibre, and by degrees substituted the wheel-lock for the match-lock and adopted the paper cartridge.

Of cavalry he employed two types, cuirassiers and dragoons. The first were partially armoured and the second were mounted infantry. The cuirassiers were formed into squadrons of three instead of ten ranks deep, and were trained to charge with the sword at the gallop instead of the trot, using their pistols only in the mêlée.

In spite of the excellence of his infantry and cavalry, it was on the power of his artillery that his great battles of Breitenfeld (1631) and Lützen (1632) were founded. He was the first to gauge the true value of the field gun. In order to render this weapon mobile he cut down its length, lightened its carriage and reduced the number of calibres. He adopted three main types—siege, field and regimental. The first two consisted of 24-, 12- and 6-pounders: the siege weighing

60, 30 and 15 cwts., and the field 27, 18 and 12 cwts. The third were 4-pounder pieces weighing 5 cwts., two to a regiment, provided with fixed ammunition in wooden cases, which enabled them to fire eight rounds to every six shots of a musketeer. These regimental pieces replaced his famous leather guns,[39] which he had used in his Polish campaign of 1628-1629. The projectiles normally fired were grape and canister for field and regimental guns, and round shot for siege.

In this new army, which radically differed from the Spanish model, we see the pattern which with one important difference was progressively followed in military organization until the end of the nineteenth century. This difference was the substitution of the bayonet for the pike, which new weapon, coupled with the flint-lock musket, made infantry supreme.

The flint-lock, or fusil, appears to have been invented about 1635. It was less expensive than the wheel-lock and less cumbersome than the match-lock.[40] In 1646, General Monk recommended it for picked shots, and between then and the end of the century it came into general use. In 1658, at the battle of the Dunes, of the 3,000 English musketeers in Turenne's army 400 were armed with the flint-lock.

The first mention of the bayonet[41] is made by the elder Seigneur de Puységur, a native of Bayonne, in his *Memoirs*, published in 1747. In them he informs us that at Ypres, in 1647, his musketeers fixed daggers into the muzzles of their muskets.[42] This particular weapon became known as the plug-bayonet. In 1671 it was issued to French Fusilier regiments, and in 1685 to the English Royal Fusiliers. How unsatisfactory it was was clearly demonstrated at the battle of Killiecrankie (1689), where Mackay's infantry, having fixed bayonets, were unable to fire and in consequence were routed by Dundee's Highlanders.

Shortly after this defeat Mackay invented a socket bayonet which could be fastened to the muzzle of a musket by means of two rings.[43] It was not a new invention, because the younger Puységur mentioned ring-bayonets in 1678.

Soon after the Peace of Ryswick (1697) the English and Germans abolished the pike and adopted the socket-bayonet, so also did the French in 1703.[44] This change revolutionized infantry tactics. First, it reduced infantry from two types to one and simplified fighting; secondly, it enabled infantry to reload under cover of their bayonets; thirdly, to face cavalry; and fourthly, to protect themselves in wet and windy weather when firing was restricted. Colonel Hime goes so far as to say: "The introduction of the bayonet marks the end of medieval and the beginning of modern war. . . . Tactics were revolutionized by a dagger some 12 ins. long. . . ."[45] I should prefer to say it ended the first lap of the gunpowder age by wedding the medieval to it; for the spear was now mated with the musket.

This radical change in armament coincided with as radical a change in the outlook on war itself, which was brought about by the realization that unless the horrors of war could be restricted by rules, as the crimes of peace are by law, society must founder. The general result was that, whereas in medieval times honour existed between feudal knights, and foot soldiers took little part in battle, now honour was established between armies led by aristocrats and the common folk were excluded from the fray. During the greater part of the eighteenth century wars were looked upon as royal games in which highly drilled soldiers were the counters or pieces, and because they were costly to maintain, armies remained small and bloody encounters were generally avoided. The masses of the people were excluded from the struggle and depot supply replaced pillage and foraging. Further, and what was the wisest change of all, the rules of the game laid down that "neither justice nor right, nor any of the great passions that move a people should be mixed up with wars,"[46] because the bullet is no answer to an idea, and should it be considered an answer, then there could be no termination to a war other than total collapse or total exhaustion.

As war became more and more regulated, military thought turned from experimental tactics, as seen in the days of

Gustavus, Cromwell and Vauban, towards tactical forms, such as the interminable argument of columns *versus* lines and *vice versa*. Nevertheless, this age was one of great generals; for as all armies were of one model and fire and shock were well balanced, genius, when in command, dominated the field—*e.g.*, Charles XII, Marlborough, Eugene, Marshal Saxe and Frederick the Great. Thus it came about that few centuries have witnessed so many decisive battles—Blenheim, 1704; Ramillies, 1706; Poltava, 1709; Leuthen, Rossbach and Plassey, 1757; and Quebec, 1759, to mention the more outstanding. Also it was an age of noted sieges.

Between 1703 and the outbreak of the War of American Independence in 1775, when ideological war was reintroduced, though the sole improvement in infantry arms was the substitution of an iron for the wooden ramrod by Leopold of Anhalt Dessau in 1740, vast strides forward were made in artillery.

Technically, the most notable suggestions were those of an Englishman, Benjamin Robins, in his book *New Principles of Gunnery*, published in 1742. Though he advocated the breach-loading rifled gun and breach-loading musket, which were a hundred years before their day, his most noted invention was the ballistic pendulum. This instrument enabled the gunner to measure the velocity of his projectile, and, in consequence, improve his powder.

Only during the last quarter of the century do we find new projectiles being devised—namely, Mercier's "operative gun shell" during the siege of Gibraltar (1779-1783), a 5·5-inch mortar shell with short fuze fired from a 24-pounder gun; and Lieutenant Henry Shrapnel's "spherical case" as he called it, but better known as shrapnel shell. The one was destined to render obsolete the wooden battleship, and the other to revolutionize battle tactics. Though Shrapnel invented his shell in 1784, it was not adopted by the British Ordnance Committee until 1803.

Tactically, the most noted innovation was the introduction of horse artillery by Frederick the Great (1740-1786) in

1759. And only second to it the extensive use he made of field howitzers, a weapon first employed by the Dutch at Nerwinden in 1693. At Burkersdorf, in 1762, Frederick massed 45 howitzers in one great battery.

The greatest progress was, however, made in France under the direction of Gribeauval (1715-1789), who, in 1776, was appointed Inspector-General of Artillery. Though he was unable to persuade the King to create horse artillery,[47] he introduced limber-boxes and reorganized French artillery from top to bottom.

His field artillery was restricted to 4-pounders as regimental guns; 8- and 12-pounders and 6-inch howitzers as reserve, or what would now be called divisional guns; and for garrison and siege 16- and 12-pounders and 8-inch, 10-inch and 12-inch mortars. All carriages were constructed on a uniform model, parts being interchangeable so far as it was possible. Horses were harnessed in pairs instead of in file.

These changes as radically influenced artillery as the introduction of the bayonet had infantry, with the result that the cannon began to dominate the musket.

Two other effects remain to be noted. The first is that the increasing use of artillery involved an increase in the number of horses and wagons, consequently the lengthening of columns on the march, and, therefore, also it raised the problem of their protection. This gave rise to the formation of light infantry and light cavalry units—*Chasseurs à pied* and *à cheval*. Thus infantry began to be split again into two types, varying in functions but not in arms. Many "free corps" were recruited, and towards the end of his reign Frederick raised three regiments of Light Infantry and a Jäger Regiment of two battalions, one of which was armed with rifles.[48]

The second effect was the rise in the cost of armies, due mainly to the increase in artillery, and the ever-increasing demands on industry for standardized arms and equipment, which, as Mumford points out, hastened factory organization.[49] Military demands fostered mass production, which, in turn, stimulated the growth of armies and the advance of

Capitalism. The quality idea, upon which eighteenth-century fighting power was based, was, in the last lap of that century, steadily giving way to the quantity idea, and at the very moment when steam power—quantity energy—was being introduced. Like gunpowder, steam was destined to revolutionize warfare, and by doing so to open a new chapter in the history of *The Will to Power*, called "The Nation in Arms."

REFERENCES

1. *History of European Morals*, William Edward Hartpole Lecky (1902), vol. i, p. 126.
2. *Sartor Resartus*, Thomas Carlyle, chap. viii.
3. *The Art of War in Italy*, 1494-1529, F. L. Taylor (1921), p. 11.
4. *Discourses*, chap xl, bk. iii.
5. On this question Sir Charles Oman writes: "There was some protest against it even among the French nobility: but the feeling of the man in the street was undoubtedly expressed by the old swashbuckler Montluc when he wrote: 'Christian princes on the other side made much ado about our master calling in the Turk to his aid. But against one's enemy one may make an arrow of any sort of wood. For my own part, I would call up all the devils of hell to help me break my enemy's head, when he is trying to break mine. I would do it cheerfully, and then may God pardon me.' This outburst refers to the time when Barbarossa's corsairs were driving off thousands of Christian men and women, to be sold in the slave market of Constantinople, while their French allies looked on, content to have handed over to them the depopulated walls (1543)" (*A History of the Art of War in the Sixteenth Century*, 1937, pp. 10-11).
6. *The Origin of Artillery*, Lieut.-Colonel Henry W. L. Hime (1915), pp. 112-113. "If Bacon were in possession of such secrets, why, it may be asked, did he not publish them openly? The reason was, as he explains repeatedly and at length, that he firmly believed scientific knowledge to be hurtful to the people. He protests in his works again and again against the diffusion of scientific information. 'The crowd,' he says, 'is unable to digest scientific facts, which it scorns and misuses to its own detriment and that of the wise. Let not pearls, then, be thrown to swine' (*Compendium Studii*, p. 416). Elsewhere he says: 'The mob scoff at philosophers and despise scientific truth. If by chance they lay hold upon some great principle, they are sure to misinterpret and misapply it, so that what would have been gain to everyone causes loss to all' (*De Secretis*, cap. viii). 'It is madness,' he goes on to say, 'to commit a secret to writing, unless it be so done as to be unintelligible to the ignorant, and only just intelligible to the best educated' " (*Gunpowder and Ammunition: Their Origin and Progress*, Lieut.-Colonel Henry W. L. Hime, 1904, p. 142).
7. See Oman's *A History of the Art of War* (1924), vol. ii, p. 21.
8. *Ibid.*, vol. ii, p. 211.

9. *Les Chroniques de la Ville de Metz*, J. F. Huguenin (1838), pp. 44-45.

10. Hime, *The Origin of Artillery*, p. 128.

11. Oman's *A History of the Art of War*, vol. ii, p. 216.

12. *Ibid.*, vol. ii, p. 222.

13. *Reliquiæ Antiquiæ*, Wright and Halliwell, 1841. Quoted by Hime in *Gunpowder and Ammunition*, p. 200.

14. *Constantine, the Last Emperor of the Greeks*, Chemodil Mijatovich, p. 150.

15. Two stone balls still exist in Constantinople of 46 inches diameter. Machines throwing much larger balls were in use just before the invention of great cannon. At the siege of Zara, in 1346, shot of 3,000 lb. were hurled by the Venetians. And, in 1373, the Genoese used nearly as large ones at the siege of Cyprus. *Mons Meg* at Edinburgh, cast in 1455, threw granite balls of 21 ins. in diameter. When attempting to force the Dardanelles in 1807, Sir John Duckworth's squadron was repeatedly struck by stone balls of enormous size (*The Evolution of Naval Armament*, Frederick Leslie Robertson, 1921, p. 67).

16. See *La Siège la Prise et le Sac de Constantinople par les Turcs en 1453*, Gustave Schlumberger, p. ii.

17. *A History of the Art of War*, vol. ii, p. 226.

18. *Ibid.*, vol. ii, p. 227.

19. *The Art of War in Italy*, 1494-1529, F. L. Taylor (1921), p. 90.

20. For a full account of this extremely interesting battle, see Taylor, Appendix A.

21. *The Prince* (Everyman's Library), chap. xii, p. 98.

22. Systematic sapping was first introduced at the siege of Padua in 1513, and explosive mines were first used by Charles VIII at the siege of Naples in 1495. They were highly developed by the great Spanish engineer Pedro Navarro, who became a scourge to French and Italian garrisons. Counter-mining was also developed. To detect mining operations,Philippe de Clèves recommended the suspension of needles over basins of water. Also bells and rattles placed on drums were sometimes used.

23. *The Art of War in Italy*, 1494-1529, F. L. Taylor, p. 61.

24. *Ibid.*, p. 62.

25. *Don Quixote*, pt. i, bk. ii, chap. 11.

26. *Orlando Furioso*, bk. i, canto 9, Engl. trans., John Hoole (1783).

27. *I Henry IV*, I, iii.

28. *A Brief Discourse concerning the Force and Effect of All Manual Weapons of Fire, etc.* (1594), p. 14. Nevertheless, in 1625 Neade published his *Double-Armed Man*, recommending the reintroduction of the longbow, and so late as 1798 Richard Oswald Mason did the same in his *Considerations of the Reasons that exist for reviving the use of the Long Bow with the Pike*. The pike had even a longer championship. In 1815 Sir Samuel Auchmuty, K.B., urged its return, as also did Major-General Sir William Morison, K.C.B., in 1850, in his *Notes Explanatory of the Advantages of the Pike-Musket and Pike-Rifle as compared with the Arms at Present in Use*. In the panic of 1940 pikes were issued to the British Home Guard.

29. "Machiavelli: The Renaissance of the Art of War," in *Makers of Modern Strategy*, edited by Edward Mead Earle, 1943, p. 10.

30. *A History of the Art of War in the Sixteenth Century* (1937), p. 351.

31. *The Evolution of Naval Armament*, Frederick Leslie Robertson (1921), p. 77.

32. *State Papers Relating to the Defeat of the Spanish Armada*, edited by John Knox Laughton, vol. i, p. 156.

33. *Historie of the World*, Sir Walter Raleigh (1736), vol. ii, p. 565.

34. Quoted by Alfred Vagts in *A History of Militarism* (1938), pp. 44-45.

35. In 1890 "the power of the Masai was waning, and a new power, that of the Akikuyu, seemed in the ascendant; for a once peaceful agricultural tribe had become a warring one, losing its native culture in exchange for a pastoral and foreign one. It is unquestionable that in this change the borrowed assegai proved a main and impelling factor. A more efficient weapon taken over, at first, as a means of self-preservation became in turn an impetus to a new field of endeavour, acquisition by means of conquest" (Walter Dyk, quoted by Quincy Wright in *A Study of War*, vol. i, p. 86).

36. *Technics and Civilization* (1934), p. 76.

37. *Ibid.*, p. 88.

38. See Gibbon's remarks in *The Decline and Fall of the Roman Empire*, vol. ii, chap. xxi.

39. They were invented by Colonel Wurmbrant and consisted of a copper tube bound with iron rings and rope and covered with leather. Without its carriage it weighed 90 lbs.

40. The flint-lock was easier to aim with as its butt could be brought to the shoulder, whereas that of the match-lock was placed against the chest six inches below the chin. Its time in loading was half that of the match-lock: by 1700 at least one round a minute could be fired. The priming of the match-lock was more liable to be deadened by wet and blown away. Risks of accidents were greater (*e.g.*, see Beaumont and Fletcher's *Knight of the Burning Pestle*, Act V, Scenes 1 and 2). In presence of the enemy the match had to be kept burning, which at night-time gave positions away. Worst of all, immense quantities had to be carried. Professor Firth quotes that the garrison of Lyme, 1,500 men, often used five hundredweights in twenty-four hours (*Cromwell's Army*, p. 83).

41. Probably derived from the town of Bayonne, where short daggers called "bayonettes" first made their appearance towards the end of the fifteenth century.

42. An earlier claim is 1643, see Gaya's *Traité des Armes*, 1678. Edited by Charles ffoulkes (1911), p. xiii.

43. Makay's *Memoirs of the Scottish War* (1833), p. 52.

44. This bayonet remained in the British Service until 1805, when Major-General Sir John Moore introduced the spring-clip bayonet.

45. *Stray Military Papers* (1897), p. 23.

46. *Peace and War*, Guglielmo Ferrero (1933), p. 7. On this question Vattel writes: "The first rule . . . is, that *regular war, as to its effects, is to be accounted just on both sides*. This is absolutely necessary . . . if people wish to introduce any order, any regularity, into so violent an operation as that of arms, or to set any bounds to the calamities of which it is

productive, and leave a door constantly open for the return of peace"
(*The Law of Nations*, 1834, p. 382).

47. Adopted by the French and Swedes in 1791 and the English in 1793.

48. For Light Infantry during this period see my *British Light Infantry in the Eighteenth Century* (1925).

49. *Technics and Civilization*, p. 90.

CHAPTER V
THE AGE OF STEAM

BENEATH the ordered absolutism of the eighteenth century there lurked powerful exlposive forces, some of the most violent of which had sprung into being during the Puritan Revolution in England. There, the divine right of kings was jettisoned; mercantilism was vastly fortified by Cromwell's Navigation Act of 1651, and a new political philosophy was planted by Thomas Hobbes (1588-1679) and John Locke (1632-1704).

This revolution had barely ended when, in 1694, the Bank of England was created by a group of men of high mercantile standing, to be followed four years later by the introduction of Thomas Savery's steam pumping engine.

The first of these creations, and later on the second also, went far to strengthen the mercantile system, in which war was endemic, because its main object was to extract wealth from other nations. Wars were now increasingly fought on credit, their aim being the capture of markets in order to compel foreigners to buy and prevent them to sell. In 1776 this was noted by Adam Smith. In his *Inquiry into the Nature and Causes of the Wealth of Nations*, he wrote: "The capricious ambition of kings and ministers has not during the present and preceding century been more fatal to the repose of Europe than the impertinent jealousy of merchants and manufacturers."[1]

The circle was indeed a vicious one. Mercantilism meant war; war to support itself demanded manufacturing power, and manufactures fortified mercantilism.

Until 1757, when Clive's victory at Plassey unleashed the hoarded treasure of Bengal, money in sufficient quantity was lacking to finance manufacture. Then, as Brooks Adams writes, " probably nothing has ever equalled the rapidity of the change which followed. In 1760 the flying-shuttle appeared, and coal began to replace wood in smelting. In

1764 Hargreaves invented the spinning jenny, in 1779 Crompton contrived the mule, in 1785 Cartwright patented the power-loom, and, chief of all, in 1768 Watt matured the steam-engine, the most perfect of all vents of centralizing energy."[2]

The industrial revolution which now set in synchronized with the preaching of a new way of life by a host of philoso-phers—Montesquieu (1689-1755), Burlamaqui (1694-1748), Voltaire (1684-1778), Rousseau (1712-1775), Beccaria (1735-1794), and Condorcet (1743-1794), to mention a few, their central doctrine being that natural society is a state of equality and liberty. In its turn, this philosophy demanded a people's army to safeguard it against tyranny, a demand voiced by Guibert in his *Essai général de tactique*, published in 1772. In it he proclaimed that European hegemony would fall to whichever nation first created a true national army.[3] Also, in his *Esquisses d'un tableau historique des progrès de l'esprit humain*, Condorcet connected the rise of infantry with the rise of democracy, though it would have been more correct to have reversed this sequence, because the musket made the infantryman and the infantryman made the democrat. Power to kill, and, therefore, to enforce freedom, was the essence of the question.

The first demonstration of this new form of war was held in America, to become known to history as the War of the American Revolution or Independence. Ideologically, it was a revolt against tyranny, a people's war and a war of loose rather than of parade movements.[4] Shooting to kill and trickery to deceive, so thoroughly indulged in by the Americans, were as contrary to the rules of eighteenth-century warfare as they were patent to Indian fighting. Incidents such as pretence to surrender and then to continue fighting, as happened at Huberton, and of swearing alle-giance one day and attacking on the next, as occurred at Bennington, were typical of this new form of warfare. Even Washington on one occasion instructed some of his soldiers who wore red coats to sew onto them the buttons of an English regiment, pass through the English lines and kidnap General Clinton.[5]

During this war there struggled into daylight not only the spirit of democratic nationalism, but also its logical sequence —the mass army. More truly may it be said that the birth of nineteenth-century warfare dates from the signing of the Declaration of Independence on July 4, 1776, than from the storming of the Bastille on July 14, thirteen years later.

Carried into France, the ideology of the War of the American Independence gave birth to the "sans culottism" of the French Revolution—the antithesis of "courtiership." Terror became a weapon under the Jacobins, and in theory at least war was rendered total and in consequence brutal. In ideal, war was no longer a royal gamble to settle a frontier or a dynasty. Instead, its aim was the destruction of the enemy until the moment arrived when "the death of an enemy soldier became useless to liberty."[6] In February, 1794, Carnot made it a rule "to act in mass formation. . . . Give battle on a large scale and pursue the enemy till he is utterly destroyed."[7] All *émigrés* when caught were to be killed, and Robespierre decreed that "no quarter be shown to British and Hanoverian soldiers."[8] Thus all rules of war were rendered absurd.

The first practical step taken in establishing this return to unrestricted warfare was the introduction of conscription by General Jourdan and the Council of Five Hundred in 1798. As Colonel Maude wrote in the eleventh edition of the *Encyclopædia Britannica*, this power to enrol a nation "alone rendered the Napoleonic policy of conquest possible. 'I can afford to expend thirty thousand men a month'; this boast of Napoleon's, made to Metternich at Schönbrunn in 1805, has determined the trend of events from that day forward, not only on the battlefield but also in the workshops."[9]

As the training of the French conscripts was negligible, tactics were irregular and based on man and musket. The skirmishers were, as Sir Robert Wilson said, "as sharp-sighted as ferrets, and as active as squirrels."[10] And the Duke of York's aide-de-camp wrote: "No mobbed fox was ever more put to it to make his escape than we were, being at times nearly surrounded."[11] Other nations followed suit, and light infantry became a permanent service in every army.[12]

Under Napoleon, armies were quadrupled in size and battles in slaughter, power being sought through multiplication, until, as it was said, God Himself had no choice but to side with the biggest battalions. Reviewing this development, Jomini was of opinion that war would become "a bloody and most unreasonable struggle between great masses equipped with weapons of unimaginable power. We might," he commented, "see again wars of peoples like those of the fourth century; we might be forced to live again through the centuries of the Huns, the Vandals, and the Tartars."[13]

This was prophecy, indeed, for a hundred years later we find Spengler writing: "For this is the century of gigantic permanent armies and universal compulsory service. . . . Ever since Napoleon, hundreds of thousands, and latterly millions of men have stood ready to march. . . . It is a war without war, a war of overbidding in equipment and preparedness, a war of figures and tempo and technics, and the diplomatic dealings have not been of court with court, but of headquarters with headquarters."[14]

In Napoleon the Power Age found its prophet: hence onwards a new Islamism was to engulf the Western World. Its Koran was written by Karl von Clausewitz (1780-1831), a Prussian general. Dying in 1831, his writings were edited and published by his widow, and the first three volumes, containing his master work, an unfinished exposition on the philosophy of war, was entitled *Vom Kriege* (On War). In succeeding years it moulded the German military mind and carried the Prussian armies to victory in 1866 and 1870. Since when it has become the war creed of all nations.

Accepting the quantity idea as the heart of the Napoleonic system, Clausewitz based his war philosophy on the syllogism: A soldier is a fighting man; a nation is a mass of potential fighting men; therefore maximum fighting power demands that all men be trained as soldiers. The following

quotations from his great work will give a fairly clear picture
of his philosophy:

(1) "War belongs not to the province of Arts and Sciences,
but to the province of social life. . . . State policy is the
womb in which war is developed, in which its outlines lie
hidden in a rudimentary state, like the qualities of living
creatures in their germs."

(2) "War is nothing but a duel on an extensive scale."

(3) "War should be waged with the whole might of the
national power."

(4) "War is . . . a continuation of political intercourse,
with a mixture of other means."

(5) "War is an act of violence pushed to its utmost
bounds."[15]

The aim of this "Spartanism" was to turn the State into
a military machine, and at the very time when steam power
was beginning to turn it into an industrial machine. Hence
onwards, both armies and factories increasingly ceased to be
the servants of the people to become their masters. Henceforth, the mass struggle dominated life (1859, *The Origin of
Species*), work (1867, *Das Kapital*) and war (1832, *Vom
Kriege*), Darwin, Marx and Clausewitz becoming the ruling
trinity of the nineteenth and twentieth centuries.

Nevertheless, without steam power there could have been
no radical change, because the struggle for existence, as
popularized by Darwin, would never have been carried into
the factories and thence on to the battlefields. In a little over
a hundred years all was transformed.

Until about 1730 British manufacture depended on foreign
inventions. Ten years later smelting with coal and coke,
instead of with charcoal, was introduced. In 1740 the annual
output of iron in Great Britain was 17,000 tons; in 1800 it
was 150,000 tons, and in 1840, 1,400,000. In the second
half of the eighteenth century machines began to make
machines: this was the true beginning of the industrial
revolution. In 1769, the year Napoleon and Wellington were
born, Cugnot, in France, invented the first steam carriage.
And in 1815, the year Napoleon was finally defeated, the

first steamship made her passage from Greenock to London,[16] and four years later the New York built *Savannah* was the first steamer to cross the Atlantic.[17] Six years later still, the first true railway was constructed by George Stephenson between Stockton and Darlington.

Here were Cyclopean forces which were about to change the face of the world, and, in changing it, raise war from the cockpit of gladiatorial armies to the grand amphitheatre of contending nations.

Nevertheless, until the middle of the nineteenth century the influence of steam power on the development of armaments was comparatively slight, mainly because peace between the greater Powers prevailed until 1848, when the first rumblings of a new period of war were heard. I will now turn to this development.

The two outstanding military inventions of the first half of the nineteenth century were the percussion cap and the cylindro-conoidal bullet, which gave further impetus to the quantity theory of war. The first was impossible until the discovery of an explosive which detonated on concussion, and it was not until L. G. Brugnatelli, in 1798, produced "fulminating silver" that this became practicable. Next, in 1800, Edward Charles Howard discovered fulminate of mercury. Seven years later, the Rev. A. Forsyth patented a percussion powder for priming,[18] and in 1814, Thomas Shaw of Philadelphia invented a steel percussion cap, substituting for it a copper one in 1816.[19]

It was this cap which made the percussion musket and rifle possible. Yet, in England, it was not until 1834 that experiments were made with the percussion system. In 1839, these led to the conversion of flint-lock muskets to the percussion principle.[20]

The next improvement came in 1823. That year Captain Norton of the British 34th Regiment designed a cylindro-conoidal bullet with a hollow base, so that when fired it would automatically expand and seal the bore.[21] In 1836, Mr. Greener, a gunsmith, improved upon this bullet by inserting a conoidal wooden plug in its base. Though both inventions were rejected by the British Government, the idea was taken up in France, and in 1849, working on Greener's design, M. Minié produced the Minié bullet. Thereupon it was adopted[22] by the British Government and a rifle of the Minié pattern was issued to the army in 1851.

This rifle was first used in the Kaffir War of 1852, during which it was discovered that "at a range of from twelve to thirteen hundred yards small bodies of Kaffirs could be dispersed."[23]

These two inventions—the percussion cap and the cylindro-conoidal bullet—revolutionized infantry tactics. The first rendered the musket serviceable in wet weather, reducing missfires in each 1,000 rounds from 411 to 4·5, and raising hits from 270 to 385 in 1,000 shots. The second caused the rifle to become the most deadly weapon of the century.

Yet another development springing from the percussion cap must be noted. It made possible the expansive cartridge case, which, in its turn, rendered practicable the breech-loading system.[24] This case completely revolutionized the art of gunnery by preventing the escape of all gases at the breech. First came Houiller's (a Paris gunsmith) pin-fire cartridge in 1847; next the rim-fire cartridge, and lastly Daw's central fire cartridge case in 1861.

While these changes were in progress, steam propulsion, in the forms of the marine engine and the locomotive, was laying the military foundations of an intensified power politics which in the twentieth century was to disrupt the world. The one enabled Great Britain to extend her dominion of the seas; the other enabled first Prussia and later on all the Continental Powers to put Clausewitz's theories into practice. I will now examine these in turn.

As we have seen, the paddle-wheel—known since the days of the Romans and experimented with during the sixteenth and seventeenth centuries—was first adapted to steam propulsion towards the end of the eighteenth century. In 1813, Robert Fulton, an American engineer of vision, built the first steam-propelled armoured ship, the *Demologos*, later renamed the *Fulton*. She was of twin hull construction with a central paddle-wheel between the hulls, and was protected by a belt of timber fifty-eight inches in thickness. This monstrous vessel clearly showed that two things were required: a less vulnerable system of propulsion and a less clumsy means of protection.

The first of these problems was solved by the introduction of the screw propeller, for which, in 1836, patents were taken out in London by F. P. Smith and Captain John Ericsson (a Swedish military officer). The second was solved by the substitution of iron for wood: the first iron vessel—a pleasure boat—had already been built in England in 1815.[25]

Strange to say, the British Admiralty was opposed to these "newfangled" ideas. For instance, when in 1828 the Colonial Office asked Lord Melville, First Lord of the Admiralty, for a steam packet to convey mails from Malta to the Ionian Islands, the following reply was received: "Their lordships felt it their bounden duty to discourage, to the utmost of their ability, the employment of steam vessels, as they considered that the introduction of steam was calculated to strike a fatal blow at the naval supremacy of the Empire."[26]

Thus it came about that, when twenty-six years later Great Britain was involved in the Crimean War (1853-1856), except for a few warships fitted with auxiliary engines and a number of steam tugs, her entire fleet consisted of wooden sail-propelled vessels.

What is so astonishing is that the shell guns, particularly the Paixhans gun,[27] had, since 1821, rendered the wooden ship so vulnerable as to deprive her of nearly all her fighting power. Paixhans saw this clearly, and, as Sir William Congreve had done in 1805, the following year he suggested that warships should be belted with iron plates.

At the very opening of the Crimean War this prevision was justified, for at the battle of Sinope, in November 1853, a squadron of Turkish frigates was almost blown out of the water by the shell fire of the Russian ships.[28] The upshot was that immediately after France entered the conflict, Napoleon III issued an order for the construction of a flotilla of floating batteries protected by armour, which would resist not only solid shot but also explosive shell. Five were built, protected by 4 inches of iron plate. They mounted sixteen 56-pounder shell guns and were equipped with auxiliary steam machinery. Their success was complete. Not only was the need for the armouring of ships proved beyond all doubt, but also that armouring would necessitate the introduction of more powerful ordnance. This led to the general adoption of rifled cannon.

Shortly after the Crimean War ended, France and Great Britain laid down the first two armoured steam warships, *La Gloire* and the *Warrior*. These vessels were launched in 1859 and 1861. The *Warrior* was 380 feet in length; 8,830 tons displacement; engine, 6,000 initial horse-power; speed, fourteen and a half knots. Her armament consisted of twenty-eight 7-inch 6½-ton guns, and her armour belt was 4½ inches in thickness.[29]

At length, on March 9, 1862, during the American Civil War came the first trial between ironclads. That day, in Hampton Roads, the Confederate *Merrimac* met the Federal *Monitor*,[30] and for three hours they pounded and rammed each other without a decision being gained. Nevertheless, this action proved decisive. Henceforth it was clear that no wooden ships could stand up to an ironclad. And of this engagement the British Admiral Sir John Hay said: "The man who goes into action in a wooden ship is a fool, and the man who sends him there is a villain."[31] Metaphorically, on March 9, 1862, the wooden fleets of the world were sunk in Hampton Roads.

Instead of striking a fatal blow at the naval supremacy of Great Britain, once a turn over from sail to steam became imperative, her superior industrial power enabled her dockyards to outstrip those of the next two greatest naval powers combined. This would not have been practicable had the wooden ship continued, for already in 1838 the combined fleets of France and Russia were superior to her own.[32] What was most fortunate for her was that this change occurred before and during, instead of after, the locomotive had placed Prussia in a supremely powerful position on the continent of Europe.

It is no coincidence that the nation which produced Clausewitz was the first to grasp the supreme importance of the railway in war. Even before a line had been laid in Prussia we find civil thought turning to the military importance of railways. Thus, in 1833, F. W. Harkort pointed out that a railway between Cologne and Minden and another between Mainz and Wesel would add enormously to the defence of the Rhineland, and C. E. Pönitz urged the general building of railways in order to protect Prussia against France, Austria and Russia. Simultaneously, Friedrich List (1789-1846), an economist of unique genius, pointed out that from the position of a secondary military power, whose weakness lay in her central position between powerful potential enemies, Prussia could be raised by the railway into a formidable one. "She could be made into a defensive bastion in the very heart of Europe. Speed of mobilization, the rapidity with which troops could be moved from the centre of the country to its periphery, and the other obvious advantages of 'interior lines' of rail transport would be of greater relative advantage to Germany than to any other European country."[33] List himself wrote: "Every mile of railway which a neighbouring nation finishes sooner than we, each mile more of railway it possesses, gives it an advantage over us . . . it is just as little left in our hands to determine whether we shall make use of the new defensive weapons given us by the march of progress, as it was left to our forefathers to determine whether they should shoulder the rifle instead of the bow and arrow."[34]

In 1833 this remarkable man projected a network of railway lines for Germany which "is substantially that of the present Reichsbahnen,"[35] and thirteen years later, the year of his death, the first extensive troop movement by rail was made by a Prussian army corps 12,000 strong, with horses and guns to Cracow. This experimental move led to the Prussian General Staff making a comprehensive survey of the military value of railways.

Though during the revolutionary troubles of 1848-1850 Prussia gained further experience in rail movements, as also did Austria and Russia, it was not until the Italian War of 1859 and the American Civil War (1851-1865) that troop movements by rail may be said to have become normal. Next, in the Austro-Prussian War of 1866, strategy was largely shaped by the respective railroad systems. Finally, in the Franco-Prussian War (1870-1871), in the hands of Count von Moltke (1800-1891), railway strategy was reduced to a fine art. In this war no less than 100,000 Germans were engaged upon protecting the railways behind the Prussian front, and the massing and supply of the German troops at the siege of Paris would not have been possible without the railway. Thus it came about that the genius of George Stephenson (1781-1848) gave life to the Clausewitzian theory of the nation in arms.

From 1866 onwards mass armies take the field. The long-service standing army progressively gives way to the short-service conscript. Quality is ousted by quantity and war becomes the affair of the "average man." As the professional proficiency of the soldier declines, a higher efficiency is demanded of the officer both in leadership and in administration. Command becomes so complex that it largely passes out of the hands of the individual into those of an oligarchy—the General Staff, assisted by a Quartermaster-General Staff, an Adjutant-General's Staff and an ever-increasing number of experts. Nor does change end here, for the larger armies grow the more dependent do they become on industry to equip, arm and supply them both in peace and war. Industry, the postal and telegraph system, etc., are organized for war, for a nation in arms demands a nation of armourers and technicians to sustain and maintain it. The nation which makes the greatest use of peace intervals to advance its mechanical and engineering potentials for war, and which possesses the greatest number of skilled workers as well as of trained soldiers, and the most abundant supplies of raw materials as well as of arms, is the nation upon whom victory smiles. In all this Prussia took the lead, as she also did in the development of the rifle, *par excellence* the weapon of the conscript mass army.

While other nations were arguing over the merits and demerits of the flint and percussion lock muskets, in 1841[36] Prussia took the bold step of issuing to certain regiments the Dreyse breech-loading rifle, better known as the needle gun.

Though breech-loading rifles, as we have seen, were suggested by Benjamin Robins, Johann Nicholas Dreyse (1787-1867) was the first man to produce a serviceable one, which he did between the years 1824 and 1836. Though its effective range was considerably less than that of the Minié rifle, seven shots a minute could be fired with it instead of a maximum of two. Nevertheless, its main advantage lay not in rapidity of loading, but that a breech-operated rifle can be loaded in the prone position.[37]

In the development of artillery Prussia was less progressive. Breech-loading and rifling of cannon were old as separate ideas,[38] and it would seem that combined they were first experimented with in England in 1745.[39] Next, exactly a hundred years later, an effective breech-loading 6·5-inch rifled gun was invented by Major Cavalli, a Sardinian officer, and a still more effective one by Baron Wahrendorff in 1846. Nevertheless, neither Prussia nor any other country would face the cost of re-equipment, so experiments continued. Then came the war in the Crimea, during which a number of cast-iron muzzle-loading smooth-bore 68-pounders and 8-inch guns were converted into rifled pieces on the Lanchester principle.[40] As their greater range and accuracy made the bombardment of Sebastopol a "very hideous thing," after the close of this war all the Powers began experimenting in rifled breech-loading ordnance.

In the next war—namely, the Civil War in America—the rifled gun came more and more to the fore. Yet, from the armament point of view, the main characteristic of this war was the extraordinary inventiveness displayed throughout it. During it a magazine-loading rifle and a machine gun were invented. Torpedoes, land mines, submarine mines, the field telegraph, lamp and flag signalling, wire entanglements, wooden wire-bound mortars, hand-grenades, winged-grenades, rockets and many forms of booby traps were tried out. Armoured trains were used; balloons were employed by both sides. Explosive bullets are mentioned, searchlights and "stink-shell" to cause "suffocating effect" were asked for. The use of flame-projectors was proposed and the U.S.S. *Housatonic* was sunk on February 17, 1864, by a small man-propelled Confederate submarine.[41]

Though Friedrich Engels saw in this war a "drama without parallel in the annals of military history," and Karl Marx wrote, "Just as the American War of Independence in the eighteenth century sounded the tocsin for the middle classes of Europe, so the American Civil War in the nineteenth century has sounded the tocsin for the European working class,"[42] it is astonishing to find that so intelligent a soldier as the great Moltke could see in it no more than "two armed mobs chasing each other around the country, from which nothing could be learned."

Though the Austro-Prussian War of 1866 followed too closely on its heels for the American Civil War to influence it, it showed little technical advance except the superiority of the needle gun over the Austrian muzzle-loading Lorenz rifle. The Austrian tactics were completely obsolete, reliance being placed on close formations and the bayonet.[43] Nevertheless, it is strange to learn that in this short war of seven weeks the Prussian expenditure of small arms ammunition was only 2,000,000 rounds—that is, about seven per man mobilized.

The importance of this war was that it increased Prussian man power by 24,000,000 people. This, bearing in mind the quantity theory, gave Prussia a mass superiority of 33 per cent. over France. When the next clash came, as it did in 1870, this to a certain extent made good the deficiency between the now obsolescent needle gun and the French *chassepot* which outranged it by several hundred yards. Nevertheless, it was the superiority in handling of the Prussian breech-loading rifled guns over the French bronze muzzle-loading rifled cannon which was the decisive factor. At the battle of Gravelotte the Prussians had altogether no fewer than 726 pieces. At Sedan—the decisive battle of the war—again the Prussians massed their guns, bringing all the French attacks to a standstill, and most of them at 2,000 yards distance—that is, outside effective rifle range. In this battle "a French officer who was taken prisoner described the German fire as 'five kilometres of artillery.' "[44]

In this war the field gun definitely challenged the dominance of the rifle, and in its turn the rifle finally abolished cavalry as a shock arm, for a single volley was sufficient to shatter a charge, as happened to General Gallifet's Chasseurs d'Afrique at Sedan.[45] Nevertheless, the outstanding lesson of the war was that a conflict of masses is a war of accidents in which genius is out of place. Though the general can still plot and plan, and increasingly must do so, he can no longer lead or command because the masses are too vast for his grasp. Command now passes to the General Staff, its foremost problem being the development of fire power. Thus the phalangial order—shock by bullets and shells—once again becomes supreme.

Though the European peace which followed the Franco-Prussian War was actually the longest in modern history,[46] no period since the Mongol invasions was so aggressive, and none since the industrial revolution set in so progressive in the development of armament. In the generation following that war, Great Britain acquired 4,754,000 square miles of territory; France, 3,593,580; Germany, 1,026,220, and Belgium, 900,000—that is, seventy-nine times her own size!

These enormous annexations, rendered possible by the breech-loading rifle, as those of the Conquistadores had been by the arquebus, so influenced international politics and trade that, in order to secure commercial predominance, an armament race was fostered. This was led by Germany, who in 1898 set out to establish herself as the second greatest naval power—a challenge to the maritime supremacy of Great Britain.

During this period naval construction developed so rapidly

that warships passed into obsolescence no sooner than they were launched. Three new weapons, old in idea, revolutionized naval tactics—namely, the submarine mine, torpedo and submersible ship.

The first had been used by the Americans as early as 1777; but it was not until electrically fired mines were introduced during the American Civil War that this weapon became really effective.

The second, in the form of the spar or outrigger torpedo, had been experimented with by Fulton in 1805, and was used during the American Civil War. It was followed by the Harvey, Lay, Sims-Edison and Brennan locomotive torpedoes, the first three electrically steered by a wire trailing behind. All these were superseded by the self-propelled Whitehead torpedo, which soon led to the introduction of the torpedo boat.

The third was the submarine, or submersible torpedo carrier, first successfully experimented with by David Bushnell in 1776.[47] It was not, however, until 1875 that J. P. Holland designed the first practical submarine, which in 1883 was followed by the Nordenfeldt model, a vessel of 60 tons, with a submerged speed of nine knots. Thence onwards evolution was rapid. Nevertheless, not until the opening years of the twentieth century was this type of warship generally adopted.

On land, military progress was equally intense. The theory of the nation in arms was now finally accepted by all Continental Powers, also by Japan, and the powers of conscript armies were vastly fortified by three developments in armament—the general adoption of the small-bore magazine rifle firing smokeless powder; the perfection of the machine gun and the introduction of quick-firing artillery.

The first came into general use between 1886 and 1891. The second, as we have seen, was a very old idea, dating back to the *ribauldequin* of the fourteenth century. In modern form it first appeared in the shape of the Gatling gun during the American Civil War.[48] This was a ten-barrel revolving rifle. In 1866 the French *mitrailleuse* or *canon à balle* was invented by Commandant Reffye. It had 25 barrels and could fire at a maximun rate of 125 rounds the minute. But it was not until 1884 that Hiram S. Maxim produced an automatic gun of real value,[49] a weapon destined to revolutionize small arm tactics.

The third, which was to re-establish the gun as the dominant weapon, was evolved from the proposals put forward in 1891 by General Wille in Germany and Colonel Langlois in France. They held that high rate of fire was impossible unless recoil on firing was absorbed. This led to much experimental work on shock absorption, and to the eventual introduction of a non-recoiling carriage, which carriage permitted of a bullet-proof shield being attached to it to protect the gun crew. Thus armour was once again introduced.

Until this improvement in artillery was made, the magazine rifle, on account of its range, volume of fire and portability, as well as the invisibility of the firer using smokeless powder, was the dominant weapon. Now it was challenged by the quick-firing gun, which not only outranged it and could be fired with equal rapidity, but which by indirect laying could also be rendered invisible.

During the Russo-Japanese War (1904-1905), this dominance became apparent to at least one eyewitness, Major J. M. Home, who in one of his reports wrote:

"The great impression made on me by all I saw is that artillery is now the decisive arm and that all other arms are auxiliary to it. The importance of artillery cannot be too strongly insisted upon, for, other things being equal, the side which has the best artillery will always win. . . .

"So strongly am I convinced of the immense importance of artillery that it seems almost a question for deliberate consideration whether artillery should not be largely increased even at the expense of the other arms. . . ."[50]

Thus do we see the gun gaining supremacy over the rifle, as the rifle had gained supremacy over the non-recoil gun. A new tactics was in the making which was destined to change the character of war and with it the course of history.

Looking back on this period, the outstanding fact is the emergence of an economic feudal order, in which the great financial, industrial and commercial interests take the place of the medieval barons. It is a society based on manufacture more so than on agriculture, the driving force of which is steam power and not religion. The common factor linking these two social systems is not so much war, but preparation to wage it. As from the fieldlands came the earliest weapons, the latest now come from the factories. Throughout both periods, it is war that shapes peace and armament that shapes war.

Lewis Mumford shows that it was the quantity idea underlying the conception of the nation in arms, and more still the quantity needs of such a society, that fostered industry. The massing of men for war demanded the massing of money to pay for them, and the massing of manufacture to equip them. As he writes: "In terms of the barracks, the routine of the factory seemed tolerable and natural. The spread of conscription and volunteer militia forces throughout the Western World after the French Revolution made army and factory, so far as their social effects went, almost interchangeable terms."[51] As an example, he notes that, in 1888, Bellamy "took the organization of the army on a basis of compulsory service as the pattern of all industrial activities."[52]

Military needs not only stimulated output and adventure, but frequently created new industries. Thus, Napoleon I offered a large prize to anyone who discovered a practical way of preserving field rations. "It was won by Nicholas Appert, who, though he used glass containers, may justly be said to have been the father of the canning industry."[53]

Similarly, in the middle of the nineteenth century, Napoleon III offered a reward for "a cheap process of making steel capable of withstanding the explosive force of the new shells. The Bessemer process was the direct answer to this demand."[54]

Gun-casting improved foundry technique, and the demand for high-grade iron went hand in hand with the increase in artillery bombardments and the armouring of warships. Railways were built for strategic purposes, harbours as naval bases, and colonies were conquered to guarantee stocks of warlike raw materials.

"The state of paleotechnic society," writes Mumford, "may be described, ideally, as one of wardom. Its typical organs, from mine to factory, from blast-furnace to slum, from slum to battlefield, were at the service of death. Competition: struggle for existence: domination and submission: extinction. With war at once the main stimulus, the underlying basis, and the direct destination of this society, the normal motives and reactions of human beings were narrowed down to the desire for domination and to the fear of annihilation. . . . The mine and the battlefield underlay all the paleotechnic activities; and the practices they stimulated led to the widespread exploitation of fear."[55]

But what kind of war did fear create? A war on all fronts —diplomatic, social, economic and psychological as well as military. This was foreseen by Engels and Marx, who, as Mr. Earle points out, "can rightly be called the fathers of modern total war."[56] "To them," he writes, "war was fought with different means in different fields. In the words of the later militant syndicalist Georges Sorel, a general strike could become a 'Napoleonic battle,' just as the Crimean War could be regarded as a prelude to a great international civil strife."[57] They were the apostles of the maturing wardom which was to engulf Christendom by unchaining mass man.

Who held the leash of this hydra-headed monster? Not kings, nor presidents, nor cabinets, nor parliaments; instead the giant financial interests. Even in his day Byron saw this:

> Who hold the balance of the world? Who reign
>   O'er congress, whether royalist or liberal?
> Who rouse the shirtless patriots of Spain?
>   (That make old Europe's journals squeak and gibber all.)
> Who keep the world, both old and new, in pain
>   Or pleasure? Who make politics run glibber all?
> The shade of Buonaparte's noble daring?—
>   Jew Rothschild, and his fellow-Christian, Baring.

Those, and the truly liberal Lafitte,
Are the true lords of Europe. Every loan
Is not a merely speculative hit,
But seats a nation or upsets a throne.
Republics also get involved a bit;
Columbia's stock hath holders not unknown
On 'Change, and even thy silver soil, Peru,
Must get itself discounted by a Jew.[58]

Two generations later Moltke's outlook was much the same. He wrote:

"Nowadays, the Bourse has assumed such influence that it has the power to call armies into the field merely to protect its interests. Mexico and Egypt have been swamped with European armies simply to satisfy the demands of the *haute finance*. To-day the question, 'Is a nation strong enough to make war?' is of less importance than that 'Is a Government powerful enough to prevent war?' "[59]

Later on came Foch, who is still more emphatic. Lecturing to the students of the French Staff College on "The Primal Characteristics of Modern War," he said:

"The means for a nation to obtain wealth and satisfy its cravings is found in waging war. . . . The German victories of 1870 have enriched the individual German. Every German has a *share in the profits*, and is directly interested *in the firm, in the constitution, and in victory. That is what is now meant by a people's war.*"

He quotes the Chinese and Japanese War of 1894, the Spanish-American War and the Franco-British quarrel over Fashoda, and then writes: "What were we all seeking? For commercial outlets to an industrial system which produces more than it can sell. . . . Who was responsible for the Boer War? Certainly not the Queen of England, but the merchants of the City."[60]

Yet, what neither Moltke nor Foch saw was that the growing interdependence of the industrial world was rapidly transforming war as a profitable business into a mad kind of burglary—the plundering of one's *own* house. One man, however, did see this, not a soldier but a banker, a Polish Jew, Monsieur I. S. Bloch, who in 1897 published a three-volume work entitled, *The War of the Future in its Technical, Economic and Political Relations.*[61]

"What is the use," wrote Bloch, "of talking about the past when you are dealing with an altogether new set of considerations? Consider for one moment what nations were a hundred years ago and what they are to-day. In those days before railways, telegraphs, steamships, etc., were invented each nation was more or less a homogeneous, self-contained, self-sufficing unit. . . . All this is changed. . . . Every year the interdependence of nations upon each other for the necessaries of life is greater than it ever was before. . . . Hence the first thing that war would do would be to deprive the Powers that made it of all opportunity of benefiting by the products of the nations against whom they were fighting. . . . . The soldier is going down and the economist is going up." Therefore war is no longer a profitable court of appeal.

"The outward and visible sign of the end of war," he wrote, "was the introduction of the magazine rifle. . . . The soldier by natural evolution has so perfected the mechanism of slaughter that he has practically secured his own extinction."

His description of the modern battle is exact, for it is exactly as it was fought seventeen years later. And his prediction of the coming war is no less so:

"At first there will be increased slaughter—increased slaughter on so terrible a scale as to render it impossible to get troops to push the battle to a decisive issue. . . . The war, instead of being a hand-to-hand contest in which the combatants measure their physical and moral superiority, will become a kind of stalemate, in which, neither army being able to get at the other, both armies will be maintained in opposition to each other, threatening each other, but never able to deliver a final and decisive attack. . . . That is the future of war—not fighting, but famine; not the slaying of men, but the bankruptcy of nations and the break-up of the whole social organization. . . . Everybody will be entrenched in the next war. It will be a great war of entrenchments. The spade will be as indispensable to a soldier as his rifle. All wars will of necessity partake of the character of siege operations. . . . Soldiers may fight as they please; the ultimate decision is in the hands of *famine.* . . ."

All these things emerged from out of a cloud of steam. If this is not magic—what is? Nevertheless, Bloch overlooked one item: man is eternally inventive. No sooner does he bring a system of destruction to perfection than the Constant Tactical Factor—the urge to eliminate the danger he has created—under the whip of disaster compels him to seek yet another. The steam age in war had reached its further shore, and as Bloch's prophecy was about to be fulfilled, already in the distance gleamed yet another unexplored sea—the ocean of the Age of Oil.

REFERENCES

1. *Wealth of Nations* (1904), p. 457. Alexander Hamilton held the same opinion. In No. 6 *The Federalist* he wrote: "Has commerce hitherto done anything more than change the objects of war ? . . . Have there not been as many wars founded upon commercial motives since that has become the prevailing system of nations, as were before occasioned by the cupidity of territory or dominion?" The increasing dependence of war upon credit may be judged from the following figures: At the close of the war in 1697 a debt of £21,500,000 had been incurred, £16,000,000 remaining due at William III's death in 1702. In 1713 the debt rose to £53,000,000; in 1748 to £78,000,000; in 1763 to £137,000,000 and in 1783 to £238,000,000.

2. *The Law of Civilization and Decay* (1921), pp. 313-14. The sudden release or discovery of bullion has always been followed by troubled periods —*e.g.*, the release of Persian gold by Alexander the Great (see chap. ii); the influx of gold and silver from the Americas during the sixteenth century (see chap. iv); the discovery of gold in California in 1848 and in Australia in 1851, and the opening of the Rand goldfields in 1885, are further examples.

3. See also his remarks on breaking away from conventional tactics, *Œuvres Militaires de Guibert* (1803), vol. ii, p. 253.

4. For the increase of light troops during this war, see my *British Light Infantry in the Eighteenth Century* (1925).

5. *Writings of Washington*, vol. ii, pp. 406, 557.

6. *The French Revolution*, Albert Mathiez (1928), p. 485.

7. *Ibid.*, p. 482.

8. *History of the British Army*, Hon. J. W. Fortescue, vol. iv, p. 294.

9. *Ibid.*, vol. vi, p. 972.

10. *Life of Sir Robert Wilson*, H. Randolph (1862), vol. i, p. 86.

11. *Journals and Correspondence of Sir Henry Calvert* (1853), p. 220.

12. See my *British Light Infantry in the Eighteenth Century* and *Sir John Moore's System of Training* (1925).

13. Quoted by Crane Brinton, Gordon A. Craig and Felix Gilbert in *Makers of Modern Strategy* (1943), pp. 91-92.

14. *The Decline of the West* (1922), vol. ii, pp. 428-429.

15. *On War*, Carl von Clausewitz (1908), vol. i, p. 121; vol. i, p. 1; vol. ii, p. 231; vol. iii, p. 121 and vol. i, p. 4.

16. In Great Britain the first successful attempt to apply the steam engine to the paddle-wheel was made in 1785. In 1775, James Rumsey, a Virginian, carried out the first practical trials of water-jet propulsion on the Potomac: a steam pump sucked in water at the bow and threw it out at the stern.

17. 130 feet long; displacement 1,850 tons; gross tonnage 320; knots 6. She was fitted with paddles and took 25 days to sail from Savannah S.C. to Liverpool.

18. The explosive he used was a mixture of chlorate of potash, sulphur and charcoal, later changed to chlorate of potash, fulminate of mercury and powdered glass.

19. Colonel Peter Hawker also invented a copper percussion cap in 1818 (*Instructions to Young Sportsmen*, Col. Peter Hawker, Eleventh Edition, 1859, p. 76). There are many other claimants.

20. The advantage of this may be judged from the following incident: "A company of Sepoys, armed with flint-lock muskets, which would not go off in a heavy rain, were closely surrounded by some thousand Chinese, and were in imminent peril, when two companies of marines, armed with percussion-cap muskets, were ordered up, and soon dispersed the enemy with great loss" (Dispatch of Lieut.-General Lord Viscount Gough, *London Gazette*, October 8, 1841).

21. "The idea came to him from an examination of the arrow used by the natives of Southern India with their blow-tube: an examination which revealed that the base of the arrow was formed of elastic lotus-pith, which by its expansion against the cylindrical surface of the tube prevented the escape of air past it" (*The Evolution of Naval Armament*, Frederick Leslie Robertson, 1921, p. 193).

22. In 1852 the British Government paid M. Minié £20,000 for his bullet, and in 1857 Greener received £1,000 for having given him the idea!

23. *A History of the British Army*, J. W. Fortescue (1927), vol. xii, p. 180. Rifles, as military weapons, would appear first to have been used in 1631 by the Landgrave of Hesse; but it was not until the War of the American Independence that their value became clear. In 1800 the Baker rifle was issued to the newly raised British Rifle Brigade. It was sighted to 100 yards with a folding sight for 200. Baker says he could hit a painted man on a six-foot target 32 times out of 34 shots at 100 yards. The main difficulty with all early rifles was fouling of the barrel, which impeded loading. A comparison between the hitting power of the 1842 percussion musket and the Minié rifle shows the vast superiority of the latter: for the musket at 100 yards 74·5 per cent. of hits to the Minié's 94·5 per cent.; at 200 yards

42·5 per cent. to 80·0 per cent.; at 300 yards 16 per cent. to 55 per cent., and at 400 yards 4·5 per cent. to 52·5 per cent.

24. The breech-loading principle was an old idea. The range of the needle gun was short, a paper cartridge was used, and escape of gas at the breech was considerable.

25. Iron canal barges had appeared in England during the late eighteenth century.

26. *Journal of the Royal United Service Institution* (London), vol. lxxvi, No. 502, p. 258 (1931). In 1834 Admiral Lord Dundonald wrote: "Give me a fast small steamer, with a heavy long-range gun in the bow, and another in the hold to fall back upon, and I would not hesitate to attack the largest ship afloat. . . . As large a gun as possible in a vessel as small and swift as possible, and as many of them as you can put upon the sea" (*The Autobiography of a Seaman, Thomas, Tenth Earl of Dundonald*, 1890, 9, 546).

27. General Henri Joseph Paixhans (1783-1854) was a noted French artillerist. His gun was adopted by the French Government in 1827.

28. Except for one small steamer, every one of the Turkish vessels was destroyed. "It was believed by men in authority that 4,000 Turks were killed, that less than 400 survived, and that all these were wounded" (*The Invasion of the Crimea*, A. W. Kinglake, Student's Edition, 1899, p. 63).

29. In 1910 the *Warrior* was converted into a floating workshop and was renamed *Vernon III*. The armour of *La Gloire* was 5 inches thick and backed by 26 inches of wood.

30. The *Monitor* was designed by Ericsson: 1,200 tons displacement; upper hull 174 feet long; low speed; 3 to 5 inches armour on 27 inches wood backing; single revolving turret carrying two 11-inch Dahlgren smooth-bore guns, protected by 8-inch armour. The *Merrimac* (*Virginia*) was a cut-down wooden vessel of 3,500 tons displacement; 175 feet long with sloping roof of 24 inches wood covered with 4-inch armour. She mounted ten guns and had a maximum speed of 5 knots. It took a full half-hour to turn her around.

31. Quoted by Robertson in *The Evolution of Naval Armament*, p. 263.

32. Great Britain, 90 ships of the line, 93 frigates and 12 steamers; Russia and France, 99 ships of the line, 25 frigates and 45 steamers.

33. Edward Mead Earle in *Makers of Modern Strategy* (1943), p. 149.

34. *Ibid.*, pp. 150-151.

35. *Ibid.*, p. 149.

36. This rifle was steadily improved and the whole Prussian army was armed with it between 1853-1858 (*Geschichte der Infanterie*, W. Rüstow, 1884, vol. ii, p. 375). It was bolt operated, and the 1841 model was sighted to 650 yards and was of ·607-inch calibre.

37. On June 29, 1866, during the attack of Königinhof, a captured Austrian officer said to Colonel Kessel: "Our soldiers are demoralized not by the rapidity of your fire, for we could find some means perhaps to counterbalance that, but because you are always ready to fire. This morning your men, like ours, were concealed in the corn; but in that position yours could, without being seen, load their rifles easily and

rapidly; ours, on the other hand, were compelled to stand up and show themselves when they loaded, and you then took the opportunity to fire at them. Thus we had the greatest difficulty in getting our men to stand up at all; and such was their terror, when they stood up to load, that their hands trembled and they could hardly put the cartridge into the barrel. Our men feel the advantage that the quick and easy loading of the needle-gun gives you; it is this which demoralizes them. In action they feel themselves disarmed the greater part of the time, whereas you are always ready to fire" (*Military Reports*, Colonel Baron Stoffel, French Military Attaché in Prussia, 1866-1870, English Edition, 1872, p. 64).

38. Breech-loading ordnance dates from about the end of the fourteenth century. A rifled cannon with 13 shallow grooves was experimented with in Prussia in 1661, and another in 1696 with elliptical bore—similar to the Lancaster of 1854—was tried out in Germany. In 1836 a number of experiments was made in Russia with a Belgian—the Montigny—rifled gun, but were not very successful.

39. *Tracts of Gunnery*, Benjamin Robins, p. 337.

40. "In this principle the rotation of the shell was achieved not by grooves in the bore of the gun, but by the shape of the bore, which was oval and made one turn in 360 inches" (*The Story of the Gun*, Lieut. A. W. Wilson, 1944, p. 47).

41. For these and other inventions see my *War and Western Civilization*, 1832-1932 (1932), pp. 97-99, also *Meade's Headquarters*, 1863-1865, Colonel Theodore Lyman (1922), p. 284; *Makers of Modern Strategy*, p. 289, and Spengler's *The Decline of the West* (1928), vol. ii, p. 421.

42. *Capital* (Everyman's Library, 1930), vol. ii, p. 864.

43. Reliance on the bayonet was the tactical obsession of the nineteenth century. Gen. Jomini, who fought in the Napoleonic Wars and died in 1869, "is said to have remarked that, though he had seen a position taken at shoulder arms, he had never actually witnessed a charge with the bayonet, let alone taken part in one" (*Makers of Modern Strategy*, p. 82). Major Hart, an army surgeon of the American Civil War, corroborates this by saying that he saw few bayonet wounds "except accidental ones. . . . I think half a dozen would include all the wounds of this nature that I ever dressed" (*Papers of the Military Historical Society of Massachusetts*, vol. xiii, p. 265). In 1866 a Spanish eyewitness wrote: "The Austrians displayed the greatest and most forlorn valour in the struggle to close with their opponents hand-to-hand, without ever being able to do so. The Prussians awaited the attack until the troops were at a distance of three hundred paces, then, discharging their needle guns, the troops fell instantaneously before them in the ranks. The few who survived were unable to continue the assault; the field remained completely covered with bodies, in the short space between the 300 and 150 paces which were required to close upon the Prussian ranks. Similar results were observed as regards the assaults made by the cavalry" (*A Narrative: The War between Austria and Prussia*. By a Spaniard. Translated from *La Epoca*, Madrid, September 6, 1866).

44. *Decisive Battles since Waterloo*, 1815-1887, Thomas W. Knox (1887), p. 358. "The ideal battle of cannon was never so nearly approached

as on that day" (Col. Chesney in *Edinburgh Review*, April 1871, p. 563).
"Placed on surrounding heights, the guns simply poured their shells into
a pit, as it were, full of human beings, so that each shell exploded with
the full effect among the enemy below . . ." (Colonel Collen in *Journal
of the Royal United Service Institution*, vol. xvii, p. 462).

45. As this is the last great cavalry charge in history, it may be of some
interest to quote what an eyewitness saw: "Not a needle gun gave fire as
the splendid horsemen crashed down the gentle slope with the velocity of
an avalanche. I have seen not a few cavalry charges, but I never saw a finer
one. It was destined to a sudden arrestment, and that without the ceremony
of the trumpets sounding the 'halt.' The horsemen and the footmen might
have seen the colour of each other's moustaches . . . when along the line
of the latter there flashed out a sudden simultaneous streak of fire. Like
thunder-claps sounding over the din of a hurricane rose the measured
crash of a battery of guns, and then a cloud of white smoke drifted away
towards the chasseurs, enveloping them for the moment from one's sight.
When it blew away there was visible a line of bright uniforms and grey
horses struggling prostrate among the potato drills, or lying still in death.
So thorough a destruction by what may be called a single volley probably
the oldest soldier alive never witnessed" (*My Experiences of the War
between France and Germany*, Archibald Forbes (1871), vol. i, p. 236).

46. Excepting the Russo-Turkish War of 1877-1878, the Græco-
Turkish War of 1897 and the Italo-Turkish War and Balkan Wars of 1911-
1913—all localized conflicts—no general war occurred until 1914.

47. Bushnell's submarine was worked by one man. During the War of
Independence, his vessel, shaped like a turtle, dived beneath the British
warship *Eagle*, and the operator attempted to drive his torpedo, which was
provided with a spiked screw, into her bottom. Through an error of
judgment he failed to do so. In 1801 Fulton built two submarines for
France. These vessels could remain under water for four hours.

48. Jomini in his *The Art of War* (Philadelphia, 1868), p. 48, mentions
"the Perkins steam-guns, which vomit forth as many balls as a battalion."
This weapon was invented in England, and was, I believe, tested before a
Committee of the House of Commons in 1821. Gatling guns were still in
use during the Spanish American War of 1898. "It's the Gatlings, men,
our Gatlings!" (*The Rough Riders*, Theodore Roosevelt, 1899, p. 135). He
also added: "It was the only sound which I ever heard my men cheer in
battle." In the American Civil War the Requa machine gun was also used.

49. Other machine guns of this period were the Gardner, Nordenfeldt,
Hotchkiss and Colt.

50. *The Russo-Japanese War, Reports from British Officers* (1908), vol. iii,
p. 202. Nearly thirty years before, in the Russo-Turkish War of 1877-
1878, the Russian General Oukanoff had written: "Artillery will become
the scourge of mankind. . . . The day cannot be much longer delayed
when the artillery shall raise itself from being an auxiliary to the rank of
the principal arm."

51. *Technics and Civilization* (1934), p. 84.
52. *Ibid.*, pp. 190-191.
53. "First Canned Rations," W. B. Chivers, *British Canning Industry*

Number, The Times, November 17, 1931. By the date of the American Civil War condensed milk in cans was issued to the troops. (See *The Soldier in Battle, or Life in the Ranks of the Army of the Potomac,* Frank Wilkeson, p. 80.) T. E. Lawrence wrote: "The invention of bully beef had profited us more than the invention of gunpowder, but gave us strategical rather than tactical strength, since in Arabia range was more than force, space greater than the power of armies" (*Seven Pillars of Wisdom,* 1935, p. 196.)

54. *Technics and Civilization,* Lewis Mumford, p. 91.

55. *Ibid.,* p. 195.

56. *Makers of Modern Strategy* (1943), p. 156.

57. *Ibid.,* p. 156.

58. *Don Juan,* canto 12, v and vi.

59. *The Franco-German War of* 1870-71 (English Edition, 1891), vol. i, p. 2.

60. *The Principles of War* (English Edition, 1918), pp. 36-37.

61. An abbreviated English edition appeared in 1899 under the title *Is War Now Impossible?* It is from this edition that the quotations are taken.

CHAPTER VI

THE AGE OF OIL—I

WHEN the nineteenth century was in its last lap, and during those years in which the nation in arms was entering the saurian stage of its development, inventions destined to revolutionize the conception upon which it was founded began to take practical form. The two most fateful were the internal conbustion engine and wireless telegraphy. The first was a direct consequence of the rapid production of petroleum in the United States from 1859 onwards,[1] and the origin of the second may indirectly be traced back to the year 1842, when Samuel Morse first experimented with an interrupted metallic electric circuit.

As a commercial proposition the gas engine was first introduced by Dr. N. A. Otto in 1876.[2] Nine years later Gottlieb Daimler improved upon it, and by fitting a small petroleum spirit internal combustion motor to a bicycle he produced the first petrol-propelled vehicle.[3] Next it was adapted to four-wheeled carriages, and in 1895 the first automobile race was held. It was from Paris to Bordeaux and back, the winner covering the 744 miles at a mean speed of 15 miles per hour. Lastly, came the most revolutionary of all its triumphs. On December 17, 1903, at Kill Devil Hill, Kitty Hawk, North Carolina, Orville Wright in a power-driven airplane flew for twelve seconds. Six years later Blériot in a monoplane spanned the English Channel between Calais and Dover in thirty-one minutes. Thus, after 3,000 years, did the legend of Dædalus become true history. A power had been born which within half a century was destined to change the face of war; for the thunderbolts of Jove could once again be hurled from high heaven.

The second invention—wireless telegraphy—was first given theoretical form in 1887 by Rudolf Hertz. He proved that under certain conditions an electrical spark creates an effect which is propagated out into space as an electric wave.

This led to Guglielmo Marconi turning his attention to the invention of a device which could detect these waves, and so successful was he that, in 1897, he transmitted a wireless message over a distance of nine miles, and in 1901 over 3,000 miles.

These two inventions[4] introduced warlike possibilities which went far beyond anything as yet accomplished by either gunpowder or steam power. The first not only led to a revolution in road transport and consequently in land warfare, but by solving the problem of flight it raised war into the third dimension. Whereas the second virtually raised it into the fourth; for to all intents and purposes the wireless transmission of energy annihilated time as well as space. Thus two new battlefields were gained—the sky and the ether—the one to be dominated by the airplane and the other by the radio.[5]

These changes, as well as others resulting from scores of less prominent inventions, when coupled with the strides made in the metallurgical, chemical, electrical, biological and other sciences, set in motion forces very different from those released by coal and steam. Mind more so than matter, thought more so than things, and above all imagination were struggling to gain power. New substances appeared, new sources of energy were tapped and new outlooks on life were taking form. The world was in the process of sloughing its skin—mental, moral and physical—a process destined to transform the industrial revolution into a technical civilization.

Divorced from civil progress, soldiers could not see this. They could not see that, because civilization was becoming more and more technical, military power must inevitably follow suit: that the next war would be as much a clash between factories and technicians as between armies and generals. Even M. Bloch, that far-sighted man, could not see that the sole thing impossible in war was for it to stand still.

Few soldiers and sailors were as clear-sighted as he. And those who were,[6] like him, failed to see that industry and science had already placed in their hands weapons of such power that, if rightly combined, they could prevent a war of pure attrition. The majority was hostile to novelty, nevertheless faith in a war of movement abounded, and in this respect bulk military outlook was diametrically opposed to Bloch's. For instance, in 1912, a French soldier of distinction wrote: "In a war between France and Germany we do not anticipate a battle of such a nature [*i.e.*, an entrenched battle]. . . . Battles in entrenched camps as occurred at Plevna or Mukden will never take place in a war with the French army."[7]

The godhead of this heresy was Generals Foch, Grandmaison and Langlois, who established a school of thought rivalled only by the Dervishes of the Sudan. The leading principle was that morale was the infallible answer to the bullet—a piece of pure witchcraft. Foch quoted approvingly the words of Joseph de Maistre: "A battle lost is a battle one thinks one has lost; for a battle cannot be lost physically." To which Foch added: "Therefore it can only be lost morally. But, then, it is also morally that a battle is won, and we may extend the aphorism by saying: *A battle won is a battle in which one will not confess oneself beaten.*"[8]

Coupled with this sophistry, he believed that "any improvement of firearms is ultimately bound to add strength to the offensive"; consequently in battle there was but one principle to follow—namely, attack![9] What he could not see was that, to render attack profitable, a return must be made to the essence of the Napoleonic offensive, which was—"it is with artillery that war is made."[10]

In part, Count von Schlieffen (1833-1913) saw this,[11] and to render the attack superior to the defence he increased the number of the German heavy guns; but he did not see that this in itself was insufficient, and that true superiority could only be gained by building a new fighting organization around the gun.

This was the dominant tactical problem which faced all armies after the Russo-Japanese War, and it was by no means an occult one, for it was clearly seen by myself when a student at the Camberley Staff College in 1914.

Because, in my opinion, the quick-firing field gun and the machine gun were the dominant weapons, I suggested that tactics should be moulded around them. "We can predict with absolute certainty," I wrote, "that the general who makes the truest use of these weapons—that is, so deploys his men that their fullest power is attained—will win, unless he is hopelessly outnumbered." I predicted that because the field gun "is now the master missile-throwing weapon," it would "revolutionize the present theory of war by substituting as the leading grand tactical principle penetration for envelopment." I further suggested that it should be supplied by motor transport, and that "the forces of the infantry decisive attack should be organized round the machine gun."[12]

To-day I see no reason to doubt that, had the German armies of 1914 been organized round the field gun and the machine gun—the two dominant weapons of that period—instead of round the rifle—the dominant weapon of the nineteenth century—they would have overrun France nearly as rapidly as they did by means of two very different dominant weapons—the tank and the airplane—in 1940.

Because this central tactical problem was not seen, when in July 1914 war was declared, faulty arrangement of weapon power, more so than lack of it, endowed the bullet on the defensive with such superiority over the bullet in the attack[13] that, within a few weeks of the war opening, field warfare gave way to siege. Thus was Bloch's forecast proved correct to the letter, not because he was right, but because neither he nor any of the belligerents had rightly seen the problem.

Stalemate setting in, the problem next became one of how to reinstate mobility, and its solution was sought in ever-increasing shell fire.[14] Nevertheless, as a prime mover, the shell failed badly because the effectiveness of artillery had been largely reduced by the growth of field works and entanglements, defences which barely existed in the opening phase of the war, and which could not be extensively built until fighting became static.

Though the reliance placed on volume fire—bombardments of obliteration[15]—could generally guarantee an initial success, by destroying forward communications, it created for both infantry and artillery movement and supply as formidable an obstacle—the cratered area—as the trench systems and entanglements it had destroyed. Thus, though the dominant weapon—the gun—came into its own, because it lacked mobility (range of movement) it could not play the part of a decisive weapon. Nor could the infantry, because they also were bunkered by the crater area. The upshot was that, instead of stalemate being liquidated, it became more complete.

The war having been reduced to a siege operation, reliance was placed on blockade, which on account of the range and volume of its "striking power" has always been the dominant "weapon" of the economic attack. The German answer to this was unrestricted submarine warfare.

To break the blockade was not a naval but a military problem. In the case of Germany, it was how to penetrate her enemies' fronts in order to extend her food area—that is, shorten the range of the blockade. In the case of France and Great Britain, penetration was also the problem, the aim of which was the elimination of the German U-boat bases.[16] As artillery could not solve this problem, in 1915 the Germans turned to lethal gas, launching the first chemical attack on April 22. But on account of the ease in neutralizing poison gas, the problem remained unsolved. Nevertheless, as a vesicant, such as mustard gas (dichloro-ethyl-sulphide), gas proved itself to be a formidable weapon.[17]

Both sides also resorted to air attack on their respective civil populations and industrial areas; but it was no more than a side issue, for though this form of the offensive pointed to an enormous future, air power was not as yet sufficiently developed to produce decisive results.[18]

Both these solutions were spurious, because the problem was not understood. It was how to neutralize the bullet; therefore, how to disarm the mass of the enemy's riflemen, not gradually but instantaneously. Clearly the answer was

bullet-proof armour and not an increase in projectiles—
whether bullets, shells, bombs or even gas. Quite early in the
war this was seen by Colonel E. D. Swinton and others[19] in
Great Britain. Further, they saw that though the soldier could
not carry bullet-proof armour, he could be carried, as the
sailor is, in a bullet-proof armoured vehicle, and as this
vehicle would have to travel across country it must move on
caterpillar tracks instead of on wheels. Thus was the tank,
a self-propelled bullet-proof landship, conceived. On
September 15, 1916, it first went into action on the shell-
blasted battlefield of the Somme.

Ever since the introduction of firearms, the two outstanding difficulties in battle tactics had been how to har-
monize movement and fire and movement and protection.
These were now overcome by the tank. (1) It increased
mobility by substituting mechanical power for muscular;
(2) it increased security by neutralizing the bullet by
armoured plate; and (3) it increased offensive power by
relieving the soldier from the necessity of carrying his
weapons and the horse from hauling them. Protecting the
soldier dynamically the tank enabled him to fight statically;
therefore it superimposed naval tactics on land warfare.

The first time tanks were skilfully used was in the Cambrai
attack, on November 20, 1917. In this battle no preliminary
artillery barrage was employed. Instead, grouped in threes,
tanks operated as a chain of mobile armoured batteries
slightly in advance of the infantry. With certain modifica-
tions, these tactics were maintained until the end of the war,
and as the following figures go to prove, they resulted in a
vast reduction of casualties to territory gained. In the Battle
of the Somme (July to November 1916), British killed and
wounded numbered 5,277 to each square mile conquered; in
the Battle of Passchendaele (July to November 1917),
8,222; and between July and November 1918, when tanks
were extensively used, 86.

In 1917 and before the battle of Cambrai was fought, a
plan was devised by me to carry machine gunners through
the enemy defences, depositing them in the rear of them,

while his front was being attacked, and special tanks were built for this purpose. In 1918 I substituted another plan, which was accepted by Marshal Foch for the 1919 campaign.[20] Instead of launching the initial attack against the enemy's front, it was decided to launch it against his rear—his command and supply system—by suddenly and without warning passing powerful tank forces, covered by aircraft, through his front. Next, directly paralyzation of his rear had disorganized his front, to launch a strong tank and infantry attack of the Cambrai pattern against that front.

Thus, what twenty years later became known as the "Blitz" attack was born; and had the war continued into 1919, seeing that the Germans had no properly ordered anti-tank defence, these tactics would have produced even more startling results than they did in 1939-1940.

This world-wide war, the origins of which were mainly financial and economic, was, as M. Bloch had foreseen, finally decided by famine, bankruptcy and the break up of the whole social order in the defeated countries. Blockade was its master weapon, as it cannot fail to be when time is sufficient to permit of its range taking effect, because the "volume" of its "striking power" is total, hitting every man, woman and child, as well as every factory and frequently all farm lands in the area laid under siege. Second to it came the tank, the moral effect of which vastly exceeded the physical damage done, because in face of its assault the German soldier felt himself to be, as he actually was, impotent. Ludendorff was right when he christened the great tank victory at Amiens, on August 8, 1918, "the black day of the German Army."

The revolution following the war was complete. Politically it destroyed three empires—the German, Russian and *and* Austrian. Economically and financially it ruined the defeated *Turkish* nations, and, with the exception of the United States, it bled white the victorious.

The character of the war itself was as revolutionary as its results. During it morality and common decency were cast to the winds. In this respect it differed essentially from both the Napoleonic and the Franco-Prussian Wars, for in these conflicts the contending sides had guarded against fostering revolution.[21] The use of atrocity as a weapon of propaganda became universal. "Terrify in order to terrify and destroy. The immediate object of fighting is to kill and to go on killing, until there is nothing left to kill," was advocated by a French soldier before the war,[22] and put into practice during it. As the British Captain Charles Ross had pointed out years earlier: "War is a relapse into barbarism. There is no disloyalty in war save that which forbears to spare; no morality save that which ends quickly. Love and sentiment are out of place in the struggle for existence. . . . It is the exercise of the sterner barbaric qualities which governs the day. Atrocities are the last resource of strategy in its efforts to force an enemy to its knees."[23]

The means of fighting were also revolutionary, because for the first time in the history of war battles were as much tussles between competing factories as between contending armies. The production of weapons more so than the conscription of men was the deciding factor in battle. God had marched with the biggest industries rather than with the biggest battalions, and with the tank and the gun more so than with the rifle and the bayonet. As J. T. Shotwell writes: "During the years 1914 to 1918 . . . war definitely passed into the industrial phase of economic history . . . the industry of war combines two techniques: the technique of peace which supplies war with its resources, and the technique of destruction."[24] Meanwhile the pecuniary profits of war shifted from plunder by the generals and troops to the gains made by financiers, war contractors and manufacturers.

As is nearly always the case in great wars, it was the losing side which learnt most. Whereas the victors looked upon the war as an incident which had been liquidated, the vanquished saw in it a consequence of faulty actions. To the U.S.S.R., to Germany and to Italy in a lesser degree, the four supreme war lessons were: the increasing necessity (1) for political authority in war; (2) for national discipline in war; (3) for economic self-sufficiency in war; and (4) for technology in war. And if in war, then in peace-time also, in order to be prepared for war.

This led to autocracy, regimentation, autarchy and mechanization. Together, to a new conception of civilization. In the U.S.S.R. and Germany military power was no longer looked upon as the protector of national existence, but as its regenerator. Thus it came about that the vanquished nations inverted Clausewitz's famous saying that "war is a continuation of peace policy." They replaced it by "peace is a continuation of war policy." Meanwhile, like medieval sorcerers, the victorious sought to attain their end —a return to the *status quo* of 1913—by solemn conjurations. They anathematized war, and, like the Lateran Council of 1139, attempted to interdict the newer weapons.

During the war these weapons—the airplane, tank and lethal gas—had been used experimentally. What did experiments point to? In each case to an extension of gun power, the gun being the dominant weapon. Thus, the tank had been used as a self-propelled armoured gun, the airplane as a long-range gun or machine gun,[25] and lethal gas as molecular shrapnel. Had these experiments been carried further, as they would have been had the war lasted another year, it would have become apparent that in themselves tanks and aircraft were not weapons, but instead vehicles in which anything could be carried up to their maximum load. Further, that as their dominant characteristics were new means of movement, rendered practical by the common prime mover, petroleum, entirely new fighting organizations could be built around them—namely, self-propelled armoured armies and airborne armies, and not merely self-propelled armoured guns and airborne artillery.

In this evolution the essential factor was oil, as in the nineteenth century it was steam. Nevertheless, though as General Denvignes pointed out after the war, "without a national carburant there is no national independence," and though Lord Curzon said, "Who has the petrol has the Empire," for purposes of war, oil cannot be fully exploited as a prime mover unless fighting power is organized around it. Fighting organization and not merely an extension of gun-power was the problem.

This was not appreciated by any single nation, and in spite of the fact that the tank tactics devised by myself for the 1919 campaign could only be developed by a self-propelled armoured army supported by a powerful air force.[26] The first was to comprise the following machines: three types of fighting tanks; an armoured infantry carrier; two types of bridging machines; an engineer tank; a mine-sweeping tank; a lethal gas tank; a recovery tank; a radio tank and a supply tank.[27] The sole important weapon lacking was an armoured self-propelled field gun; unarmoured self-propelled 60-pounder guns and 6-inch howitzers were already in existence.

In spite of its juvenile imperfections, such was the first combined land and air army planned to fit the war demands of an advancing technical civilization. In idea and in armament it was as different from the Napoleonic mass armies as were the armoured feudal levies from the armed barbarian hordes they replaced. Tactically, there was a closer relation-ship between the feudal and the technical orders than between the technical and the Napoleonic, because in the feudal and the technical the tactical elements were more closely integrated. In the one, armour (protection) and the *arme blanche* (offensive power) were co-ordinated by the horse (motive power); in the other, armour and projectile powers were co-ordinated by the internal combustion engine. Therefore, as in both the central idea was the development of protected mobile offensive power, logically I urged the study of medieval warfare.[28]

The problem was how to integrate the three tactical elements, and it was not clearly seen by either Russia or Germany—the two leading military powers in 1939. Instead of integration, in the main they adhered to the separation which during the First World War had existed between what may be called the old "handicraft" army and the new "machinecraft" forces. This led to the adoption of a neo-Napoleonic organization—that is, an army based on the principle of the nation in arms, to which were attached as appendices the new technical arms and services, co-operating instead of being combined with it. A mistake, however, which the Russians and Germans did not make was to separate their air forces from their land forces. They were not misled by the theory of absolute air warfare as expounded by Douhet, Mitchell, Seversky and others, who looked upon the airplane as being so dominant and so decisive a weapon that its powers rendered those of all other weapons nugatory.

It is of importance to outline this theory, because the misuse of a weapon, as much so as its correct use, by influencing war influences history.

On account of its range no one will dispute the dominance of the airplane; but that it is a master weapon as once was Greek fire, or for a brief moment Charles VIII's cannon, or as the rifle still is to-day against ill-armed savages, is clearly an exaggeration.[29]

In brief, the Douhet theory was as follows: As fighting power is based on industrial production and civil morale, once it is deprived of these two sources of energy it must automatically collapse. Therefore, all that is necessary is to gain command of the air and then bomb these two fountain-heads out of existence. Land forces, sea forces, and even anti-aircraft defences, whether mobile or static, meant nothing to Douhet, because *"National defence can be assured only by an Independent Air Force of adequate power."*[30]

His error was Bloch's in reverse. Whereas Bloch saw total stalemate through fire power, he saw total annihilation. Both overlooked the supreme fact that the sole thing impossible in war is for it to stand still. That directly a weapon approaches or enters the master stage, the Constant Tactical Factor comes into play—that is, every improvement in armament is eventually met by a counter-improvement which gradually or rapidly whittles down its power. Were this not true, war would have come to a Blochian or Douhetian conclusion in the Stone Age or before. The secret which Douhet could not grasp was that inventive genius when stirred by the instinct of self-preservation knows no bounds. He was a wonderful salesman, and like many such people—a prophet of the ridiculous.[31]

It was not the airplane as is so generally held which rendered war total. Instead it was science—technology generally—which in its many forms transcends all political frontiers and is to-day steadily obliterating them and in consequence integrating or, perhaps, disintegrating human society.[32]

Though in the welding of civilizations the airplane is playing a great part, in range and speed of "striking power" it is vastly inferior to the radio, the reach of which is global and the volume of its striking power—"atomic." Without exaggeration, it may be said that to-day the radio provides us with an inexhaustible supply of mental food which, like the manna of Exodus, is for immediate consumption. Whereas print can attack the literate only, the radio attacks literate and illiterate alike.[33]

Because among the vanquished war was the uppermost thought, by means of the radio the nation in arms was transmuted into the total war state. Whereas among the victors, who anathematized war, it was used to propagate pacifism.

Meanwhile, in the years following the war, technology, advancing by leaps and bounds, led to such overwhelming production that, restricted as they were by the shortage of currency inherent in a financial system shackled to gold, the peoples of the world were unable to purchase and therefore consume the plethora of goods produced. This lack of purchasing power resulted in world-wide unemployment, which led to two tentative solutions: in the victorious countries to the "dole" system and the subsidizing of non-production, and in the vanquished to a return to conscription and the establishment of war industries, the product of which could only be consumed on the battlefield.

Thus arose two opposed conceptions of peace: on the one hand that of the New Orders, the aim of which was to create economically self-sufficient blocks of nations linked together by a currency based on capacity to produce, and on the other hand that of the Old Order, whose aim was to maintain the existing status of nations, trusting that the old financial system would in some undefined way solve the economic problems which technology had created and was daily multiplying. Thus it came about that, once again, the world was faced by an irresistible force confronting an irremovable object, and the inevitable result was the Second World War, which was opened by the German invasion of Poland on September 1, 1939.

The war which now burst upon Europe, though technically and tactically less experimental than the one which preceded it, was nevertheless essentially a testing ground of theories, each of which was intimately related to armament. Of these theories six are outstanding—namely: (1) The value as a fighting instrument of the nation in arms as conceived by Clausewitz. (2) The value of mechanized armoured forces as visualized by myself and others. (3) The value of linear defence as represented by the French Maginot Line. (4) The value of the blockade as held by the British. (5) The value of the Douhet theory of the attack on industry and the civil will. (6) The influence of air power on land and sea power.

These technical-tactical problems were set in a strategical frame, also largely theoretical, and it is important to have a clear conception of it before the six problems are examined.

Not only for statesmen and soldiers, but also for history, it is tragic that Clausewitz did not live to complete his philosophy of war. Had he done so there can be little doubt that his claim that the military aim of war is the annihilation of the enemy's fighting forces would have been modified by his belief that at times the goal should be more limited.[34] Of his many students, Delbrück was the first to point out in his *Geschichte der Kriegskunst* that as there were two forms of war—limited and unlimited—it follows that there must be two forms of strategy. These he called the strategy of annihilation (*Niederwerfungsstrategie*) and the strategy of exhaustion (*Ermattungsstrategie*). Whereas in the first the aim is the decisive battle, in the second battle is but one of several means, such as manœuvre and economic attack, whereby the political end is attained.[35]

Were Clausewitz and Delbrück alive to-day, both, I think, would see that in the present technological age the strategy of annihilation demands not so much the destruction of the enemy's army as the destruction or occupation of his vital area of operations, that part of his country essential to the maintenance of his forces in the field—his coalfields, oil wells, industries, etc. Therefore, should it be sufficiently shallow to permit of the momentum of a mechanized attack being maintained without break across it, its occupation will prove even more decisive than the enemy's defeat in the field, for without it his armed forces cannot for long exist.

This shallowness was to be found both in Poland and France, whereas in Russia it was not, for there the vital area stretched from the river Bug deep into Caucasia and far beyond the Urals. Therefore the German strategy of annihilation which succeeded in France failed in Russia, because the condition of depth demanded the strategy of exhaustion.[36]

Between the poles of this dual strategy revolved the main events of the war, and to their six major problems I will now return.

(1) *The Value of the Nation in Arms.*—This order of power was not only extended but also vastly modified. On account of ever-increasing industrial demands, the conscription of labour, including women as well as men, was introduced even in the democratic countries. On account of the constant threat of air attack, an unarmed *levée en masse* was made, that of civil air defence workers—fire watchers, fire brigades, demolition squads, police, ambulance units, etc. And on account of the danger of airborne invasion, militias were raised, such as the British Home Guard and the German Volkssturm. But in offensive value the nation in arms declined, for though in battle infantry still played a notable part, the striking power of armoured troops, of artillery and of aircraft, was the dominant offensive factor. Otherwise put, fighting power was derived from the machine arms far more so than the hand arms: from technology and quality rather than from quantity and man power. Such are a few of the

outstanding differences between the people in arms of
to-day and the nation in arms as visualized by Clausewitz
and as seen in the nineteenth century. The one is mainly
in arsenals, the other in barracks.

(2) *The Value of Armoured Forces.*—Throughout the war
mechanized armoured forces more than justified the expec-
tations of their adherents. Poland was conquered in three
weeks, Holland in five days, Belgium in eighteen, France in
thirty-five, Yugoslavia in twelve and Greece in eighteen.
Such consistent rapidity of conquest was utterly novel. As
the author of *The Diary of a Staff Officer* wrote of the invasion of France: "The French General Staff have been para-
lyzed by this unorthodox war of movement. The fluid
conditions prevailing are not dealt with in the textbooks and
the 1914 brains of the French generals responsible for
formulating the plans of the allied armies are incapable of
functioning in this new and astonishing layout."

What was behind it? The answer is—machine power!

Though in Holland, Belgium and France, as in Poland,
the Germans deployed a large number of infantry divisions,
the decisive fighting fell almost entirely on the armoured and
air forces. In spite of exact figures being unobtainable, it is
improbable that the tank and aircraft personnel exceeded
200,000 men. France, a first-class power, was in the main
conquered by this minute force and at a cost to her enemy of
27,074 killed, 111,034 wounded and 18,384 missing, or at
considerably less than one-third of the British casualties in
1916 during the Battle of the Somme. In Poland it had been
the same, the German losses numbering 10,572 killed, 30,333
wounded and 3,400 missing, or a little more than two-thirds
of those the British sustained on the first day of the above
battle. Never had great modern campaigns been so bloodless, so rapid and so decisive.

Tactically, the conquest of Yugoslavia and Greece was
even more remarkable than that of France; for, as both
these countries are mountainous, they are formidable anti-
tank areas. Nevertheless, when tanks and aircraft work in
close combination, it was proved that such regions are no

more difficult to conquer than are open plain lands. Mountains are no real obstacle to a flying machine, and as all major operations are in the valleys, aircraft can even more easily concentrate against the enemy and his communications than in plain warfare.

Though in North Africa, in the Russian counter-offensives of 1943-1944, in the Anglo-American invasion of France and in the final Allied operations in Germany, tanks, again and again, proved themselves to be the decisive land weapon, in the German 1941 and 1942 campaigns in Russia, faulty strategy and inadequate cross-country supply limited their success. In so vast a theatre of war the tactical problem was much the same as in running. A runner who can run 100 yards in 10 seconds would not expect to run 1,000 in 100 or a mile in 176. Only in a relay race can such speeds approximately be attained.

The crucial German error was that they had no relays. To conquer Russia rapidly demanded vast reserves of machines, supply as well as fighting, meticulously organized to overcome space at high speed. They had not thought out the spacial problem, and not having the necessary machine power at hand, they fell back on man power, and not only clogged their communications, but presented the Russian armoured forces with magnificent slow-moving targets to encircle and destroy.

(3) *The Value of Linear Defence.*—Though in armoured warfare all field defences should be mobile—that is, transportable, as in a rudimentary way many of the German "hedgehogs" were in Russia and the British "boxes" in North Africa—permanent fortifications, if built from an anti-tank and anti-aircraft point of view, are as essential to tank forces as once were castles to armoured knights.[37] Even the much abused Maginot Line could have been turned into a formidable barrier, not by continuing it from Longwy to the sea, but by assembling on its left flank a powerful armoured force to act to it as sword to shield. In mobile warfare, the point to note is that static defences should be built in order to develop mobility, even more so than to impede it.

It is a remarkable fact that, though elaborate linear systems of defence, such as the German West and Atlantic Walls, were constructed, and that frequently armoured forces in the field sought to secure themselves by field defences and mine-fields, as in 1942 was notably the case in North Africa, in every instance the side with the superior armour broke through.

The reason is that, in armoured warfare, defence is strategical, more so than tactical. This means that it depends more on space as a factor of exhaustion than on obstacles as factors of resistance. For example, in the German Russian campaign of 1942-1943, once it became apparent that the initiative had been lost, instead of gradually falling back westwards from the Volga in accordance with what was called "the elastic defensive"—really a morcellated semi-mobile and extemporized Maginot Line—the German High Command should, as rapidly as possible, have withdrawn the whole of the front west of the Dnieper. There the armoured forces should have been rested and refitted, and directly the Russians, exhausted by their long approach and hampered by the length of their communications, gained contact, a powerful armoured counter-offensive should have been launched against them. Also, in October, 1942, at El Alamein, when it became clear that General Montgomery was about to attack, or at the moment he opened his offensive, General von Stumme, who was in temporary command of Rommel's army, instead of awaiting the attack, should, under cover of a screening force, have withdrawn his army to Sollum, and from there, as Montgomery approached, have vigorously counter-attacked him.

The truth is that in armoured warfare there is no linear or even reliable static defence. Two operations alone are practical—namely, in the offensive to advance, and in the defensive to retire, in order to compel the enemy so to exhaust himself in the follow-up that the initiative is regained. Therefore, as was the case in former cavalry warfare, both the offensive and defensive depend on mobility.

(4) *The Value of Sea Blockade.*—Blockade by sea power reaches its maximun effect when defensive warfare predominates on land—that is, when the enemy's land forces are denied liberty of movement, as they were throughout the greater part of the First World War. Conversely, its value falls in proportion as land warfare becomes mobile, either because the enemy is rapidly defeated on land, when blockade becomes useless, or because by vanquishing his opponents and occupying their countries the enemy increases his food and supply area, as was the case in the Second World War. Further, the advance made in the production of synthetic substances has gone far to blunt the edge of blockade. The most remarkable example is synthetic oil, without which the Germans could not have declared war, let alone wage it.

Though it is indisputable that the blockade of Germany did deprive her of certain essentials and many luxuries, the point to note is that, in highly mobile warfare, blockade itself should be highly mobile. In 1937 I pointed this out in my book *Towards Armageddon.* "In 1914," I wrote, "we opened our blockade of the Elbe, its primary object being to stop the exit of the High Sea Fleet, and its secondary to prevent contraband entering Germany. A little later on the Germans retaliated with their U-boat counter-blockade, and in spite of our surface supremacy they all but drove us out of the war. The difference between these two forms of blockade is that whereas the first was mainly passive, the second was highly active . . . the essence of ours was strangulation, the essence of theirs was sinking at sight. When we compare these two methods there is no doubt that the second is superior, because successful attack is the quickest and surest means of defence. In this method the point to note is that the weapon used—the submarine—possesses three-dimensional powers of movement, restricted to operating *below* its opponent; therefore its tactical superiority lies in its ability to hide and so indirectly to defend itself. When, however, we turn to the airplane, we find that no such limitation exists, for of necessity it is compelled to operate *above* its opponent: therefore its tactical power is incomparably more offensive; therefore, in this respect, it is incomparably superior to the submarine. Further still, being equally well able to fly over sea or land, it can vastly widen the range of blockade, until, as in our own case, it includes the entire country."

The point to note is this, that blockade by sea is increasingly being replaced by blockade by air, because aircraft are more mobile than ships. Whereas the aim in the one method is to block the enemy's ports and prevent merchandise entering them, the aim in the other is to destroy by aerial bombardment the ports themselves and the ships as they are being unloaded. Clearly, to strike at the ports is both easier and more economical than either to clear the seas of enemy shipping or to strike at the enemy's industrial cities and manufactories which receive the raw materials imported, because ships move and manufactories can be moved, whereas ports are permanently fixed.

(5) *The Value of the Douhet Theory.*—As a speedy means of bringing the war to an end, bombing attacks on the enemy's industrial centres and civil population were a costly failure; for not only did they prolong the war, but they knocked the bottom out of eventual peace. Though between 1939 and 1942 each great offensive had clearly shown that rapid conquest, and, therefore, the shortening of the war, depended on the integration of land and air power, from 1942 onwards the British and Americans relied mainly on what was called "strategic bombing." So fully was the Douhet theory accepted that, in 1944, when speaking on the Army Estimates the British Secretary of State for War said: "We have reached the extraordinary situation in which the labour devoted to the production of heavy bombers alone is believed to be equal to that allotted to the production of the whole equipment of the Army." The result was that, instead of one co-ordinated offensive, two separate battles were fought: the one on land with inadequate air power, and the other against the enemy's cities with a superabundance. In these latter attacks the cultural, domestic and human damage done

was appalling. No consideration was paid to the fact that in an industrial civilization the annihilatiom of the enemy's industries must inevitably unhinge eventual peace. To have warranted the name "strategic," once the army's air needs had been met, the residual bombing power should have been directed, not against the enemy's industrial centres, but against their sources of energy, also his communications. Had the German coal-fields and synthetic oil plants been from the earliest moment possible kept under *constant* bombardment, in time, without damage to themselves, all the German heavy industries would have had to be closed down. Not until the last lap of the war in Europe was this system of attack systematically resorted to, when shortage of oil brought Germany to total collapse.

(6) *The Influence of Air Power on Land and Sea Power.*—When used as an independent weapon, the tactics of the air assault were as brutally simple as those of the old cavalry charge, and on occasion were as overwhelming, as in the great attack on Hamburg in July 1943.[38] Nevertheless, as cavalry only attained its full effect when combined with infantry, and later on with artillery, so did aircraft only attain theirs when combined with armies and fleets. Whenever this was done on land, as notably in the German invasion of France in 1940, in the British campaign of El Alamein in 1942-1943, and in the Allied invasion of Normandy in 1944, integration of air and land power proved overwhelming. Similarly at sea, for though on occasion independent aircraft gained spectacular victories, as in the sinking of the *Prince of Wales* and the *Repulse* in December 1941, it is in integrated battles such as those of the Coral Seas and Midway Island in 1942, and in the great battles of the Philippine Seas in 1944, that their fullest effect is seen.[39]

Nevertheless, it is as carrier—flying vehicle—more so than as long-range gun that the greatest tactical and administrative revolutions are effected. Examples of the first of these revolutions are the airborne attacks on Norway in 1940 and on Crete in 1941, the Wingate Burma campaign of 1944, the invasion of Normandy and the battle of Nijmegen-Arnheim that same year. To have attempted to bomb Norway or Crete into submission would have taken months, possibly years. But granted surprise, then, when occupation by ground or airborne troops coincides with cover by bombing —as was conclusively proved—conquest can be effected in days and even in hours.

The second revolution—supply by air—was as radical. Thus, in April 1945, during the final Anglo-American advance into Central Germany, without air transport it would have been impossible to have kept the armoured forces mobile. Each armoured division consumed 100,000 gallons of petrol a day, and the average daily quantity supplied by air was roughly 500,000 gallons. On April 4, 669,465 gallons were transported by nearly 2,000 aircraft.

An even more remarkable example of this revolution in supply is the Burma campaign of 1944-1945. In fact it could not have been conceived apart from aircraft. In 1944 Allied transport aircraft made more than 90,000 flights, carried into the fighting zone over 270,000 tons of freight and brought back 60,000 casualties at a cost of only one or two transports intercepted by the Japanese. This was rendered possible by Allied command of the air, which command simultaneously was daily paralysing the Japanese ground communications.

These various problems, as well as the normal demands of war, backed as they were by industry and technology, led to a progress in armament so all-embracing that many years will be needed to codify and digest it.

Since 1939, new weapons, as well as new means of waging war, such as radio location, direction and control, have literally poured on to the battlefields. Innumerable improvements have been made in aircraft and in anti-aircraft devices, in submarine and anti-submarine warfare, and in armoured vehicles and anti-tank weapons.[40] Of these many inventions, probably the most radical, revolutionary and portentous are those of the German flying-bomb[41] and war rocket, because both, and more particularly the second, promise an ever-increasing range of action, until striking power may actually become global. Further, both cut the human element in war down to its irreducible minimum, an achievement hastened by aircraft and tank. As one writer has written, the portent is "blind-annihilation at an ever-lengthening range."[42]

It is strange that the rocket, now the newest, is yet probably the oldest of all explosively propelled projectiles, for it is supposed to have been first used by the Chinese against the Tartars in 1232.[43] Anyhow, it is known to have been used by Timur in his great battle of Delhi in 1399, and it was the Indian rocket employed by Tipu Sultan at the siege of Seringapatam in 1799 which the British gunnery expert, Colonel Sir William Congreve, took as his model and improved upon. He informs us that he made rockets of from two ounces—"a species of self-motive musket ball"—to three hundredweights.[44] In 1806 they were first tested out at the siege of Boulogne, when, as Congreve writes: "In less than ten minutes after the first discharge the town was discovered to be on fire."[45] Of this weapon he predicted: "The rocket is, in truth, an arm by which the whole system of military tactics is destined to be changed."[46]

This prediction is one of the most remarkable in military history, for though as a weapon the rocket was abandoned by the British Army in 1885, and by all continental armies still earlier, to-day the prophecy is being fulfilled by this weapon in three separate forms: as a short-range projectile, as a long-range projectile and as a propulsion engine.

In the first form it is being used in the air, on land and at sea, by aircraft, such as the British Typhoon machine, because high projectile power can be gained without the use of a heavy cannon. On land, the short-range rocket has taken a large number of forms, such as the American Bazooka rocket gun, the Russian multiple rocket thrower called Katyusha, and the German Nebelwerfer,[47] a six-barrelled weapon which fires six 55-pound rockets to a range of 6,000 yards.

As a naval weapon its importance is now fully recognized. It proved so successful in the Pacific waters that, on

December 13, 1944, the U.S. Navy Department announced that rocket production was to be increased by 300 per cent. In these operations rocket-equipped landing craft formed the spear-head of nearly every invasion, and we read that, as a covering weapon, it has become "a vital factor in landing on enemy-held beaches."[48]

So far, as a long-range projectile, it has been solely used by the Germans. Though a cumbersome weapon, some 46 feet in length and weighing between 12 and 15 tons, considering that it is still in a purely experimental stage, at ranges of 200 miles and under it has proved itself to be a formidable weapon which, should a less bulky propellent than alcohol and liquid oxygen be discovered, will, as Congreve foresaw, entirely revolutionize tactics.

Also, when used as a propulsion engine,[49] its possibilities are as great, because, as certain types of fighter planes are already propelled by rockets at speeds exceeding 600 miles per hour, before the present century has run its course there is nothing fantastic in suggesting that complete armies will be transported through space hundreds of miles above the earth's surface, to speed towards their enemy at thousands of miles per hour.

Indeed, we live in extraordinary times, in days of strange and violent possibilities. Daily war is becoming even more a struggle between inventors than between soldiers. So much is this so that the highest inventive genius must be sought, not so much among those who invent new weapons, as among those who devise new fighting organizations; who by shaping all instruments of war, old and new, round the dominant weapon, invent new fleets and new armies. Whereas one category of inventiveness is related to the imagination, the other is related to ratiocination. Thus, the man who first perceived that by linking together the ends of a bended stick with a twisted gut he could fashion a weapon—a bow—which would outrange an enemy armed with a javelin was a man of imagination. Also he who first thought out how to combine bowmen and spearmen in such a way that their united powers would exceed their individual endeavours was a reasoner.

An outstanding example of this latter form of inventiveness is the Normandy invasion of June 1944. What was the problem? Not merely to cross the English Channel, but to cross it on a wide front in deployed fighting order, land a highly motorized army, its equipment and stores with the utmost speed, and on landing supply it with the utmost rapidity.

In the past the major difficulties were: (1) That there could be no deployment in order of attack, because the vessels used reduced the troops to passenger freight, which could only assume a tactical order after landing. (2) Before this change over from a tripper to a fighting footing could be effected, a transhipment from transports to lighters had to be made in order to span the gap between ship and shore—this was the crucial sub-problem. (3) That unless a well-found port was immediately occupied, the invading forces could not be adequately supplied. In brief, in face of an alert enemy, protected by powerful coastal defences, an overseas invasion was not a practical operation of war.

All these problems were solved by inventions their difficulties suggested. The three outstanding were: (1) The construction of special landing craft which enabled the sea passage to be made in tactical order. (2) The waterproofing of the vehicles—fighting and administrative—in such a way that, under their own power, they could span the sea gap between landing craft and shore. (3) The prefabrication of a transportable port of disembarkation.[50]

By these three inventions, each suggested by the analysis of the problem, under cover of the dominant arm—the airplane as flying gun and carrier—the problem was not only solved as if by magic, but its solution has revolutionized naval strategy and tactics, for it has bereft a maritime power of at least half its shield.

In the Pacific theatre an even more intricate inventiveness is to be seen, and as there the problem of invasion is a threefold one—namely, to maintain command of the sea, to gain command of the land and to supply vast numbers of vessels, machines and men—the instrument is also a threefold one.

It consists of a battle fleet, a floating army and a floating base. The first is organized round the aircraft carrier—its out-fighting arm—and also comprises light coastal vessels, either towed or carried on parent ships, for island fighting —its in-fighting arm. The second consists of a vast number of transports and special landing craft. And the third of various vessels, many of which have never before been seen at sea. Among these are to be found escort aircraft carriers, aircraft tenders and repair ships—floating workshops which take the place of shore dockyards—minesweepers, supply ships, oilers, ammunition ships, water ships, store ships, food ships, hospital ships, salvage ships and recreation ships.

This vast instrument, an integration of air, sea and land power, is a creation rather than an invention. Like a great city it is the product of innumerable brains and hands, and it requires a vast staff of technicians, engineers, mechanics and craftsmen to maintain it. In it armament has all but completely grown out of the tool stage and has entered its machine life—a weapon of a million parts working as one part and vivified by oil.

Technology is now in complete command, and the effect this is likely to have on history and civilization I will attempt to outline in the next chapter.

REFERENCES

1. The production of crude petroleum was 2,000 barrels in 1859; 4,215,000 in 1869; 19,914,146 in 1879 and 126,493,936 in 1906. Since 1870 the industry has spread all over the globe.

2. In idea the gas engine was old. The first constructed would appear to be Christian Huygens' in 1680; it was worked by gunpowder and air.

3. This same year (1885) Butler in England propelled a tricycle by means of an internal combustion engine using vapour of benzoline exploded electrically.

4. There were of course many other inventions which I have no space to examine. A few were: 1876, Bell's electric telephone; 1884, Pearson's steam turbine; 1888, Dunlop's pneumatic tyre; and from this date onwards, and more especially so in America, tractors fitted with endless chain tracks instead of wheels. The most interesting is the Batter tractor patented in the U.S.A. in 1888. It was furnished with two tracks, their contour closely

resembling those of the British Medium Mark A (Whippet) tank of 1918. Another invention of this period which was prodigiously to influence propaganda, and, consequently, both peace and war, was the development of the moving picture from 1890 onwards. Yet, as Lewis Mumford points out, "the technique of temporary sterilization—so called birth-control—was perhaps the most important to the human race of all the scientific and technical advances that were carried to completion during the nineteenth century" (*Technics and Civilization*, 1934, p. 260). The practice of abortion went far to destroy the vigour of Rome (see *Society in Rome under the Cæsars*, Dr. W. R. Inge, 1888, and *The Fate of Empires*, Arthur John Hubbard, 1913). Also, I think, contraception sapped the fighting vigour of France between 1870 and 1940. A nation faced by a stationary or falling birth rate intuitively fears war, because war hastens biological extinction.

5. Broadcasting was first initiated in the United States in 1920.

6. In 1902, Emile Mayer in the *Revue militaire suisse* wrote: "Putting face to face two human walls, only separated by the depth of danger, and this double wall will remain almost inert, in spite of the will of either party to advance. . . . Exterior circumstances will bring the end of the purely defensive war of the future." In 1907, Colonel à Court Repington, Military Correspondent of *The Times*, told Sir Ernest Swinton of "the likelihood of a preponderance of siege operations in the next great European war" (*Eyewitness*, E. D. Swinton, 1932, p. 62). In 1912 the French Colonel Montaigne wrote: ". . . war will assume the features of a siege war. . . . The battle will be decided by exhaustion" (quoted by A. Vagts in *A History of Militarism*, 1938, p. 383). Early in 1914 I put forward a similar view (see my *Memoirs of an Unconventional Soldier*, 1936, pp. 23-27).

7. *A Critical Study of German Tactics*, Major de Pardieu (American translation, 1912), p. 117. The outlook of the French on the approaching war is summarized by General Herr in his *L'Artillerie* (1923), pp. 4-5. Among other things he says: "The war will be short and one of rapid movements, where manœuvre will play the predominant part; it will be a war of movement. The battle will be primarily a struggle between two infantries . . . the army must be an army of personnel and not of *matériel*. The artillery will only be an accessory arm. . . . The necessity for heavy artillery will seldom make itself felt. . . . It will serve no useful purpose to encumber oneself with an over-numerous artillery. . . ."

8. *The Principles of War*, Marshal Foch (1918), p. 286.

9. *Ibid.*, p. 32.

10. *Correspondance*, vol. xxx, p. 447.

11. In England Admiral Sir John Fisher saw it, hence the laying down of the first Dreadnought battleship in 1905.

12. See my *Memoirs of an Unconventional Soldier*, pp. 23-26.

13. So long ago as the American Civil War, Colonel Theodore Lyman had seen this: "Put a man in a hole," he wrote, "and a good battery on a hill behind him, and he will beat off three times his number, even if he is not a good soldier" (*Meade's Headquarters*, 1863-1865, 1922, p. 101). This was in the days of the muzzle-loading rifle.

14. One thing this did was to open the eyes of the General Staffs to the intimate relation between tactics and munitions (industrial) production.

Example: In Great Britain 3,000 18-pounder shells were produced in July, 1914, and 1,104,812 in October 1915. The total British expenditure during the war was 170,385,295 shells.

15. The growth of preliminary artillery bombardments was rapid: in the battle of Hooge in 1915, 18,000 shells; in the first battle of the Somme in 1916, 2,000,000; in the battle of Arras in 1917, 2,000,000; and in the third battle of Ypres in 1917, 4,300,000. Contrary to what was believed at the time, battles of *matériel* instead of economizing personnel squandered life. The battles of the Somme in 1916 and of Ypres in 1917 cost the British Army 800,000 men.

16. The third battle of Ypres, or Passchendaele, was fought for this purpose.

17. The American gas casualties in the war were 74,779, or 27·3 per cent. of the total. Of these, only 1·87 per cent. were fatal.

18. One hundred and eleven air attacks were made on England, in which 8,500 bombs weighing about 300 tons were dropped; 1,413 people were killed, 3,407 injured and £3,000,000 of property was destroyed. In Germany, according to German figures, 720 people were killed, 1,754 injured, and damage to property amounted to £1,175,000.

19. See *Eyewitness*, Major-General Sir Ernest D. Swinton (1932). On account of the development of missile power, as early as 1837 Jomini had predicted the introduction of armour. "We may see again," he wrote, "the famous men-at-arms all covered with armour, and horses also will require the same protection" (*Summary of the Art of War*, American Edition, 1854, p. 60). For *The Nineteenth Century Review* of July, 1878, Colonel C. B. Brackenbury contributed an article entitled "Ironclad Field Artillery," in which he wrote: "If . . . we add the use of defensive armour which can be carried by artillery and cannot be carried by cavalry and infantry, a power will be created which must seriously modify the tactics of the battlefield. The development is as sure to come as the day to follow the night. We may hope that England will set the example instead of following other nations" (vol. iv, pp. 40-50). This was not to be, for the idea was taken up in Germany by Colonel Schumann, and was tested out in the autumn manœuvres of 1889 and 1890. His invention consisted in 37-mm. and 53-mm. guns mounted in bullet and splinter proof steel turrets, which were transported on special vehicles. The turret weighed approximately one and a half tons. The Rumanian army bought several hundreds (a lecture given by George Saunders, *Morning Post* Berlin Correspondent, on "The Employment of Large Cavalry Masses, of Smokeless Powder, and of Movable Fortifications as Illustrated by the German Autumn Manœuvres of 1889," *Journal of the Royal United States Service Institution*, vol. xxxiv, pp. 867-889 and 1029-1035).

20. For this plan, see my *Memoirs of an Unconventional Soldier* (1936), chap. xiii. It was based on range of striking power, technology, and psychology. A complete tracked army was in the process of being built up around it.

21. Napoleon could have and to his advantage unleashed the "pent-up animality" of the Russian serfs and Ukrainians in 1812, and have called up the Revolution in France during the Hundred Days; yet he refrained

from doing so (*Napoleon*, Eugene Tarle, 1936, pp. 289, 381). The Duke of Wellington once said: "I always had a horror of revolutionizing any country for a political object. I always said—if they rise of themselves, well and good, but do not stir them up; it is a fearful responsibility." In 1871 Bismarck did not befriend the Paris Commune.

22. Quoted by Alfred Vagts in *A History of Militarism* (1938), p. 250.

23. *Representative Government and War* (1903), pp. 4, 6, 8.

24. *War as an Instrument of National Policy* (1929), pp. 34-35.

25. Though as auxiliaries to the older arms airplanes were employed for reconnaissance, observational and photographic duties, the idea growing dominant towards the end of the war was their independent use as bombers protected by fighters—that is, of escorted long-range artillery. There was no idea of organizing an airborne army.

26. The aircraft duties were: (1) To act as an advanced guard to the tanks; (2) to assist tanks in disorganizing the enemy's headquarters; (3) to guide tanks on to their objectives; (4) to protect tanks from hostile gunfire; (5) to supply advanced squadrons of tanks with petrol, etc.; (6) to act as messengers between tanks and their headquarters, and (7) to carry forward tank brigade commanders.

27. The British quota of cross-country supply machines was 7,296.

28. See my *Lectures on F.S.R. III, Operations between Mechanized Forces,* 1932, annotated editions published under the title of *Armoured Warfare,* 1943.

29. It is of course true that, were a nation in possession of an over-whelmingly strong air force, to attack an enemy possessing none, and in no way prepared or equipped to face obliterating bombardments, the airplane would be a master weapon. Or again, were it possible in a brief period of time to drop a bomb on every acre of the enemy's territory, the same would hold true. Among technically-minded nations, such suppositions carry air power into the realm of the ridiculous.

30. *The Command of the Air*, Giulio Douhet (1943), p. 31.

31. To see this, all that is necessary is to compare the events of the Second World War with his theory as expounded in *The Command of the Air.*

32. "Every technological improvement applied to the machinery of destruction tightens the grip which modern war has on the common man's life. The scope of war has become as large as that of peace, or indeed even larger, since under modern conditions it is the interest of efficient war to militarize peace" (*War in Our Time*, Hans Speier and Alfred Kähler, 1939, p. 13).

33. For psychological warfare see *Makers of Modern Strategy*, "Epilogue," by Edward Mead Earle; *Hitler Speaks*, Hermann Rauschning, 1939; *Spreading Germs of Hate*, George Sylvester Viereck (1931); *British Propaganda at Home and in the United States,* James Duane Squires (1935); *Falsehood in War Time*, Arthur Ponsonby (1928), and *Propaganda Technique in the World War*, Harold D. Lasswell (1938).

34. This may be gathered from book viii, chaps. v, vii and viii of *On War.* They are no more than notes, which, had he lived, would have been elaborated.

35. As representatives of these two strategies, Delbrück lists Alexander, Cæsar and Napoleon as strategists of annihilation, and Pericles, Belisarius, Wallenstein, Gustavus Adolphus and Frederick the Great as strategists of exhaustion.

36. It is interesting to note that, according to Max Werner, the present Soviet concept of *blitzkrieg* "comes at the end of the war, not at the beginning." This is certainly true of Russia *vis-à-vis* any neighbouring power, but it is not true of Germany *vis-à-vis* France or Poland. For Russia, the right course was undoubtedly to begin with a strategy of exhaustion and end with a strategy of annihilation. No other nation in the Old World is so well placed to combine the two strategies.

37. I point this out again and again in my *Armoured Warfare*, an annotated edition of *Lectures on F.S.R. III, Operations between Mechanized Forces*, first published in 1932.

38. Used as an independent weapon, the airplane proved less effective than the submarine; yet when combined with anti-submarine craft it went far to master that weapon. As was the case with lethal gas, the defence soon caught up with the attack. The most effective means was to scatter the target, just as infantrymen assume artillery formation when coming under gunfire.

39. In 1937 I wrote on this subject: ". . . it seems to me that a radical change will have to take place in our idea of the capital ship, around which present battle tactics revolve. In my opinion she will no longer be a gun-ship but a bomb-ship. In other words, our present aircraft carriers, which are looked upon as adjuncts to battleships, will, in more efficient form, replace them as the master ships of our fleet, and all other ships—cruisers, destroyers, submarines and possibly also battleships—will become their auxiliaries, the moving sea-fortress from which their aircraft will operate. . . . Bomb-power is the key, because air-carried bombs vastly outrange gun-fired shells. As this is so, it follows that naval warfare will be very different from what it was in 1914-1918" (*Towards Armageddon*, 1937, p. 196).

40. A few: flail tanks for exploding mines; saw tanks, an American invention for cutting paths through woods; recovery tanks for hauling vehicles out of deep water; flame projector tanks of great power; engineer tanks armed with a heavy mortar and equipped to carry and place in position carpets of flexible tracks to enable following vehicles to cross beaches, sand dunes and marshes; the American Locust tank, for airborne troops; and such allied instruments as various types of bulldozers, and the American "Water Weasel," a sort of amphibious jeep, and the British "Duck."

41. A jet-propelled flying torpedo (*Vergeltungswaffe Ein*, or V1), with a warhead of approximately 1,000 kg., gyro controlled and driven by petrol of which 180 gallons were carried. The range of the first model was about 150 miles; speed approximately 400 miles per hour.

42. *The Times*, December 1, 1944. The first time I wrote on this type of warfare was in the London *Radio Times* of July 6, 1928. I amplified it in my book *The Dragon's Teeth*, published in 1932; and for Sir Oswald Mosley's paper *Action* of October 19, 1939, I wrote an article entitled "Hitler's New Weapon: Rockets in War," in which I said: "Therefore, I

suggest it is possible that in this present war, and highly probable should it be a long one, we shall see cities bombarded by rockets. . . . Also . . . as a stepping-stone to this war of annihilation, aircraft will be fitted with rocket-bombs. . . ."

43. *The Origin of Artillery*, Lieut.-Colonel Henry W. L. Hime (1915), p. 144.

44. *Congreve Rocket System as Compared with Artillery*, Maj.-Gen. Sir W. Congreve, Bart., M.P. (1827), p. 39. Eventually four types were adopted by the British Army, a 3-, 6-, 12- and 24-pounder. They were made of sheet steel with a bombing charge in their heads. They had a range of 1,000-3,000 yards, and were fired from a rocket tube mounted on a tripod.

45. *Congreve Rocket System*, p. 18. Rockets were again used and with considerable effect at Walcheren and Copenhagen in 1807, and at the battles of Leipzig (1813), Waterloo and New Orleans (1815). In the last, writes Major A. Lecarrière Latour, "a cloud of rockets continued to fall in showers during the whole attack" (*Historical Memoir of the War in West Florida and Louisiana in 1814-15*, 1816, p. 154).

46. *Congreve Rocket System*, p. 42. Marshal Marmont considered that the rocket "may become the first arm . . . such as it now is . . . must exercise an immense influence on the destinies of armies" (quoted by Captain Boxer in his pamphlet on Congreve rockets, 1860, pp. 65, 66).

47. Called after Herr Nebel, the inventor. He claims that a rocket can be made to land within a 200-yards circle over a distance of 1,300 miles.

48. *The Times* (London), December 14, 1944. The growing importance of rocket projectiles is shown by the following U.S.A. expenditures on them: in 1942, $309,000; in 1944, $97,764,000, and in 1945 (estimated) over $1,000,000,000.

49. Unlike a shell, the rocket needs no explosive force behind it, and, unlike the flying bomb, no atmosphere against which to push. In fact, it attains its highest efficiency when moving in a vacuum. This was Ziolkowsky's great discovery in 1903. The reason is that it acts by reaction in accordance with Newton's third law of motion—"To every action there is an equal and contrary reaction." This may be explained as follows: Place a machine gun on a frozen lake. Fire one round and the gun will jump back a certain distance. Next, fire a succession of rounds, so that the recoil of each shot fired boosts on the recoil of the last shot fired; then, in a few seconds, recoil accelerating recoil will send the gun racing backwards over the ice. Lastly, imagine all friction with the ice removed, and you have a simple picture of how a rocket works.

50. The size of the port was roughly that of Dover, sufficiently large and well equipped to permit of 12,000 tons of supplies and 2,500 vehicles of all kinds being landed daily.

CHAPTER VII

THE AGE OF OIL—II

ARMAMENT is the outstanding product of the Age of Oil. Never before in all history has man so fervently bent his will towards destruction. From the opening of the present century onwards the sums spent on the means and weapons of war have exceeded those of all previous ages combined. The labour squandered has been incalculable and the damage done immeasurable. Only by imagining that had these sums and this labour been spent on construction, instead of on destruction, are we able to picture the immensity of the influence of armament on the age in which we live.

Nevertheless, in spite of the ever-increasing power to destroy, weapon development has never deviated from the path it has followed since the dawn of history; for to-day, as yesterday, perfection is sought through ever-increasing range of action, striking power, accuracy of aim, volume of fire and portability, or now better defined as "power-propelled means of mobility." The sole fundamental difference between present and past development is that to-day it is scientific, whereas formerly it was haphazard or by rule of thumb.

Therefore there can be no doubt that, now that military research has been placed on as highly an organized footing as industrial research has for long been, not only will progress in armament be stupendous, but its influence on civil industry will be equally so. As far back in the war as 1942 this fact was noted by Dr. M. A. Stine, research adviser to the American firm of Dupont. Addressing the Convention of the American Chemical Industry he said:

"The war is compressing into the space of months scientific developments which, without the spur of necessity, might have taken half a century to realize. As a result, industry will emerge from the war with a capacity for making scores of chemical and other raw materials on a scale that, only two years ago, was beyond comprehension."[1]

Yet this is by no means the most significant characteristic of the armament revolution. Instead it is the enormous stimulus destruction has given to production. Thus, in the United States—the outstanding example—in spite of the withdrawal of some 15,000,000 men from civil life and their enrolment in the fighting services, we read in the *Washington Post*: "For the first time in American history the men who control production are dealing with an unlimited market, and the results have been amazing. Next year, it seems, this country will make as much civilian goods as it did before the war, and on top of that it will make as much war goods as civilian goods. 'We are going to double the national output over 1939,' says Mr. Stuart Chase, which means that we can double the 1939 standard of living any time we want to."[2]

Of course it means a great deal more than that, because the 15,000,000 men now serving in the fighting forces have been left out of the reckoning, and when, with the ending of the war, they cease to be destructively employed, the question will arise, can they be productively employed? If they can, then, to keep them in full employment, the peace-time consumption of goods will have, at least, to be trebled. Should this be impossible, then, seeing that foreign markets are but a temporary vent for over-production, for the goods exported must sooner or later be paid for by goods imported, which means a reduction in the man power supplying the home market, either these 15,000,000 men, and probably more, will have to be relegated to the ranks of the unemployed, or else they must continue to serve in the fighting forces, which will become vast alms-houses.

As this holds good in practically all countries, whether belligerent or non-belligerent—for in the latter, world-wide blockade has stimulated the growth of their industries to a degree only second to war production in the former—in order to mitigate unemployment an all-round increase in armed forces is to be expected. In brief, as technology advances, militarism advances too.

Thus war becomes the prime mover in a technological civilization. And as in power industries the object of the machine is not only to produce, but to do so with an ever-decreasing amount of human labour, war is essential to the health of such a civilization; for in its preparation it absorbs much labour, and in its execution it finds employment for the unemployed by regimenting them into armies which liquidate each other. Further, by devastating entire countries and reducing their cities to rubble, it automatically creates a demand for employment on its termination.

It is this difference—war to solve unemployment in order to ensure against internal anarchy, instead of war solely to protect employment (ordered life) against external aggression—which has raised the problem of warlike production to the first place in our civilization. To-day the dependence of industry on war has become even more vital to our economic system than the dependence of war on industry. And because war is the sole corrector of over-production in an economy governed by under-consumption,[3] the military organization of entire nations in peace-time is now essential, not only that preparation for war may be complete, but that internal peace may be assured.

Thus we arrive at the war state, which in conception differs radically from the nation in arms. Whereas the latter is no more than the military aspect of collectivism (Socialism), which long ago Herbert Spencer foresaw must inevitably lead to the growth of military communities organized for a state of constant war,[4] the former demands the constant threat of war, because, as Mr. Walter Lippmann has pointed out, "there is only one purpose to which a whole society can be directed by a deliberate plan. That purpose is war: there is no other."[5] Therefore, should an enemy not exist, he will have to be created.

This is what happened in the U.S.S.R. and Germany after the last war. In order to build their total war states on the four supreme lessons the war had taught them, the one persuaded its people to believe that the destruction of Communism was the avowed aim of all the capitalist powers, and the other that the annihilation of the Third Reich was the aim of Communism, Judaism and international finance.

It was this fear which enabled these two great powers to develop into total war states, and though in the present war the proclaimed aim of the Allied Powers—one of whom is 100 per cent. totalitarian—is the destruction of the war state in its forms of Fascism and National Socialism, the certainty is that both the United States and Great Britain will become more and more totalitarian.[6] Already, in order to fight the war on equal terms with their enemy, it has become necessary for them to adopt one totalitarian measure after the other. Also it will be necessary for them to maintain many of these measures after the war, if not add to them, not only because unemployment will compel them to do so; but, unless they do, they will be unable to live alongside, let alone compete with the U.S.S.R. and the countries they have Sovietized.

Clearly the circle is a vicious one: machine power induces unemployment; unemployment increases fighting power; fighting power needs an enemy to justify it, politics create him; and war systematically follows and for the time being solves the unemployment problem.

So long as the machine governs peace and war, this sequence of events is inevitable. As Mumford points out, whereas the tool lends itself "to manipulation," the machine demands "automatic action."[7] Which, when translated into political terms, means that the one is a democrat and the other a communist. In a tool civilization individual thought and skill are essential; in a machine civilization it is collective effort. Like in an army, each human part must not only fit into the general plan, but all parts must be subservient to a single will. Therefore a technical civilization demands the war state,[8] which in turn demands centralized authority. Therefore such a state is autocratic and non-democratic, or at least non-liberal.

The moral effect of this is summed up by Lewis Mumford as follows: ". . . War is the supreme drama of a completely mechanized society . . . for those actually engaged in combat war brings a release from the sordid motives of profit-making and self-seeking that govern the prevailing forms of business enterprise, including sport; the action has the significance of high drama. . . . The death or maiming of the body gives the drama the element of tragic sacrifice, like that which underlies so many primitive religious rituals: the effort is sanctified and intensified by the scale of the holocaust. For peoples that have lost the value of culture and can no longer respond with interest or understanding to the symbols of culture, the abandonment of the whole process and the reversion to crude faiths and non-rational dogmas is powerfully abetted by the processes of war. If no enemy really exists, it would be necessary to create him in order to further this development.

"Thus war breaks the tedium of a mechanized society and relieves it from the pettiness and prudence of its daily efforts, by concentrating to their last degree both the mechanization of the means of production and the counter-ing vigour of desperate vital outbursts. War sanctions the utmost exhibition of the primitive; at the same time it deifies the mechanical. In modern war the raw primitive and the clockwork mechanical are one. . . .

". . . As long as the machine remains an absolute, war will represent for this society the sum of its values and compensa-tions: for war brings people back to earth, makes them face the battle with the elements, unleashes the brute forces of their own nature, releases the normal restraint of social life, and sanctions a return to the primitive in thought and feel-ing. . . . War, like a neurosis, is the destructive solution of an unbearable tension and conflict between organic impulses and the code and circumstances that keep one from satis-fying them.

". . . A society that has lost its life values will tend to make a religion of death and build up a cult around its worship—a religion not less grateful because it satisfies the mounting number of paranoiacs and sadists such as a dis-rupted society necessarily produces."[9]

This spiritual return to the Dark Ages is in its own par-ticular way leading to the establishment of a new feudalism. First, by reducing the masses to a servile proletariat, and secondly, by exalting over them the State as supreme over-lord with a vast bureaucracy as its baronage. Examine what is happening to-day, and then compare it with what Monsieur P. Boissonnade has to say on medieval feudalism —namely:

"In the name of the protection which they claimed to secure for the masses, the feudal classes chained men to the soil or to the workshop, claimed to regulate every sort of activity, divided the fruits of labour as they pleased, and weighed down the multitudes under the yoke of a capricious and tyrannical authority, though obliged to allow them a minimum of material advantages."[10]

To-day, in order to extinguish class differences, the avowed aim of Socialism is to create a proletarian (serf) community by exalting the State to the position of the supreme money power[11]—the creator and destroyer of financial values. In its scheme of things the State takes the place once occupied by the medieval Papacy—the creator and destroyer of spiritual values—and, in consequence, what may be called the Theocracy of Money will be estab-lished.

In this transformation the main weapon is taxation, and its object is to equalize the distribution of money in order to obliterate the power of the wealthy. Taxation may, therefore, be compared to a blockade of the richer classes, and, like mutual blockade, though its range is all-embracing, its pro-cess of reduction is slow. Here war assists, for at one and the same time it is tax gatherer and leveller, and never more so than to-day because of the range and striking power of aircraft.

By attacking the enemy's cities and centres of industry the airplane reduces their inhabitants to a common level of poverty and distress, and, what is far more important, as I will show, even when destruction is made good, it establishes a state of intellectual and moral communism which will profoundly influence future society.

"The city," writes Lewis Mumford, ". . . is the point of maximum concentration of the power and culture of a community. . . . Cities are the product of time. They are the moulds in which men's lifetimes have cooled and congealed. . . . In the city, time becomes visible: buildings and monuments and public ways, more open than the written records . . . leave an imprint upon the minds even of the ignorant or the indifferent. . . . By the diversity of its time structures, the city in part escapes the tyranny of a single present . . . life in the city takes on the character of a symphony. . . . With language itself, it remains man's greatest work of art."[12]

Cities are histories fashioned of brick and stone. We are what our cities make us: living histories—unconsciously so—fashioned by the petrified history in which we are encased. Then falls the bomb, and in thirty minutes the work of thirty generations is heaped into dust.

What does this mean to history, to civilization, to the future, to the way of life Western man will have to tread once the war ends, and he sets forth to rebuild his shell? It means that the dwellers in the new cities will be different from ourselves, because their cities will take on the character of a monotony—the symphony will be no more.

If we conjure up before us the destruction that Western man has wrought, and then ponder, we shall at once see that we are fighting for the things our cities give us: liberty, democracy, parliamentary government, wealth and trade. Yet in their destruction these very things are being destroyed, and far more surely so than any hostile ideology could ever do.

For instance, take cities like Berlin, Hamburg and Cologne —great cities of four million, two million and one million inhabitants. The first rose from out of a Wendish village, the second began its life as a Carlovingian fortress, and the third as a Roman colony—hence its name—planted by the Emperor Claudius. Like plants, they grew gradually; now, for the greater part, they will have to be rebuilt in a handful of years. No doubt they will be meticulously planned, yet monotonously so; for their architects will be of one generation and of one architectural impulse. Their cities will be utilitarian in form and communistic in character. They will be human hives rather than homes; rapidly built, for man must have cover, and those who dwell in them will become bees: symmetrically minded, efficient, but historically soulless.

Under no democratic or individualistic system can these cities be rebuilt: solely under a tyranny and by slave labour. The virtue of a democracy is that it never hurries, it argues as well as works. But when millions of people have to be housed and thousands of factories resurrected in a moment, work will be the order of the day and words will be silenced at the pistol point; for what thirty generations did at their leisure will now have to be done by one through toil and sweat. It will be the building of the pyramids over again, and the crack of the lash will be heard throughout Europe.

Thus, on account of the discovery of flight, the whole social, economic, financial and political life of Western man is changing. Strange though it may seem, day by day and hour by hour, the very things we are fighting for are being silted up by the rubble and dust created by the very means of war which we imagine will liberate the nations and secure for all time our own freedom. Such is in all probability the dominant influence of armament on our way of life: it is reducing us to the serfdom of the Middle Ages.

It is out of these "barbaric invasions" that the new feudalism is steadily taking form. And as a proletariat, whether medieval or modern, agricultural or industrial, is incapable of governing itself, power over it inevitably passes into the hands of the manipulators of psychological and physical forces. Once these manipulators were ensured by irresistible armoured knights, to-morrow it would seem that they are to be guaranteed by irresistible armoured machines, in face of which popular risings will be impotent.[13] If so, then, after five hundred years, armour will once again be the central fact in the social system.

This advance towards autocracy is not only to be seen within nations, but also within the community of nations. Whereas, in 1776, Adam Smith pointed out that "in ancient times the opulent and civilized [the soft] found it difficult to defend themselves against the poor and barbarous nations [the hard], in modern times the poor and barbarous find it difficult to defend themselves against the opulent and civilized."[14] To-day this remains true, if for "soft" and "hard" are substituted "technical" and "non-technical." On this question Quincy Wright remarks: "Nations skilled in modern military techniques have an overwhelming advantage over those not so skilled."[15] This advantage has already demilitarized the smaller nations, such as Holland, Denmark and Belgium, and in time must inevitably lead to their absorption by the greater powers. Already we see this happening in Eastern Europe. Poland, the Baltic States and the Balkan countries are each too lacking in material resources to wage mechanized war; therefore they are being swallowed up by the U.S.S.R., not only to add to the strength of the Soviets, but to deprive Europe as a whole of strength to wage war against the Soviets. Thus it comes about that it is not so much unattackable frontiers which the greater powers are now seeking to establish, as ever-increasing armament resources—mines, oil wells, coal-fields, etc. This, of course, is the true meaning of *lebensraum*.

On this question Mr. Ely Culbertson has written:

"The nature of modern fighting machines and the vast amount of them needed are such that the industrial giant states require the resources of continents to wage a winning war. For the first time in history the battle for loot has become the battle for weapons. From time immemorial, men fought against men, and weapons were but accessories; in this and in future wars, machines fight against machines and men are all but auxiliaries. Vast mechanized blocs of workers and soldiers fight under their leaders to produce and use still more of the engines of destruction which devour their substance. The strategy of war and the strategy of economics and politics will be built around the central mathematical fact that the greater weight of organized metal and scientific chemicals will prevail. Unless something equally revolutionary is done to segregate the fighting machines, even this war may be but an incident in the continuous struggle for the monopoly of heavy weapons. To the winner must eventually go the dominion of the world."[16]

There is much truth in this statement; yet it will be remembered that, when the rise of Feudalism was examined in Chapter III, we noticed much the same. Then armour fought armour, the unarmoured being pure auxiliaries; many of the Viking raids were hunts for armour, and again and again Charlemagne prohibited traffic in armour in order to keep it within his realm. Then the dominant impulse was valour, now it is money as power. Then the one led to a war period known as the Crusades, the supreme gesture of spiritual thought between the years 1095 and 1204. Now the other has led to a period of economic crusades which may well last as long, should 1914 be substituted for 1095.

Looking at this grim situation, two points clearly stand out. The first is that in former days, when the simplicity of army organization may be compared to the handicraft period in industry, the invention of a new and powerful weapon frequently led to decisive results. The second is that to-day, when army organization is progressively catching up with industrial machine-craft, the decisive effect of such inventions is becoming more and more circumscribed.

At the opening of this the Second World War it may still be said that the then recently discovered processes of radio location had a decisive effect on the air defence of Great Britain. Yet, later on, so novel a weapon as the self-propelled bomb, and in spite of its effective range, had practically none, because time was insufficient wherein to build around it a highly organized machine tool. In itself it was but another projectile.

Therefore the conclusion is that, to attain their maximum utility, inventions should be suggested by the problems of war, not as they arise but by their being foreseen. In other words, through prolonged contemplation, and not as has normally been the case by sudden inspiration. Though this does not mean that intuitive flashes, such as the vision of the use of gunpowder as a projectile propellant, or of fulminate of mercury as a cartridge detonator, have lost their values, it does suggest that the problems of war, rather than some sudden inspiration, should fructify them.

This means that as each major war problem can more rapidly and economically be solved by an instrument specially built to solve it, the day of general purposes armies is drawing to a close. Such organizations are static and consequently conservative, and in a progressive scientific age are generally completely out of date when most needed. They are Jacks of all trades and masters of none, and are terrified by novelties because they upset their inertia.

To create a special purposes army first demands a new type of General Staff, an organ which, like the management of any great business, is not only concerned with maintenance and discipline, but above all with service, and to serve it must keep up to date in all its departments. A separate section of this Staff should deal with each special problem, constantly reviewing it in the light of scientific and industrial progress, and as constantly turning over to inventors the specifications of weapons and means it wants designed.

Had such an analytic war brain existed in Great Britain in 1919, the embryonic mechanized army then in formation would not have been scrapped, and the probabilities are that the whole course of the war would have been changed. Had Germany before the war been in possession of such an organ, it would have been seen that at bottom the conquest of Europe was not a land but a sea problem, because conquest could never be complete until the English Channel was successfully stormed. Therefore, to go to war before an instrument had been invented to storm it was to gamble with fate. As such an instrument was not devised, England remained unconquered, with the result that each continental nation Germany overran became a liability instead of an asset to her.

Again, had the Germans possessed the type of General Staff I have in mind—a technical as well as a tactical organ—would not it have immediately seen that, in so vast and ill-roaded a country as Russia, the crucial problem was cross-country supply, and that, without it, the larger the armoured forces put into the field the more road-bound they must become?

In these three cases, and others could be added to them, the key to inventiveness is range of action governed by the dominant weapons, those of most effective range—the airplane and the tank.

On land this range has been gained by the tank, and at sea by the airplane. In the one case, because on land the main purpose of a weapon is to enable its wielder to occupy an area or deprive the enemy of its use, whereas at sea it is to annihilate or compel the capitulation of the area the enemy is fighting on—namely, his ship. Whereas a warship is an armoured machine from which missiles are propelled, whether shells, torpedoes or rockets, and the aircraft launched from its decks are but an extension of its fighting range, the tank is an armoured machine which by its movement coupled with its fire power reduces the enemy's fighting space until insufficient is left of it for him to fight on.

Throughout the war the governing principle has been the integration of fighting power, not only of arms, but also of the fighting services. Thus, on land, only when air power has been combined with land power has the greatest effect been attained.

Also, at sea, no fleet can be considered a fighting instrument unless it is combined with air power. Co-operation is now no longer sufficient, therefore integration has not only become the key to battle but also to organization, and in consequence to invention—the invention of organizations in the shape of vast machine tools or weapons.

In their turn these organizations require vast industries to maintain them. These must be planned and built for war, and not merely be convertible for war production after the outbreak of hostilities, because the ever-increasing range of aircraft and self-propelled projectiles prohibits mobilization. This was seen clearly in the Japanese attack on Pearl Harbour, which is likely to become the classic example of the declaration of future wars. Like fire brigades, fighting forces will have to stand in a permanent state of readiness, as did the knights in the Middle Ages, no more than a trumpet blast being necessary to call them forth in fighting array. Incidentally, in those ages the above industries were represented by the armourers, the most highly skilled technicians of that period.

Whereas in Christendom the ideal was an unending spiritual conflict, in Wardom the real is an unending physical conflict, a return not so much to barbarism as to animalism in its crudest Darwinian form. In the one we see a spiritual autocracy, a spiritual regimentation and the establishment of vast instruments of spiritual propaganda. In the other we see a military autocracy, a military regimentation and also the establishment of vast instruments of military propaganda.

As the old feudalism gave rise to the burgh, the castle and the walled city to protect Christendom against the sudden invasions of barbarians, already in the new we have seen the introduction of the deep air-raid shelter and the placing of entire factories underground in order to protect them against the barbarians of the air. Thus, as Wardom advances, we may expect to see all great cities and industrial centres duplicated: the surface buildings constituting the peace and the underground the war establishments, so that like burrowing animals—rats and rabbits—their inhabitants may find immediate security and work may not be interrupted.

Well may it be asked, will men and women tolerate such restrictions of their liberties and comforts? I think the answer is that they will support anything so long as their animal instincts are first aroused. Proof of this is to be found in all totalitarian states, also in all non-totalitarian, which to fight totalitarianism have adopted totalitarian methods and, above all, totalitarian propaganda.

Man is what he thinks, and in an autocracy what he thinks is what his government decides he should think. Propaganda is therefore the master "weapon" of the new feudalism, as it was of the old, and to-day both intellectually and morally it is an all-obliterating weapon. As the machines of war are driven by oil, so is the will of man to wage war driven by lies. Thus the once sublime maxim, "The truth shall make you free," has been inverted, for to-day it reads, "The lie shall make you fight." As Georg Brandès once said: "War means the assassination of truth"; and as G. S. Viereck has written: "The object of propaganda in war-time is to make men see red," and "without hate there can be no propaganda. Give me something to hate and I guarantee to organize a powerful propaganda campaign anywhere within twenty-four hours."[17] Propaganda is the poison gas of the soul, for as Mr. Culbertson has truly said: ". . . the will of the masses is divided by far-reaching distortions and the mass mind is corrupted by a knowledge worse than ignorance because it is false. In the totalitarian countries millions marched with hypnotic exaltation to an inglorious death."[18]

Whether it is a coincidence or not, it is nevertheless a fact that this decreasing moral sense has steadily kept pace with the growth in armament; for as explosives have gone up, morality has gone down. Treaties are now scraps of paper; war aims, weathercocks which change with each political breeze; pledged words are sugared lies; honour between allies, veiled deceit; and obligations towards neutrals, implements of betrayal. Allies change sides, enemies become friends, friends become enemies and the leaders of the opposing nations bawl at each other like fish-wives, until war dissolves into a howling pandemonium in which every kind of atrocity is applauded when committed against the enemy and execrated when perpetrated by him. It would be invidious to quote examples, for all belligerents, in a greater or a lesser degree, have been party to them. Yet the most significant fact is not the universality of these barbarities, but the popular gloating over them, which shows the degradation into which humanity has slumped. Out of the scores of examples which flood the daily press, I will quote one as typical of the prevailing Satanism:

"Aachen is the biggest German town in our hands. It is the most exhilarating sight I have seen for years. The town of some 170,000 inhabitants . . . has now not a single

habitable house left in it. I have never seen such destruction.
. . . Ten thousands of them [the inhabitants] are living
like rats in cellars among the debris . . . one air raid alone
caused 3,000 deaths. . . . And it is good to think that what
happened in Aachen happened and goes on happening in
almost every German town. . . ."[19]

This was published on Christmas eve! The only lines I
can recall which compare with its brutality are those of
Byron:

> "And what shall I ride in?" quote Lucifer then—
> "If I follow'd my taste, indeed,
> I should mount in a wagon of wounded men,
> And smile to see them bleed."[20]

War ceasing to be a struggle between life values becomes
a blind destructive death force, like an earthquake, a volcanic
eruption or a typhoon. Whole populations are now attacked,
wiped out, enslaved or herded from one country into another
like cattle. As Quincy Wright says: "The entire life of the
enemy state comes to be the object of attack. The modern
doctrine of conquest even extends to the elimination of that
population and its property rights in order to open the space
it occupied for settlement."[21] And so it comes about that we
find writers, such as the late Morley Roberts, an Englishman,
advocating complete extermination of the enemy: "But if
the Germans are again overcome," he wrote in 1941, "it must
be held that the massacre of a whole population is justified
if no other means can secure an inoffensive nation or
nationality."[22]

Were the Germans the sole people who had ever caused a
war, or the sole aggressive nation remaining in the world,
there might be some sense in this suggestion. Clearly this is
not so, therefore it logically follows that to establish peace
on these lines, each succeeding aggressor nation, actual or
alleged, will have to be massacred, until but one nation is
left in the world—a saurian monster, all metal and no mind,
which will perish through its own stupidity.

This total mechanization for destruction (war) instead of
for construction (peace), for "illth" instead of for wealth,

for death instead of for life, is something totally new in Western civilization. Even during the hideous Thirty Years' War nothing approaching it was to be seen. Yet it is child of man's intelligence, and because science is all-pervading and because everything including the soul of man is now stretched and lopped to fit the Procrustean bed of techniques, wars which once were conflicts between nations are no longer so, instead they are struggles within civilization itself. Few exactly know what they are fighting for, and in this nescience nations tear each other to pieces like beasts in rut.

Yet one and all are fighting a universal disease: it is the mechanization of life, the blind dominance of the machine over man.

> We are greater than the Peoples or the Kings—
> Be humble, as you crawl beneath our rods!—
> Our touch can alter all created things,
> We are everything on earth—except the Gods![23]

Not until this dominance is shattered, and the machine and all it begets, politically, economically, socially and financially, ceases to be the master of man and instead becomes his servant, war will remain constant in our civilization. As William Blake long ago exclaimed: "Art Degraded, Imagination Denied, War Governed the Nations."[24]

To beget and build in order to kill and demolish is lunacy. And the more powerful becomes the war machine, the more certain is it that war will bring losses far in excess of gains, not only to the vanquished but also the victors. This is the uncontradictable fact the Second World War has revealed to all who still are sane. The truth is this:

"If the institutions and activities of a civilization do not reciprocally support each other, but instead destroy each other, the civilization is in peril. The signs of disintegration in modern civilization are manifest. The grave contradictions must be resolved in a higher dialectic if more frequent and more destructive wars are to be avoided. Can this vast and multiplex civilization be grasped as a whole in the minds of men so that those values can be perceived and accepted which both contribute to the civilization and result from the application of the best procedures which the civilization has yet developed? Can the spontaneous desires and behaviours of men deriving from the past be adjusted to the technologies and needs of society of the present and future?"[25]

This was the problem which faced the early Christian Church: how to adjust what remained of Roman culture to the "technique" of barbarism. It was also the problem which faced Western Europe after the Thirty Years' War: how to adjust what was left of medieval culture to the "technique" of rationalism. The first attempted to solve the problem by ennobling barbaric valour and converting the warrior into a soldier of the Church. The second attempted to solve it by classifying all soldiers as ruffians and by disciplining the scum of society in penal settlements called regiments. Neither sought to eliminate war; both sought to restrict its ravages, and of the two there can be no question that our forebears in the seventeenth and eighteenth centuries came the nearer to solving the problem.

Can we emulate them? I doubt it, because the conditions we are now called to work in are utterly different.

In the eighteenth century nations were self-sufficient so far as the necessities of life went; in consequence foreign trade was a negligible factor, and therefore the struggle for raw materials and markets was insignificant. Secondly, the ruling class in each country was composed of gentlemen who, in spite of their many failings, did maintain a code of honour both in peace and in war. Thirdly, armament development was all but stationary and armies limited in size; consequently success in war depended more on skill in generalship than on force of arms, and as battles depended on manœuvre more so than on slaughter, the damage done was correspondingly slight. Fourthly, the masses of the people were excluded from war, and protected against its ravages by rules and conventions; consequently war psychosis was kept within bounds.

All these conditions were changed by the French and Industrial Revolutions. The bourgeoisie came more and more to the fore, introducing into politics and war a *furor loquendi*, and dementing the masses through their newspapers, which began to take on their present propaganda form with Marat's *Ami du Peuple*. Weapons were multiplied, conscription enormously stimulating their production. The ruling class was liquidated or proscribed, and replaced by politically minded upstarts who, having neither position nor rank and frequently little wealth, had everything to gain by turning events to their personal advantage. Finally, with the advent of steam power the economic foundations of autarchic civilization began to crack and crumble.

Nevertheless, the nineteenth century was the most peaceful in European history since the days of the Antonines. Between 1815 and 1914 no war corresponding in dimension to the War of the Spanish Succession, the Seven Years' War, and the Revolutionary and Napoleonic Wars disturbed the peace of the world. All wars were localized, the main reason for this being the establishment of the *Pax Britannica*. It meant, as Britain ruled the oceans and the seas, by her sea power alone she could confine a European conflict and so prevent it assuming world-wide dimensions.

Notwithstanding, the age was one of ever-increasing military power, due largely to the rapid development of armaments, and a maritime empire does not fit securely into an epoch of mammoth armies. Consisting mainly of sea communications, which, unlike land communications, are uninhabitable, a maritime empire is primarily a trading and not a fighting community, and its people are, therefore, unmilitary.

The massive strength upon which the *Pax Britannica* was built was founded on steam power and remained virtually unchallenged until the advent of the Oil Age. Far more so than steam, oil favours the growth of armies because, when fully exploited as it is to-day, it does for land traffic what steam power does for sea traffic: it enables land forces to move in any direction over a plane surface, whereas the railway only permits of movement in one dimension. Further, though possessing vast supplies of coal, Great

Britain has no extensive natural sources of oil. Further still, the airplane—*par excellence* the petrol-driven fighting machine—is the dominant weapon at sea, and though in the oceans it still needs ships to operate from, as its range increases, more and more will it operate from land bases. Already the narrow seas are entirely dominated by air power, and it is on their command that British sea power is based, and far more so than on the command of the oceans, because the keys to them are to be found in the straits, channels and narrow seas.

It was the decline in British naval power which unhinged the peace of the world, as in its day it was the decline in Roman land power which unhinged the peace of the Latin world. This weakening set in at the opening of the present century, when Germany, foolishly, set out to challenge Britain's command of the sea. Had William II refrained from doing so, the probabilities are that Great Britain would not have declared war on Germany in 1914, and that, in spite of Russia, the Franco-German war would once again have been localized, as it was in 1870.

Now that the *Pax Britannica* is no more, the problem of the future is whether some other instrument can fill its place. In spite of hypothetical leagues of nations and world security pacts, all of which scout the fact that man is essentially a quarrelsome and pugnacious animal, it seems to me that there are only two possibilities: either a *Pax Sovietica* or a *Pax Americana*. Which is the more likely? The answer largely depends upon armaments, for they are the ultimate arbiter in an Age of Power.

Since the days of Darius and Xerxes the fundamental power problem in the Old World has been the struggle between Europe and Asia. Geographically, Europe is but a promontory of Asia; ethnographically, a brewhouse of virile and quarrelsome peoples. Normally Europe is at war within herself. Nevertheless, until the outbreak of the present war, whenever Asia has threatened her existence as a Continent, her turbulent peoples have called off their quarrels and have marched against the Asiatic invaders.

Until 1917 Russia was largely an Occidental Power with an empire in Asia—a "pseudo-morphosis" as Spengler calls it. Since then she has become more and more pronouncedly an Asiatic—that is, an Oriental Power. Bolshevism (not to be confused with Marxian Communism—a problem of cashiers) is an Asiatic cult steaming up from the steppelands of Asia. It is profoundly anti-Occidental;[26] yet, in 1941, the two greatest maritime powers of the West, Great Britain and the United States, by pledging full support to the U.S.S.R.—though they may have little realized it at the time—opened the gates of Eastern Europe to the Russian hordes. No more portentous event has occurred in Europe since August 24, 410, when some unknown hand unbarred the Salarian Gate and let Alaric and his horde into the Eternal City—"Adest Alaricus: trepidam Romam obsidet, turbat, irrumpit."

At Tilsit, in 1807, Napoleon exclaimed: "Within a hundred years Europe will be Republican or Cossack!"[27] Though wrong in time it would appear that his prediction is about to be fulfilled, and that Europe is once again to become no more than an Asiatic promontory, as she was when the all-conquering Aryans came from the steppelands with horse and sword.

Should this be, then the Soviet Imperium will stretch from the Pacific to the Atlantic and from Cape Chelyuskin to the Cape of Good Hope. That such a conglomeration of power will last for long is unlikely, for empires like their makers are mortal.[28] Yet, so long as it does last, what does this colossus mean to the United States? It means that three-quarters of the war potentials of the world will be in Soviet hands, and oil power favours land power more so than sea power, and the shortest distance between the U.S.S.R and the U.S.A. is but a little more than twice the breadth of the English Channel at its narrowest!

In these circumstances is peace possible? Though no man can answer this question, Stalin, approvingly quoting Lenin, has said:

"We are living, not merely in a State, but in a system of

States, and it is inconceivable that the Soviet Republic should continue to exist interminably side by side with imperialist States. Ultimately one or the other must conquer. Pending this development, a number of terrible clashes between the Soviet Republic and the bourgeois States must inevitably occur."[29]

Granted that Stalin is right, then "he who has the petrol has the Empire." Therefore, until a new prime mover[30] is discovered, more so than all other war potentials, oil[31] will decide whether the *Pax Sovietica* or the *Pax Americana* is for another brief space of time to give peace to the world.

REFERENCES

1. As reported in *The Times* (London) of November 9, 1942.
2. As reported in *The Times* (London) of October 28, 1943.
3. Lewis Mumford is highly illuminating on this important point. He writes: "An army is a body of pure consumers . . . not merely a pure consumer but a negative producer; that is to say, it produces illth, to use Ruskin's excellent phrase, instead of wealth; misery, mutilation, physical destruction, terror, starvation and death characterize the process of war and form a principal part of its product . . . for the army is the ideal consumer, in that it tends to reduce toward zero the gap in time between profitable original production and profitable replacement. The most wanton and luxurious household cannot compete with a battlefield in rapid consumption. . . . Mechanized warfare, which contributed so much to every aspect of standardized mass production, is in fact its great justification. . . . Quantity production must rely for its success upon quantity consumption; and nothing ensures replacement like organized destruction" (*Technics and Civilization*, 1934, pp. 43-44).
4. In *The Man versus the State* (1884), which first appeared in the *Contemporary Review* of May 1884. He predicts the coming of the war state. To him "all Socialism involves slavery," and trade unionism militarism in the form of "industrial armies under State control." He points out that in militant communities the individual becomes "a slave to the community as a whole."
"In ancient Greece the accepted principle was that the citizen belonged neither to himself nor to his family, but belonged to his city—the city being with the Greeks equivalent to the community. And this doctrine, proper to a state of constant war, is a doctrine which Socialism unawares reintroduces into a state intended to be purely industrial" (p. 41).
5. *The Good Society* (1937), p. 90.
6. The same is to be seen during the French Revolutionary and Napoleonic Wars. The English set out to fight Jacobinism in a Phrygian cap, and ended by adopting it in a Manchester topper.

7. *Technics and Civilization*, p. 10.

8. "In the past half-century, the economic and propaganda aspects of war technique have so gained in importance that the diplomatic and military advantage of highly centralized and militarized states appears to have increased" (*A Study of War*, Quincy Wright, vol. i, p. 271).

9. *Technics and Civilization*, pp. 309-11. Mumford also writes: "The difference between the Athenians with their swords and shields fighting on the field of Marathon, and the soldiers who faced each other with tanks, guns, flame-throwers, poison gases, and hand-grenades on the Western Front, is the difference between the ritual of the dance and the routine of the slaughter-house. One is an exhibition of skill and courage with the chance of death present, the other is an exhibition of the arts of death, with the almost accidental by-product of skill and courage" (p. 310).

10. *Life and Work in Medieval Europe* (1937), p. 333.

11. Lenin defined his system as "Socialism plus electrification." It would have been more correct to say "Socialism plus moneyfication" (state capitalism). The cash-box is God, the Party his priesthood and the socialized the servile congregation.

12. *The Culture of Cities* (1938), pp. 3-5.

13. This would seem to be one of the possibilities arising out of the Dumbarton Oaks proposals.

14. *An Inquiry into the Nature and Causes of the Wealth of Nations* (Edwin Cannan's Edition, 1904), vol. ii, p. 202.

15. *A Study of War*, vol. i, p. 313.

16. *Total Peace* (English Edition, 1944), p. 46.

17. *Spreading Germs of Hate*, George Sylvester Viereck (1931), p. 16. The most noted example is the Bryce Report on alleged German outrages in Belgium in 1914.

18. *Total Peace*, p. 44.

19. Mr. John Gordon in *The Sunday Express* (London), Dec. 24, 1944. Though it is highly probable that similar utterances have appeared in the German Press, it would surprise me to learn that any German editor would consider Christmas Eve an appropriate date for their publication.

20. *The Devil's Drive.*

21. *A Study of War*, vol. i, p. 310.

22. *The Behaviour of Nations* (1941), p. 161.

23. *The Secret of the Machines*, Rudyard Kipling.

24. "The Laocoön." He adds: "Where any view of Money exists, Art cannot be carried on, but War only." Also: "The unproductive Man is not a Christian, much less the Destroyer. Christianity is Art and not Money. Money is its curse."

25. *A Study of War*, vol. i, pp. 370-371.

26. It has always seemed to me that Mikhail Toukhatchevski, who was shot by Stalin in 1937, was the perfect example of what Bolshevism means, for in him lived the soul of Genghis Khan, of Ogdai and of Batu. Autocratic, superstitious, poetic and ruthless, he hated Christianity and Christian culture because they had obliterated paganism and barbarism and so had deprived his fellow-countrymen of the ecstasy of the god of war and the glamour of "the carnival of death." Also he loathed the Jews, because they

had helped to inculcate Russians with "the pest of civilization" and "the morale of money capitalism." When incarcerated in Ingolstadt, to Pierre Fervacque, a fellow-prisoner, he said: "A demon or a god animates our race. We shall make ourselves drunk, because we cannot as yet make the world drunk. That will come." Once Fervacque found him painting in discordant colours on a piece of cardboard the head of an atrocious idol. "What is that?" he asked him. "Do not laugh," replied Toukhatchevski. "I have told you that the Slavs are in want of a new religion. They are being given Marxism; but aspects of that theology are too modern and too civilized. It is possible to mitigate that disagreeable state by returning to our Slav gods. . . . For long I have hesitated to choose my particular god, but, after reflection, I have accepted Pierrounn [god of war and of lightning], because, once Marxism is thrust upon Russia, the most devastating wars will be let loose. . . . We shall enter chaos and we shall not leave it until civilization is reduced to total ruin." In his eyes, destruction alone justified everything, because it unlocked the door to the road back to Seljuk, Tartar and Hun. "Seriously," he said, "it would be a good thing for humanity were all books burnt, so that we could bathe in the fresh spring of ignorance. I even think that it is the sole means of preventing humankind becoming sterile." What he yearned for was a return to the days of Ivan the Terrible, "then Moscow will become the centre of the world of barbarians." "Had Nicholas II but followed in the footsteps of Peter the Great and Catherine II, how docile the Russians would have been, for they love a despot." "If Lenin is able to disencumber Russia from the old scrap-iron of prejudices and de-Westernize her, I will follow him. But he must raze all to the ground, and deliberately hurl us back into barbarism." The quotations are from *Le chef de l'armée rouge, Mikail Toukhatchevski*, Pierre Fervacque.

27. Quoted from *Problems of Power*, Wm. Morton Fullerton (1913), p. viii. When at St. Helena, Napoleon said: "Is not Russia the head of the Hydra, the Antæus of the fable, which can only be subdued by seizing it bodily and stifling it in the embrace? But where is the Hercules to be found? Should there arise an Emperor of Russia, valiant, impetuous and intelligent, a Tzar with a beard on his chin, Europe is his own. . . . When I am dead and gone my memory will be esteemed and I shall be revered in consequence of having foreseen and endeavoured to put a stop to what will yet take place. I shall be revered when the barbarians of the North possess Europe, which would never have happened had it not been for you (the English)."

28. Few empires have lasted longer than 300 to 400 years, and not a few considerably less. The longest lived, the Byzantine (330-1453), was of all the most unprogressive.

29. *Leninism*, Joseph Stalin (1928), vol. i, p. 56.

30. Possibly the rocket.

31. "The Soviet Union is credited by its specialists to possess a potential reservoir of oil equal to two-thirds of the entire oil wealth of the world. . . . It would seem far simpler for the Soviet Union to improve and develop the exploitation of its own oilfields than those of a foreign country. But Moscow prefers to obtain concessions in all the neighbouring States. The

Curzon line continued to the Carpathians is drawn so as to bring within the Soviet Union the Galician oilfields; in Rumania the U.S.S.R. has declared its desire to buy out the oilfields from Western companies; now it is the turn of Persia" (*The Patriot*, November 30, 1944). Clearly the reasons for this are (1) to preserve Soviet oil and (2) to deny oil to potential enemies. This is corroborated by Commander Stephen King-Hall, M.P., in his *National News-Letter* of March 8, 1945. On his return from an official visit to Russia he wrote: "Does Russia want the oil in North Persia? Answer: Yes. Why? A big Russian oil chief in Baku told me that Russia's internal demand will absorb her production capacity for five years. Secondly, in a world of power politics, oil is Power, and even if one does not use it oneself, it is a good thing (in a world of power politics) to control as much oil as possible."

CHAPTER VIII

THE AGE OF ATOMIC ENERGY

TWENTY years ago, in an article on " Atomic Energy," Professor F. W. Aston wrote: "Within a tumbler of water lies sufficient energy to propel the *Mauretania* across the Atlantic and back at full speed . . . if only ten per cent. of the hydrogen in the sun were transformed into helium, enough energy would be liberated to maintain its present radiation for a thousand million years. . . . How long it will be before man can release and control this energy, and to what uses he will put such vast potentialities, are subjects for the philosopher. . . . It may be that the highest form of life on our planet will one day discover supreme material power, or cataclysmic annihilation, in the same ocean wherein, we are told, its lowest forms originally evolved."[1]

There is one point in this statement I would question. It is that it should have been as apparent to Professor Aston, as it was to Roger Bacon in the case of gunpowder, to what uses man would put atomic energy, once the secret of its release was his. This ought to have been quite clear to him, for since the day Leonardo da Vinci banished from his mind the thought of designing a submarine, because he realized the uses to which such a vessel would be put, nearly every great scientific discovery has either been turned to profit-making or to war, and profit-making is a breeding ground of war because in itself it is so largely war in the making.

In the Second World War, as in the First,[2] but on a vaster scale, scientists were regimented for war, and so thoroughly did they place their knowledge at the service of destruction and death that, as instruments of war, they and their laboratories are fast ousting the generals and their armies. This fact was pointed out by Professor H. H. Dale, President of the Royal Society, two days after the first atomic bomb was dropped. In *The Times* of August 7 he wrote:

" In any case, is it not obvious that, with the closing stages of this war, scientific discovery and invention are becoming the essential combatants? Science, an unwilling conscript,[3] is becoming the direct agent of undiscriminating devastation at long range, needing only a minimum of military apparatus or personnel—witness the German V weapons, and now the atomic bomb."

This is startlingly true when we consider the second of these weapons from the points of view of scientific production and military use.

Its design and manufacture entailed the enrolment of hundreds of leading scientists and skilled technicians as well as 125,000 workers. The money spent on this " the greatest scientific gamble in history," was $2,000,000,000, and the bomb produced "had more power than 20,000 tons of T.N.T., and more than 2,000 times the blast power of the British 'grand slam' (22,000 lb.) bomb, which until now was the largest ever used in the history of warfare."[4] We have also been told: "Theoretically, provided it can be manufactured in sufficient quantity, the atomic bomb has multiplied the destructive power of the American bomber fleets about 3,000 times.   Equipped with the new weapon, a fleet of 800 Super-Fortresses such as recently raided Japan would have the blasting effect of 2,500,000 such airplanes carrying T.N.T."[5]

Compared with all this, the military use is truly trivial. One airplane, a B29, carrying a crew of eleven men, set out on August 5 and, when at an altitude of some 20,000 feet above the city of Hiroshima, one of these men, the bomb aimer, manipulating a lever, released a bomb attached to a parachute; whereupon the airplane raced away out of range of the forthcoming blast. Then we read: "What had been a city going about its business at a quarter-past nine on a sunny morning, went up in a mountain of dust-filled smoke, black at the base and towering into a plume of white at 40,000 feet."[6] Next, on the 9th, the same infantile performance was repeated over Nagasaki.

In the first of these operations four and one-tenth square

miles out of almost seven of built-up area were completely obliterated; 160,000 people killed and injured, and 200,000 rendered homeless. And in the second 120,000 were killed and injured, but, as the report added, "many bodies remain uncounted under ruins of buildings."[7] Therefore it may be accepted that no less than 300,000 people were killed and injured by the two bombs dropped, and at no single casualty to the attacker. In other words, battles as destructive in life to the "defender" as had been the Battle of the Somme in 1916 and the Battle of Ypres in 1917 were lost and won, not in months but in seconds. Battles carried out by a section of men to whom generalship, strategy, tactics or any kind of fighting meant nothing at all. And, be it remembered, this is but the beginning of atomic warfare, for we are told that an atomic bomb can eventually be made "a thousand times more powerful, and that, if only a few per cent. of atomic mass can be converted into energy instead of the present o·1 per cent., mankind will be in a position to commit suicide at will."[8]

Excluding for the moment this grim possibility, the question I will first ask myself is: How far does the power of this new weapon affirm or disprove what I have already written?

(1) Clearly it supports my statement that "tools, or weapons, if only the right ones can be discovered, form 99 per cent. of victory. . . . Strategy, command, leadership, courage, discipline, supply, organization and all the moral and physical paraphernalia of war are nothing to a high superiority of weapons . . . at most they go to form the one per cent. which makes the whole possible."

(2) Though it does not contradict what I have called "the law of military evolution"—namely, that "civilization is environment, and, consequently, armies must adapt themselves to its changing phases in order to remain fitted for war," for the time being at least it reverses this law by making war the environment to which civilization must be adapted in order to survive. Thus a return is made to the conditions prevailing in the days of the Vikings.

(3) It both supports and contradicts my contention that in present-day warfare " quality beats quantity and not merely a greater quantity a lesser." (*a*) It deproletarianizes war by rendering the conception of the nation in arms or in arsenals absurd, for in atomic battles the quantity of fighting man power is reduced to its irreducible minimum. (*b*) Its striking power is so great that quantity rather than quality of weapon power is, in a given time, more likely to achieve the enemy's annihilation. This, it would seem, will become absolute once the bomb becomes an atom-propelled rocket, for then, to all intents and purposes, the soldier will retire from the contest to become the fearful spectator of a war fought between fearless robots. As I wrote in Chapter IV: "With the discovery of gunpowder . . . we pass into the technological epoch of war, the hidden impulse of which is the elimination of the human element both physically and morally, intellect alone remaining." To-day the highest practical form of intellect is scientific thought, and from now onwards its óne aim is to discover how the atomic bomb can be countered.

(4) This leads directly to the question of the "Constant Tactical Factor": will science discover a means of neutralizing it? Thus far in the history of armaments each new weapon has eventually been mastered. Not necessarily by a more destructive weapon and sometimes not even by a weapon at all. Thus, in 1494, though few Italians, if any, could see an answer to Charles VIII's bombards, within fifteen years of their use a new defensive system laughed them to scorn. Against this may be set that, from 1519 onwards, the Aztecs and Incas empires went down before the Spanish arquebus and cannon because they could find no answer to these weapons. Whether today we are placed in a similar position it is impossible to say. Nevertheless, even should the Constant Tactical Factor have run its course—which is yet to be proved—should man regain his sanity as regards the purpose of war—that is, should he revert to war as a political instrument (a subject I will return to later) instead of regarding it purely as a cataclysmic instrument,

he may eventually abandon so destructive a weapon, as Goth, Vandal, Lombard and Seljuk in the end found that to enjoy their conquests was more profitable than to devastate and pillage their enemies' countries on primitive Potsdam lines.

Sane though such a change would be, so long as the tribal instincts of mass man are free to dominate both peace and war, there is little prospect of it taking shape. Never since the introduction of firearms, which started the proletarianization of war, has morality sunk to such depths of degradation as in the recent conflict. Had this catastrophic decline ended with the war itself, there might be some hope for sanity; but this is far from being the case, because what may correctly be called the strategy of frightfulness was carried over into the peace in the peculiarly repulsive form of the trial of alleged war criminals.

Though in all wars atrocities have abounded, and after some, more particularly those of a religious origin, massacres and reprisals have followed, no single one, so far as my knowledge goes, has ended in a wholesale proscription of an enemy's government, its statesmen, officials, police officers, bankers, scientists, industrial magnates and generals, for crimes actual or alleged perpetrated during and even before the war.[9] Were justice the aim, then justice would be impartially administered, which in the case of Germany and Japan it clearly has not been, since from the start of the witch hunt it was postulated that only the enemy were subject to criminality, and in spite of the monstrous actions on the part of their conquerors, such as the massacre of Katyn, the obliteration of scores of cities, and the mass deportation of from twelve to eighteen million Germans. "Justice, being destroyed, will destroy; being preserved, will preserve." These wise words of Manu cast a portentous shadow over the length and breadth of Europe.

This travesty of justice is nothing other than the upthrust of primitive cruelty[10] in a society which has lost all sense of moral values.[11] Therefore it would appear that the Western World is fast retrogressing to the vilest period of the Roman

Empire, in whose gladiatorial games the victims were torn to pieces in order to propitiate or appease the blood-lust of the rabble, now the newspaper and cinema fed masses. And, as Lecky points out when considering these games ". . . in every society in which atrocious punishments have been common, this side of human nature [indifference to the sight of human suffering] has acquired an undoubted prominence."[12] Further, "One of the first consequences of this taste was to render the people absolutely unfit for those tranquil and refined amusements which usually accompany civilization."[13]

The trial of war criminals and massacring of Jews, as well as the exultation over war atrocities when perpetrated by one side and their execration when identical ones were committed by the other side, show that both during and after the war nations were mentally and morally so completely unbalanced that, had they been individuals, they would have been considered insane. Is it, therefore, likely in a world which morally has reverted to the circus that sanity in the use of the atomic bomb is to be expected? How can it be in a world of propaganda-fed masses who for six years had it dinned into them that annihilation of the enemy is the sole aim in war? This is corroborated by the most popular of the justifications for the use of the atomic bomb— namely, that it saved the lives of Americans by destroying the lives of Japanese, as if saving and destroying lives were aims of war; if so, why go to war at all? Clearly, could a war be won without any damage to life and property, the easier would it be for the victor to establish peace on whatever terms he desired. Peace and not saving or taking life is the aim of war.

An equal lack of balance is to be seen in the suggestions made to control the manufacture and use of the new weapon: the most popular, and, therefore, the most irrational, was that civilization can only be prevented from committing *felo de se* by handing the invention over to an international authority with sole powers to manufacture it. But how can an authoritative Super-State be founded on a moral vacuum? And, until this chasm in civilization is filled up, is it rational to suppose that the United States will agree to scrap their existing atomic plants and hand all uranium over to such a reptile of a world power? Also, is it likely that Russia will agree to forgo experimentation in the production of atomic energy, now the greatest potential prime mover in the world? Should these things happen, then they will only show that the nations are madder than they actually were when these suggestions were first made; for the whole idea of maintaining peace through power to destroy is unadulterated madness. "From whence come wars and fightings among you? come they not hence, even of your lusts that war in your members?"—thus St. James.

Such grasping at straws by a world drowning in its own immorality is fantastic. Instead, what may be expected is that hence onwards uranium (or whatever element is found more destructive), now the most essential raw material for war, will be fought for by the nations, as in the past they have fought for gold, iron, coal and oil. Therefore it may be accepted that, so long as greed for material things dominates the lives of men, peace is only likely to last the time necessary for the nations to recover from the last war and prepare for the next one.

Accepting the likelihood of this, what are the probable influences the atomic bomb will exert on war?

First, let us consider this problem from the point of view of the recent war. Though, as we now know, Japan was approaching collapse before the atomic bomb appeared, there can be little doubt that had it been used at any time in the Far East war it would have brought it to an abrupt termination. Therefore we may accept as certain that, had the Germans possessed a dozen of these bombs on D-Day, not a vessel of the vast armada which sailed from England would have reached the Normandy coast. Further, had they had a few score in April, 1945, in one gulp they could have swallowed the death rattle then choking them, and in a fortnight have imposed unconditional surrender upon Russia, France and Great Britain, if not the United States as well.

From these two possibilities alone it is clear that already the recent war is as out-moded as the Trojan, and that so long as the aim of war remains destruction, every military, naval and air quantity of to-day must be relegated to the scrap heap. For in a war of laboratories what place is there for navies, armies and air forces; for conscription, militia or voluntary service; for tanks, artillery and infantry; for fortifications, defended frontiers and strategic railways; for military academies, schools and staff colleges, and for generals, admirals and air marshals?

These statements are in no way exaggerated, as the following facts will show. Because it is known that the first model of the atomic bomb, when detonated at an altitude of 1,800 feet, obliterated a built-up area of over four square miles in extent, it is obvious that no army could exist if attacked by even a small squadron of atomic bomb carrying aircraft. The same applies to a fleet at sea, even should it consist of submersible vessels, because depth charges equivalent to the detonation of 20,000 tons of T.N.T. would prove irresistible. Also the same applies to aircraft, when the bomb in conjunction with radar (radio location) is used as a "height-charge" instead of a depth charge. Because it was possible by means of radar on a foggy day and at a range of from 28,000 to 30,000 yards to score three 9-inch shell hits out of thirty-three rounds fired by the Dover batteries on the *Scharnhorst* sailing at 30 knots, it should be as possible to do the same with atomic shells or rockets against aircraft at equal or greater ranges, and, be it noted, in this case scoring direct hits is quite unnecessary. As this is so, it may be accepted that the rocket, eventually propelled by atomic energy and carrying an atomic war head, will become a master weapon with "Blast" as its sole aim. Warfare will then take on a Krakatoan aspect.

Instead of cities being walled in as happened in the Viking age, we can picture whole countries girt about by radar sets, ceaselessly "listening-in" for the first jazz note of the broadcast of annihilation. In the vicinity of these instruments will be hidden away two tactical organizations of atom charged and propelled rockets—the one offensive and the other defensive. The first will be ranged on every great foreign city in the world, because before war is launched—to declare it would be sheer madness—no single nation will know who among the rest is its true enemy. The second organization will be directed by the radar sets, and so soon as they signal a flight of offensive rockets speeding towards them, the defensive rockets will automatically be released by radar, to speed into the heavens and explode in whatever cubic space in the stratosphere radar decides the enemy's offensive rockets will enter at a calculated time. Then, hundreds of miles above the surface of the earth, noiseless battles will be fought between blast and counter-blast. Now and again an invader will get through, when up will go London, Paris or New York in a 40,000 feet high mushroom of smoke and dust, and as nobody will know what is happening above or beyond, or be certain who is fighting whom—let alone what for—the war will go on in a kind of bellicose perpetual motion until the last laboratory blows up. Then should any life be left on earth, a conference will undoubtedly be held to decide who was victor and who was vanquished, the latter being forthwith liquidated by the former as war criminals.

At the moment this picture of Mars "gone barmy" is as good as any other. But the point to note in it is that it does not matter how atomic wars are fought; for the sole thing which does matter is that all nations will be prepared to fight them, because in the age of atomic energy the small will be as puissant as the large. Therefore this potential fact will dangle like the sword of Damocles over the world's head. Its thread may be cut wilfully, but on account of the tension in which all nations will live, it is far more likely to be severed accidentally: perhaps a maniac may press the button, or a defective fuse set the whole thing off.

The absurdity of this situation is patent, and even should it not awaken wisdom, at no distant date it must make man laugh. To found civilization on the destructive power of war is as idiotic as to found health on the destructive power

of surgery. That for centuries this topsy-turvy outlook has
been glimpsed is proved by man's gropings after a warless
world state. And, as is to be expected, this aim began to take
visible shape shortly after the general adoption of firearms,
since such a state required power to police it. These gropings
are worth a moment's enquiry, because thus far each has
failed. The war devil has refused to be exorcised by good
intentions, nor can his shield be cleft by a weapon wielded
by many hands.

The first proposal of note was Sully's "Grand Design."
Sully (1560-1641) proposed a federated Europe of fifteen
states with an army and a navy at the disposal of its Senate.
"To succeed in the execution of this plan," he optimistically
wrote, "will not appear difficult, if we suppose that all the
Christian Princes unanimously concurred in it." The next
scheme was put forward by William Penn shortly after the
close of the Thirty Years' War. It, like the League of Nations,
was backed by moral sanctions without police power. In
1713 this proposal was followed by the Abbé de St. Pierre's
Projet de Paix Perpétuelle, of which Frederick the Great
said: "The thing is most practicable; for its success all that
is lacking is the consent of Europe and a few similar trifles."[14]
Next, in 1761, came Rousseau's *Jugement sur la paix Perpétuelle*; then, in 1795, Immanuel Kant's treatise entitled
Zum ewigen Frieden;[15] after which came the first actual
though far from practical peace organization, the Holy
Alliance of 1815, which, as Metternich called it at the time,
soon proved itself to be a "loud-sounding nothing." Lastly
came the League of Nations in 1919. It also failed, yet, as
hope springs eternal in the human breast, we now have
Dumbarton Oaks and San Francisco, and, in the imagination of the multitudes, a Super-State is in the making. All
this State need do is to brood over the atomic eggs, when,
through fear of their hatching, the lion will lie down with
the lamb and the wolf of war will cease its howling.

Is this likely? "Yes," should these Elders of Zion, or
whatever they call themselves, eliminate the causes of war,
and "no" should they fail to do so, because so frequently

foreign wars are waged in order to prevent these causes leading to internal revolutions and civil wars. Should it be "no," then all that will happen is that one type of conflict will be exchanged for another—a type universally accepted as the very worst. Instead of the human world blowing up like one immense volcano, it will be shaken to pieces by an unending series of disruptive social earthquakes, in which knuckle-dusters, tommy guns, razor blades and coshes will prove more practical though less immediately destructive than atomic bombs. In fact, a state of affairs may actually arise in which wars of atomic energy will be looked upon as a blessing rather than a curse.

Clearly, then, a World State which relies on force alone is no solution. Therefore we are back at our starting-point, for war is a peculiar kind of baby—it cannot be thrown out with the bath water.

To build on reason and not on force is our only hope; therefore let us attempt this.

In an age in which we are told that the Great Architect of the Universe is beginning "to appear as a pure mathematician,"[16] it is in no way strange that man is obsessed by quantities, magnitudes, volumes and measurements, and that, in consequence, the immense, the monstrous, the enormous and the prodigious inform his mind. During six years of war he was taught to measure out victory in terms of material things—their tonnage or dollarage—until with Attila (the Flail of God) he saw physical destruction as the one and sole aim in war. Thus, logically, "Unconditional Surrender" became his slogan: admitting of no argument, it compelled annihilation.

Such is the popular framework in which war is now set; yet the historic framework is very different, for it has to do with causes and aims and not merely with measurements and numbers. War, in whatever form it may have taken, has until recently and with few exceptions been fought to achieve a more profitable peace than the one it broke. What does profitable mean? The answer depends on the state of society at the time. Should it be utterly barbarous, as in a primitive hunting community, the military aim is to exterminate the enemy and the political aim is to occupy his land. If less barbarous, as in a primitive agricultural community, then the first becomes the capture of the enemy —killing being purely incidental and to be avoided—and the second his enslavement. At once it will be seen that in both the fundamental cause of war is economic, in the one case the want of hunting fields and in the other of field hands. It has always been so; and though there are many other causes, economics are at the bottom of war.

In our existing and highly integrated industrial civilization the struggle has progressed several steps farther on. In it the main causes of war are raw materials, foreign markets and their riders, tariffs, embargoes and favoured nation clauses, not forgetting the minus factors—unfavourable trade balances, debts and unemployment. Therefore the aim of war is still the acquisition of wealth. But there is this difference, whereas in an agricultural civilization wealth is autarchic, in an industrial it is interdependent, the wealth of one nation depending on that of all other nations, as in a community the health of one individual depends on the health of all other individuals. Therefore to obliterate an enemy's wealth is as foolish as it would be in a slave hunt to kill off the enemy, or in a hunting field hunt to fail to occupy the conquered lands.

Clearly, then, granted that the atomic bomb can win a war, it must also be granted that, in a machine civilization, it cannot win a profitable peace unless the enemy capitulates at once, which he is unlikely to do should he be similarly armed. Even war as a whole cannot do so, unless it be looked upon as a surgical operation and not as mere butchery. Whereas the aim of a surgeon is to cut out a tumour, etc. (causes of war) at the least loss of blood and vitality (wealth) to his patient (enemy), the aim of a butcher is to kill an animal (enemy) as quickly as possible in order to get all blood and vitality out of it. But should the butcher slaughter his stock in such a way that good mutton and beef are reduced to molecules, rightly he would be certified insane, because the result (victory) would not be porterhouse steak (a profitable peace), but a meat famine (an unprofitable one). Yet this is the very position the world faces to-day.

Had statesmen only consulted Clausewitz, they could not have fallen into what I will call the Churchillian error of mistaking military means for political ends. For Clausewitz, war to the statesmen and war to the soldier are different things. For the former, "war is a continuation of state policy by other means"; for the latter, "war is nothing but a duel on an extensive scale." In the one case, war is a "continuation of political commerce," and in the other, the "destruction of the enemy's military forces is the object of all combats." Though these aspects of war are complementary, their respective aims are antagonistic. That of the first is moderation; that of the second is violence. Therefore, should the second eclipse the first, it will cease to be its instrument and instead become its master, and a return to the moderation which peace demands will become impossible.

Clausewitz made this perfectly clear as follows:

"That the political point of view should end completely when war begins is only conceivable in contests which are wars of life and death from pure hatred. As wars are in reality they are . . . only the expression or manifestation of policy itself. The subordination of the political point of view to the military would be contrary to common sense, for policy has declared the war; it is the intelligent faculty, war only the instrument, and not the reverse. The subordination of the military point of view to the political is, therefore, the only thing which is possible."[17]

Until 1914 English military policy was based on this subordination, and previous to that date all England's wars since the days of Cromwell were founded on the policy of the balance of power, the aim of which was to prevent any single continental nation establishing a hegemony over Europe. Therefore England allied herself to the second strongest, or to a group of powers, her war aim being, not to annihilate the strongest, because that would permanently have upset the balance, but instead to reduce the strength of the strongest to whatever point it was deemed would re-establish the balance, and when that point was reached to negotiate peace.[18]

The point to note is that up to 1914 all England's wars were political instruments, as were the wars of other nations, for the aim of each was a more profitable peace to the victor, and even in the most aggressive of these wars the aggressor's aim was never to annihilate the enemy by obliterating his country.[19] Consequently, the question which now faces the nations is: Can the atomic bomb be usefully employed in Clausewitzian in contradistinction to Churchillian warfare?

Should the Constant Tactical Factor remain operative—that is, should an antidote to the atomic bomb be discovered which in part or in whole neutralizes its destructive power—the probable answer is "yes." But should this not be the case, it is clear that, should future belligerents revert to war as a political instrument, the atomic bomb is so destructive that few operations in these restricted conflicts could or would warrant its use. This becomes apparent directly such a war is examined.

To repel the aggressor the defender will have to blast his own country and people into molecules, and once the defender is annihilated all the aggressor will win is a dust bowl.

Nevertheless, it is irrational to suppose, even should the nations agree not to use atomic projectiles in the next war, that they will not be prepared to use them, as in the recent war they were prepared to use lethal gas.[20] Further, that so long as amorality and propaganda remain what they are, in spite of peace-made affirmations, ratifications and solemniza-tions not to use atomic energy, directly a situation becomes critical it will be used and to its fullest extent. To think otherwise is to cast past experience to the winds.

Therefore, however desirable a return to Clausewitzian warfare may be, it is no good burking the fact that the world is to-day faced by Churchillian warfare—by bleedings, blast-ings and burnings, by devastation, obliteration and annihilation, however insane and unprofitable these may be. Therefore, the only course to take is to accept the world as it is—namely, as a gigantic lunatic asylum in which those few who are sane are its potential mental pathologists and alienists. Therefore, as power to wage wars of annihilation is generated in physico-chemical laboratories, its neutralization must be sought in their psycho-pathological counterparts. Humanity as a whole must be laid on the operating table and the causes of its international war diseases examined under the microscope.

Is this possible? Clearly it should be, seeing that today, except for the pathology of war, every conceivable science has been established. Though biologists, anthropologists, psychologists, etc., probe into man's nature and discover why he is so pugnacious, they leave unanswered the question: Why in this scientific age do nations fight nations? It cannot simply be because they are composed of individuals who are still primitively warlike, for less than a year before the outbreak of the recent war a wave of relief swept over Europe—Germany included—when Mr. Chamberlain brought back from Munich "peace in our time." No single nation wanted war; yet war came, and it came because no "scrap of paper" can charm away the diseases of peace, any more than it can typhus or cholera.[21]

This problem I have touched upon already, first in the Introduction, then when examining eighteenth-century warfare; and also I have pointed out that the diseases of war lie within our civilization, and in the main may be traced to the dominance of the machine over man. Therefore, as President B. Conant of Harvard declared in 1937, ". . . scholarship must probe the innards of the economic structure as well as the innards of the atom."[22]

This is the first essential problem, for though the causes of war are many—biological, psychological, educational, strategical, traditional, etc.—the fundamental causes in our machine civilization are financial and economic. To show that this is so, let us for a moment glance back on recent history.

What caused the rise of Hitler and National Socialism? The economic ruin to which Germany was reduced by the Treaty of Versailles,[23] coupled with the world financial crisis of 1919-1931, largely caused by the victorious nations re-implementing the gold standard, and thereby throwing millions into unemployment. Next, no sooner did this crisis place Hitler in power, than, breaking away from gold,[24] he based German finance on production and German foreign trade on a subsidized barter system. These innovations were so successful[25] that it became clearly apparent to the orthodox trading gold standard nations that, unless they ceased, their own economic systems would eventually be ruined.

For instance, on December 2, 1938, the Rt. Hon. R. S. Hudson, Secretary for British Overseas Trade, stated: "Her [Germany's] methods are destroying trade and are unsettling conditions throughout the world. They must be countered."[26] And on January 25 following the Hon. Rupert E. Beckett, Chairman of the Westminster Bank, quoted the Secretary of Overseas Trade as saying: "If the countries concerned continued to employ these unorthodox methods, then we should fight them at their own game, and if we fought we should win."[27]

Fearing economic encirclement, Hitler accelerated his *Lebensraum* policy, the aim of which was, to establish a German economic hegemony over Europe. As this struck directly at British and American foreign trade, a clash was inevitable, and in September, 1939, it came, for on the 1st of that month Hitler invaded Poland.[28]

When in the summer of 1941 Germany appeared to be winning, what did we see? The Atlantic Charter, the eight points of which, could they be implemented, would at least mitigate the economic causes of war. Then, three years later, when Germany was in full retreat, what next? Not a reaffirmation of that charter, but instead one open declaration after the other that the very causes which had led to the war were to form the foundations of peace: Bretton Woods and its gold standard; Dumbarton Oaks and its league, and Mr. Morgenthau and his pastoralisation (economic destruction) of Germany.

Next, in 1945, followed the San Francisco Conference and the Potsdam, which laid the foundations of what may be called the Morgenthau Peace,[29] for the bulk of his proposals was accepted. Geographically, Germany was to be reduced by a third and 60,000,000 to 70,000,000 Germans crowded into a territory less than the size of Great Britain, and her industries de-industrialized, which meant that she could not possibly support so dense a population.

Commenting on these decisions, the *Economist* said:

"The Potsdam settlement will not last ten years, and when it breaks down there will be nothing but the razor-edge balance of international anarchy between civilization and the atomic bomb."[30]

Thus it has come about that once again the "financial coterie," as Delaisi politely calls it, has won, and like the Bourbons its members have since 1918 learnt nothing and forgotten nothing. Having knocked out their two most formidable trade competitors—Germany and Japan—they are now busily engaged in re-establishing their old racket. Here is an example out of many of this inverted surgery:

Recently the Foreign Trade Sub-Committee of the United States Department of Commerce pointed out that, as the United States now possess half the world's industrial capacity, in order to maintain full employment 10 billion dollars' worth of goods must be exported. But that, as the American foreign market is only capable of absorbing 7 billion dollars' worth of imports, the export surplus of 3 billion dollars' worth will remain over. As this surplus will represent not an exchange of goods, but instead a source of employment in the United States, clearly it must result in an equivalent source of unemployment in the foreign countries which receive these goods. And as these countries will have to be lent the price of the goods in order to purchase them, they will not merely have workers thrown into unemployment (out of purchasing power), but will be put into unpayable debt to the United States.

As this form of usury was one of the main causes of the recent war, it cannot fail to be one of the main causes of the next war.

What chance, then, is there that the pathology of war will be encouraged? None! For even were such a science created, the pathologists would either be bribed, suborned and cajoled, or, what is far more likely, selected by the "financial coterie" to conceal instead of reveal the economic causes of war.

Is, then, the final chapter of *The Will to Power* to be entitled "The Will to Annihilation"? Are the words of Lewis Mumford, quoted in the preceding chapter, to be the final sentence in the history of armament: "A society that has lost its life values will tend to make a religion of death"? Are the aims of strategy and tactics to be terror and obliteration? Is that Europe which arose from out the valour of the ancients and the chivalry of the men of faith to sink into the mire of murder and be extinguished in the pit of blind devilry?

I do not think so. Instead, I believe that once intra-atomic energy is harnessed, civilization will be purged of its financial and economic diseases. That man's eyes will be opened and that with Malinowski it will be seen that "there is a powerful propaganda at work which attempts to foist on us the conviction that war is an expression of the struggle for existence, that it is due to man's innate and inevitable pugnacity or aggressiveness; that war as a selective agency has been, is, and will remain unavoidable as well as benefi-cent. Is this true? Give me the old warfare and I shall become as enthusiastic about war as any member of the most military propaganda organization. . . . Quite com-patible with the principle of the survival of the fittest" was the old type of warfare. But modern war is the "imbecilic expression of the domination of the machine over man. . . . You can praise the virtues of modern warfare only if you blind yourself to its realities . . . war has become . . . a de-structive anachronism, useless as a tool, unpracticable as a measure of international policy, an unmitigated waste of all that is best in our civilization."[31]

That atomic energy will open the gateway of a new epoch is no vision of a busy brain, because the process of splitting the atom is well known—it is no secret. Further, not only have scientists already transmuted one element into another, but, so it would appear, they have also discovered means of releasing intra-atomic energy other than in purely explosive form.[32] Therefore, it may be predicted with no small assurance that the day is approaching when science will give humanity not only almost unlimited power of locomotion,[33] but also the long sought philosopher's stone.

When this Age of Abundance becomes a fact, what place will there be in it for gold standards, loans, debts, foreign markets, tariffs, embargoes, full employment and all the other black magic of the Age of Snatch and Grab? Every nation will have most of the material things it wants at so low a price in human labour that the garden of the Hesperides will no longer be a myth but a reality. The dragon of toil will have been slain by the newborn Hercules—the Mighty Atom.

And, finally, what of war?

As I have shown, the present epoch of the Will to Power came into being with the discovery of gunpowder, not merely because that explosive could more readily than cold steel overcome resistance, but because it accelerated military movement. I have traced its course from the days of Roger Bacon onwards, and among other things have, I hope, made clear that firearms changed the course of history by substituting for the medieval conception of war as a trial between right and wrong the secular conception—a trial between two wills to attain what to each was considered to be a more profitable peace. Whereas to the Church war was a spiritual contest, to the secular state it is a political contest. But a war founded on split atoms is, as conceived today, purely a technical contest—a trial between contending laboratories in which the mutual aim is annihilation: an annihilation so absolute that it shatters the whole basis of present-day power politics by making power virtually omnipotent and, therefore, super-political, for all politics as hitherto conceived are obliterated.[34]

Thus it would appear to substantiate M. Bloch's vision that in an industrial civilization war is no longer a profitable court of appeal. Does this mean that the history of armaments is approaching its end: that weapon development has run its course and is about to annihilate itself by exploding the Constant Tactical Factor?

Though the future alone can answer this question, that it will be answered in the affirmative seems to me to be unlikely, and for the following reasons:

(1) That as gunpowder, by founding the secular state, went far to eliminate the religious causes of war, the harnessing of atomic energy, by drastically curtailing its economic causes, will finally found the technical or scientific state in which it will become as clearly apparent that material destruction is as unprofitable an aim in war as, in the name of religion, spiritual destruction was to the secular state.

(2) That, though gunpowder was of purely explosive value, atomic energy is also of locomotive value, for it can be used as a prime mover as well as a prime destroyer.

(3) That because electronic devices will undoubtedly be used to direct the flight of projectiles, so undoubtedly they will be employed, not only to detect their approach, but also to deflect their line of flight and thereby throw them off their targets.

These three possibilities—avoidance of economic destruction, atomic energy as a prime mover, and electronic devices as a means of defence—all point to the Constant Tactical Factor remaining in operation. Let us, therefore, examine this probability more closely.

Compared to former explosive projectiles, the atomic bomb possesses one outstanding difference. It is that its destructive force is so enormous that it cannot be neutralized by any known means of direct protection. Armour is useless, also are earthworks, and though, in order to avoid extinction it is possible to place a whole community underground, such a means of defence is really impracticable, not on account of labour and cost, but because there are obvious limits to burrowing. Further, the explosive force of the bomb is so great that it goes far to neutralize indirect protection, such as the deflection of the bomb from its course. For example, were 100 atomic rocket bombs to be fired at London, and should ninety-nine be deflected, the one which penetrates the electronic defences will in itself be sufficient to destroy the greater part of that city; whereas were 100 of the largest aerial bombs at present made dropped, and only one explode, the damage done would be inconsiderable. This is something new, because in the past all that indirect means of defence have hoped to accomplish was a reduction of the danger and not its abolition.

Defensive counter-agents are, therefore, insufficient; consequently offensive counter-agents must be sought, and if unprofitable destruction is to be avoided, these are not to be looked for in superiority of destructive power—in more or larger atomic bombs—but instead in speed of movement which will lead to the rapid occupation, in contradiction to the rapid obliteration, of the enemy's country. What, at present, is missing is ability to follow bombardments up, or to dispense with them altogether.

As the follow-up must be effected in hours or days, and not in months or years, as was the case during the recent war, any form of petrol-propelled aircraft is quite useless. In their stead an air vessel which can travel at thousands of miles the hour and lift thousands of tons from the ground is required. Such a vessel is the future rocket ship propelled by atomic energy.

With the introduction of this vessel, at once the war picture returns to normal. Forthwith occupation becomes the strategic aim and destruction of the enemy's power of resistance the means of accomplishing it. Destruction not by super-atomic bombs, but, as hitherto, by weapons of various types and powers devised to enable the rocket-ship-borne armies to accomplish what is tactically necessary: the imposition of will upon will, and not merely of force upon force or of obliteration upon obliteration, in the shortest possible time and with the least material damage, so that a profitable peace may be won.

If, in the recent war, Germany had been occupied without obliterating her cities and devastating her industries, there can be no question that peace today would be far more profitable to her victors than it actually is. In fact, the situation which now faces England and the United States is in every way less profitable, not only economically, but also politically and strategically, than the one which faced them before the outbreak of the war. A mad war can only lead to a mad peace, and to fight a war in such a way that an unprofitable peace is a certainty is clearly idiotic.

It is this idiocy which, throughout history, has made the military mind so dangerous an instrument of government, for the warrior takes to destruction like a duck takes to water—chaos is his element. It is so easy to destroy, and destruction makes so small a demnad on creative thinking. The industrialist of the present age comes a near second, for to him construction is as frequently as not an end in itself.

Both outlooks are illogical, because the governing factor in peace and war is neither construction nor destruction; instead it is usefulness. Though it may be useful to build a skyscraper 100 storeys high, it is useless to build one of 1,000 storeys; and though it may be useful to make an atomic bomb which will demolish a fortress, it is useless to make one which will annihilate an entire country—why? In the one case, because a house is something to live in and not to travel in, and in the second because war as fought today is an argument between the living and cannot be settled with the dead. To annihilate an enemy will certainly end a war, but as certainly it will not win a profitable peace.

In everything there is a mean, a middle path called "sanity," outside which man enters the jungle of madness in which monsters, zoological, spiritual, political and material, roam: dinosaurs, universal creeds, world dictators and atomic bombs. Gigantism is a sure sign that a species or a civilization is approaching its end. The secret of war is not to be sought in size, because, as Lucretius 2,000 years ago pointed out: "For whatever animals now feed on the breath of life, either craft or courage or speed has preserved their kind from the beginning of their being." And in the coming age of atomic energy, of these three essentials speed dominates.

Should this be accepted, then the two main armament problems which to-day face the world are:
(1) The harnessing of atomic energy.
(2) The shaping of the instruments of war around this new prime mover.

Not to abolish war; but, so long as the urge to fight remains part of human nature, to impose the will of the victor upon the vanquished with the least possible destruction to either, because destruction is never more than a means to the end.[35]

Therefore, in this violent age in which we live, as Thomas Fuller once said: "When our hopes break, let our patience hold." For "there is some soul of goodness in things evil, would man observingly distil it out"—so wrote a greater than he.

REFERENCES

1. *Encyclopædia Britannica*, 13th edition, vol. i, p. 267.
2. See "The Romanes Lecture, 1915," *Science and the Great War*, E. B. Poulton. "The German success in trench warfare is entirely due to the use of science. English science, at least equal and probably better, has always been longing to help" (p. 40). "The want of a scientific spirit in the army has been even more conspicuous, and has led to more tragic consequences in the use of men than in the use of material" (p. 44).
3. Whether willingly or unwillingly, more and more is science becoming regimented in the War State. As an example, we read: "With the approach of World War II the [American] scientists were mobilized with Vannevar Bush in charge, who said, 'Active organized defence effort, involving thousands of scientists, has been going on intensively for 18 months.' A 'National Roster of Scientific and Specialized Personnel' was established under President Carmichael of Tufts, which spent over $100,000,000 during the year 1943. The colleges and universities were given research contracts amounting to hundreds of millions of dollars. The Kilgore Bill, still pending before Congress, provides for the permanent mobilization of all scientists under an administrator, appointed by the President, who shall 'co-ordinate scientific facilities and personnel' and 'make and amend appropriate rules and regulations which shall have the force of law.' The Bill appropriates $200,000,000 and provides maximum penalties of $5,000 and/or one year's imprisonment for infringements of regulations set up" (*Between Two Wars*, Porter Sargent, p. 313, 1945).

4. President Truman's statement as reported in *The Times* of August 7, 1945.

5. *Ibid.*, August 8, 1945.

6. *Ibid.*, August 9, 1945.

7. *Ibid.*, August 23, 1945.

8. *The Economist*, August 18, 1945.

9. The closest historical parallel to these trials is that of Joan of Arc, who in Rouen was burnt as a witch on May 30, 1431, and who in 1904 was canonized. The executions of Colonel Labedoyère and Marshal Ney are not in the same category, because both betrayed Louis XVIII during the Hundred Days.

10. This question is illuminatingly dealt with by Alfred Machin in his *Darwin's Theory Applied to Mankind* (1937).

11. An example of this is the reduction of Reichs-Marshal Goering, Field-Marshal Keitel and General Jodl to the status of civilians—why? The following answer is to be found in the *Sunday Times* of August 26, 1945: "The Geneva Convention forbids solitary confinement in the case of war prisoners taken from the enemy's fighting services. It is, however, permissible to place civilians in solitary confinement, and it is as civilians that these three prisoners are now regarded." To avoid hypocrisy and a travesty of justice, the way to deal with such of the enemy who cannot be trusted is the way Napoleon was dealt with. Without trial he was shipped on board the *Northumberland*, under Rear-Admiral Sir George Cockburn, and sent to St. Helena. At the Admiral's table he and his staff of seven and six British officers consumed: port 20 doz.; claret 45 doz.; madeira 22 doz.; champagne 13 doz.; sherry 7 doz.; and malmsey 5 doz. It is instructive to contrast with this the treatment meted out to Goering, Doenitz, Keitel and Ribbentrop, etc.: "The bedrooms are absolutely bare, except for the prisoners' camp bed (no mattress), two blankets, a chair, and the usual hotel wash-basin . . . no kind of artificial lighting is provided. . . . There are no garbage cans, because there is no garbage. They eat all they get!" (*Daily Mail*, August 8, 1945.)

12. *History of European Morals*, William Edward Hartpole Lecky, vol. i, p. 280 (1902).

13. *Ibid.*, vol. i, p. 276.

14. *Letters of Voltaire and Frederick the Great*, R. Aldington (1927), p. 160.

15. English translation, third edition, 1917. This essay is well worth studying, as the ideas set out in it are very different from those of his predecessors. In brief, his theory is that in the long run wars tend to unite the human race, because grouping lessens the incidence of war. Nature's goal is unity and her driving force towards it is war.

16. *The Mysterious Universe*, Sir James Jeans, p. 134 (1930).

17. *On War*, Gen. Carl von Clausewitz, vol. iii, pp. 124-125 (English edition, 1908).

18. Though the Napoleonic Wars were fought to a finish, this policy was nevertheless maintained, for after the French collapse at Waterloo England prevented the dismemberment of France and took every step possible to maintain her as a great power.

19. As an exception, the invasion of the Seljuk Turks may be quoted. In the eleventh century they overran Asia Minor, and as they were a pastoral people they destroyed not only the Byzantines but also their cities, because they were useless to them. All they wanted were unrestricted field lands for their herds and flocks. The ancient Hebrews were noted for their liquidations—*e.g.*, Num. xxxi. 1-18; Deut. ii. 30-34, xx. 16-17; Josh. vi. 17-21; and 1 Sam. xv. 1-8.

20. That gas was not used can easily be explained. The most profitable use of gas is as a city taker. Tactically it would have paid the Germans to have used it in the sieges of Leningrad and Stalingrad. But they knew that, were they to do so, they would be out-gassed; further, that in Western Europe the prevailing winds are westerly. The Americans and British did not use it, because their aim was not to take cities, but instead to obliterate them in order to destroy German industrial power. Had they discovered a gas which would have accomplished this more economically, there is little question that they would have used it, as also would the Germans have used gas had they possessed gas superiority.

21. Many writers have seen this; for instance, Bernard Shaw is reported to have said: "To me war fever is like any other epidemic, and what the patients say or do in their delirium is no more to be counted against them than if they were all in bed with brain fever...."

22. Quoted by Porter Sargent in *Between Two Wars*, p. 329 (1945).

23. In 1938 Lord Lothian said: "We are largely responsible for the situation that confronts us today.... If another war comes and the history of it is ever written, the dispassionate historian a hundred years hence will not say that Germany alone was responsible for it, even if she strikes the first blow, but that those who mismanaged the world between 1918 and 1937 had a large share of responsibility for it."

24. In 1937 Hitler said: "The community of a nation does not live by the fictitious value of money, but by real production which in its turn gives value to money. This production is the real cover of a currency, and not a bank or a safe full of gold." Five years previously, Mr. Churchill had said much the same thing—namely: "Is the progress of the human race in this age of almost terrifying expansion to be arbitrarily barred and regulated by fortuitous discoveries of gold mines here and there? ... Are we to be told that human civilization and society would have been impossible if gold had not happened to be an element in the composition of the globe?" For a brief account of Hitler's financial system, see *Nazi War Finance and Banking*, Otto Nathan (1944).

25. The success of this may be judged from the table on page 212.

26. *Daily Telegraph*, December 2, 1938.

27. *The Times*, January 26, 1939.

28. In 1914 conditions were much the same. In 1915, in *The Inevitable War*, Francis Delaisi wrote: "Diplomats ... are the tools of the financial and industrial oligarchy and work to obtain for them foreign loans and foreign purchasers for their goods; the ambassadors in gold braid are today no more and no less than the agents of the banks and the great corporations. ... The great European nations are governed by men of affairs. ... They struggle for the control of the railways, loans, and mining

GREAT GERMANY'S TRADE WITH SOUTH-EASTERN EUROPE
(PERCENTAGE OF EACH COUNTRY'S TRADE)

Year	Hungary		Rumania		Jugoslavia	
	Imports from	Exports to	Imports from	Exports to	Imports from	Exports to
1929 ..	33·2	42·1	36·6	37·0	33·0	24·1
1932 ..	38·0	45·3	28·6	18·7	31·1	33·4
1937 ..	44·2	41·0	38·0	26·9	42·7	35·2

Year	Bulgaria		Greece		Czechoslovakia	
	Imports from	Exports to	Imports from	Exports to	Imports from	Exports to
1929 ..	29·8	42·4	10·6	25·6	46·2	37·9
1932 ..	31·9	41·0	11·9	18·7	40·8	33·5
1937 ..	58·2	47·1	29·6	32·2	19·7	21·0

Extracted from *Our Own Times*, Stephen King-Hall, p. 876 (1938).

concessions, etc. And if, perchance, two rivals' camps cannot agree, they make an appeal to arms." Also: "The financial coterie which are carrying on their machinations in the dens of the chancelleries is not large, but it has a most powerful ally, the popular ignorance. . . . To hinder financiers from playing with the public opinion, the people must be awakened, shaken out of their heavy sleep. And above all front must be made against preachers of peace, who lull it into a false security."

29. *Economist*, August 11, 1945.

30. Also: "The conviction that the peace proposed at Potsdam is a thoroughly bad peace . . . is based on the belief that the system proposed is in the fullest sense unworkable. It offers no hope of ultimate German reconciliation. It offers little hope of the Allies maintaining its cumbrous controls beyond the first years of peace. Its methods of reparations reinforce autarchy in Russia and consummate the ruin not only of Germany. but of Europe."

31. Quoted by Porter Sargent in *Between Two Wars*, pp. 321-322.

32. Mr. Stimson, U.S. Secretary of War, as reported in *The Times* of August 7, 1945. ". . . when U-235 is hit by a neutron that enters into its nucleus the atomic weight becomes 236, which is an exploding atom which splits easily. Merely by adding water, it is stated, energy can be released, and when all this water is converted into steam the process stops unless more water is supplied, making the energy-liberating process automatic and self-regulating" (*The Times*, August 8, 1945).

33. "The new type of bomb also gives frightening new possibilities to the rocket and developments of the flying-bomb type. If, as has long been believed in some quarters, uranium with deuterium oxide as the catalytic

agent can also be used as a propellant, it may completely revolutionize aviation and all other forms of locomotion" (*The Times*, August 8, 1945).

34. "It is an irony of history that the terms for Germany decided at Potsdam should have been published within forty-eight hours of the dropping of the first atomic bomb. One may wonder what future historians will make—in such a context—of the victorious statesmen's conception of security. If one bomb can annihilate Königsberg, do the Russians gain much by annexing it? What possible defensive importance can be attached to a frontier on the Oder—or anywhere else? Can the ban on German production of aircraft and sea-going vessels have any bearing on war-making power in the Atomic Age? Once again we are reminded of the appalling gap between man's adult scientific mind and his political infantilism. It is as though the victors, in the age of the tank, were making a peace of bows and arrows" (*Economist*, August 11, 1945).

35. To some this may seem a fantastic aim; yet, as we have seen in the days of chivalry, the object was not to kill but to obtain ransom, an economic gain. Also in the wars of the Aztecs the aim was not to kill but to capture victims to be fattened and sacrificed on the altars of their war and sun god Huitzilopochtli. Also an economic gain, for, according to their religion, unless he were fed their crops would be ruined. Though cannibals kill their enemies, they eat them, again an economic and religious gain, whereas to-day we kill our enemies and have to subsist on ration books. Who is the wiser warrior?

INDEX